Navigating West

Towards Incredible Truth

Mohammad Masud

Published On Amazon Kindle Direct Publishing (KDP).

Published on May 10th, 2024.

Reprinted with correction on May 31st, 2024.

Reprinted with correction on June 28th, 2024.

Reprinted with correction on July 22nd, 2024.

ISBN: 979-8-854-23707-9 (Paperback)

ISBN: 979-8-325-29406-8 (Hardcover)

To all who are looking for a way out of the current mess the West is spiraling into and gracefully untangle from it.

Scan for all books from the author

CONTENTS

Figures

Preface

The world of our time is full of injustice. In fact, the history of the world had no shortage of injustice and humanity will continue to have the injustice - that's what we, the homo sapiens are. But that's just one side of the coin. The other side of the same coin holds the story of another part that always stands for justice, fights evil and puts injustice in check. This book is for that bright shiny side of the coin where we seek to be part of and takes care of the earth, who are the caretaker of it, with the blessings of the highest level of intellects, ability of language that were possible due to the most optimal formation of the homo sapiens. I was searching for solutions to the widespread injustice affecting countries in both the East and West, including Palestine, Syria, Lebanon, Libya, Iraq, Afghanistan, India, Pakistan, Bangladesh, Burma, Mali, Sudan, Ethiopia, Somalia, Haiti, Ukraine, and even many parts of America. However, the most vivid examples of current injustice, corruption, and oppression are primarily found in Muslim-majority countries. While searching for the solution I found many micro actions that the Muslim world should take to solve their local problem. However, the more I dive deeper into the last several centuries, it becomes more and more clear that the problems of this world that we see today are actually seeded a century ago. The Ottoman empire, British and French colonialism, German, Austro-Hungarian and Russian empire's race for world dominion, all played a role in creating the world that we see today. So, the problems also cannot be solved in isolation. Then, my life in this America has opened up an entirely new world where this country's very formation was anti-colonialism and anti-monarchy and anti-imperialism and took sides for the right-side in the first-world-war and in the second world war. Yes, America had dark history: native-American's ethnic cleansing, taking over their lands; the trans-Atlantic slave trade from Africa that created the wealth in the South; the invasion and atrocities during Vietnam, Iraq and Afghanistan wars. Despite all that, America has in its core the declaration of independence and the constitution that sanctified human equality through the rights of life, liberty, and pursuit of happiness: "We hold these truths to be self-evident, that all men are created equal, that they are endowed by their Creator with certain unalienable Rights, that among these are Life, Liberty and the pursuit of Happiness "; to practice religion freely, to fight against tyranny, freedom of speech and individual property, etc. Finally, this is the land of immigrants welcomed throughout its history by welcoming people from various parts of the world. All these are so unique in our time that if we don't see the bright side of it then we are only looking at one side of the coin and ignoring the other.

Looking into the brighter side of America, I am convinced that holistically America can and will be the force of positive influence and can become a righteous leading position that can change the world full of injustice and oppression thus save the world from tyranny. However, before America can get into that position, it needs to be cleansed off from the current injustice, social breakdown, moral decay and all other corrupting factors from within and replenish the shiny sides of it and strengthening those. In this book I am going to focus on the problems that are destroying the American exceptionalism faster than any other civilization in the history. We will take a close look at the current trajectory and why this path would inevitably expedite the demise of this great civilization. Then, we will explore the solutions, comparing the available choices at hand, to address these underlying root causes and navigate it back to the right course to reemerge as a beacon of hope for humanity. If we miss this opportunity, the world may have to wait for decades, if not centuries, to recover from the loss. It would be a significant loss to the world if we were to slip. The world is waiting for that beacon, and the time is now.

An early disclaimer: The goal of this effort is not to hurt anyone's feelings or portray any religion negatively. The sole objective is to present the current situation and discuss available options candidly, without excessive political correctness. When our goal shifts from seeking truth to pleasing everyone, we risk missing the opportunity to present facts for a fair comparison. However, if some words seem harsher than intended, this is largely due to my limitations in English language skills. I welcome feedback to help improve my communication in the future.

Convention disclaimer

- I will use the word "verse" to translate the Arabic "*ayat,*" even though the word "verse" doesn't fully capture the essence of the Quranic "*ayat.*" The true meaning of "*ayat*" is "signs" from God. But, as most of the readers of this book likely do not have an Arabic background, I will use "verse" to make it easier for them.
- Common acronyms used in this book: *pbuh*: Peace be upon him; *a.s.*: Peace be upon him; *r.a.*: God is pleased with him.

How to contact

- You are most welcome to provide feedback and suggestions to improve this book. Email me at *mmasud.therevival@gmail.com.*

Chapter I: What is West?

In a dry academic context, the West is often defined simply as a geographic area within the Western hemisphere of the earth, west of the Prime Meridian (which crosses Greenwich, London) and east of the 180th meridian. However, if you enroll in a Western Civilization course at an American college, it begins with Mesopotamia and Egypt. Thus, in that sense, the West cannot be narrowly defined in purely geographic terms. Additionally, if you dive a little deeper, you will see how the definitions of the East, Middle East, Far East, and West have been defined and redefined many times in history. Believe it or not, in classical antiquity, "the West" initially referred to the western part of the Mediterranean, including parts of what are now Italy, Spain, and North Africa. In the context of ancient Rome, the Western Roman Empire was centered around Rome itself, contrasting with the Eastern Roman Empire based in Constantinople. In recent history, during the Cold War, the term "the West" took on a more ideological dimension, broadly referring to countries aligned with NATO and opposed to the Soviet bloc. In this context, the West was associated with capitalist democracies, contrasting with the communist states of Eastern Europe and elsewhere.

Having said that, I am using the term "West" more loosely, as it is popularly, albeit academically inaccurately, labeled on a geo-demographic basis: the Western hemisphere of the globe, primarily inhabited by Caucasian whites with a predominant Christian heritage. This ethnic identity, along with their common system of government—which derives from Greek philosophy and democratic principles—distinguishes the West from the rest of the world. Therefore, the traditional definition of the West encompasses a democratic, Christian, and capitalist economy that primarily resides in the Western hemisphere of the Earth, though not exclusively. The term "primarily" is used because countries like Australia and New Zealand, while not in the same geographical hemisphere, share key characteristics with the West and are thus considered part of it. To avoid further confusion in defining the

"West," it is important to note that the discussion would be incomplete without mentioning Israel. Although geographically located in Asia, specifically in the current Middle East, Israel is a member of many European Union institutions. It participates in the Eurovision Song Contest and the European Games, is a full member of the Union of European Football Associations (UEFA) and the European Organization for Nuclear Research (CERN), and holds observer member status in the Council of Europe. Israel is also seriously considering applying for EU membership. This underscores the fact that geography is not a strict boundary for being considered part of the West. This includes other consequential attributes such as secularism, the separation of church and state, developed economies, liberal ideology, individual freedom and rights, and military supremacy.

Going further, I consider any country that adopts Western systems, culture, and lifestyle as part of the "West," regardless of its global location. Countries like India, the capitalist regions of China, Pakistan, Bangladesh, Morocco, Egypt, Brazil, etc., are embracing the Western lifestyle, often uncritically, without considering how it aligns with their socio-cultural contexts. As a result, these countries enjoy many benefits of the Western lifestyle but also face many of its drawbacks.

If I had stopped there, the necessity for this book would not exist, and we could simply close the cover. However, that's far from the end of the story. The current reality of the "West" is predominantly a consequence of the civilization led by European countries over the last few centuries. Like many other civilizations in human history, it continued but acquired many consequential attributes, exacerbated in the fifties and sixties, and are now prevalent, especially in the USA, and similarly in other European countries. These changes motivated me to write this book. Some of the consequential attributes of the West can be illustrated by a few alarming realities currently faced by the USA, the leader of modern Western civilization:

- The collapse of traditional values such as marriage, family, and societal norms, which is contributing to a birth rate in the USA that is currently hovering at 1.64%, below the replacement birth rate threshold of 2.1%.[1]
- Widening income inequality and disparity in the distribution of wealth, with the top 0.1% in the USA holding more wealth than the bottom 50% of the population.
- Healthcare has become an unstoppable trainwreck, with 124 million out of 240 million adults being metabolically sick, and more than 50 million adults suffering from anxiety or depression. This is happening while Americans spend $4.3 trillion on healthcare, which amounts to 18% of the total GDP.
- Structural racism and systemic abuse have created a society where 38% of the entire incarcerated population is black, whereas they comprise only 13% of the total US population, and only 30% of blacks own homes, in comparison to 80% of whites who enjoy homeownership.
- The most recent surge in the LGBTQ+ and gender fluidity movement has seen young generations being indoctrinated with unscientific myths about gender and sexuality, leading to irreversible physical and psychological transformations.

The list above is by no means exhaustive; however, it provides a glimpse into the few "perks" associated with living in the West. For those born here who haven't experienced the outside world, this represents one aspect of what it means to them. For immigrants like myself, who came to this land of opportunities to live the American dream, the perspective and experience gained cannot be acquired without living in both "worlds" almost simultaneously—within a span of 15 years, and with the ability to travel back and forth between these two "worlds" every few years. I would argue that this "two worlds" perspective is valuable not only to immigrant Americans but also to the native/local citizenry.

Immigrants Dilemma

The majority of the population in underdeveloped and developing parts of the world dreams of migrating to, or at least visiting, America. This is no surprise. America has taken the torch of civilization, building from scratch in just a couple of hundred years—a feat that you would find in only a handful of examples throughout human history. Islam did something similar in a couple of hundred years (from 650 CE) and built a civilization from nothing (which I will cover in detail later in the book). When immigrants, myself included, look at the West, they see a shiny, bright life—and rightly so. Life in America comes with law and order, security, stability, civic behavior, a knowledge-based society, technological advancements, wealth and prosperity, and most importantly, the dignity and respect afforded by the American passport worldwide. If the above list seems conceptual and vague, for many of us, it translates to the tangible aspects of life: skyscrapers, the New York skyline, endless highways and shiny cars, individual single-family homes with green grassy lawns and white fences, children going to school safely, working in corporate offices, vacationing in theme parks and resorts, and enjoying a "dream" retirement. Nicely equipped hospitals and healthcare facilities contribute to this image. Much of our portrayal of the USA comes from Hollywood movies, and these are not entirely wrong either. From an outsider's perspective, I would say all these are very real. So, nothing can go wrong, right? Wrong! The promised dream comes with a package—occasional nightmares that nobody was prepared for. Let me explain how. This is from a Muslim perspective, so there may be some variation, but having lived in the West for 15 years, I can tell you that it will cover the majority of immigrants coming from the eastern hemisphere.

What immigrants fail to appreciate until they have landed and lived for a certain time is that this "dream" isn't a pick-and-choose menu like in a restaurant. It's a complete package system. It gives you a lot and, rightly so, demands a lot from you. And often, these demands are not mutually exclusive to the good things of the East compared to the West. In fact, the West had, maybe a few centuries ago, what an Eastern man left behind but now is lost or decayed in exchange for material advancements. The most important thing from that "lost" list is family value. Most of us never thought that we would have to exchange our family values, bonds, or the morality of the next generation to gain those materialistic benefits. We had thought we would just "add" the good things of the West that we were missing in our native country. But when we realize there's no free lunch, then we wake up. Some wake up early to find a solution; some wake up late in life when their kids have already left them to live their individual American dreams, and many of us never even realize it, even as we continue to pay the highest price for it through the rest of our lives with loneliness and the pipe dream of "going back". I would like to acknowledge that there is a small percentage of the population who adopt the materialistic life completely, not even taking time to ponder what they have gained and what they have paid for it. There will always be a group of people like this, in every time, every place, every nation, and this book is not for them. For them, they choose to live a constantly running life without even taking a pause for a second to reflect. Otherwise, those thoughts would come to their mind and "ruin" their living in the dream. They only live for the moment and don't take heed of the reality surrounding them. That's a life in hallucination, and I can only pray for them.

For the non-immigrants, those who were born here and grew up in this civilization, it is more challenging for you because you have lost the baseline of those missing values to compare against. It is very difficult, if not impossible, to recognize the reality unless you really choose to, and even then, it would require a great deal of effort. It's not surprising why this is difficult. Our human brains operate with a concept known as "shifting baseline syndrome." So, the baseline for populations that have lived for generations has completely shifted, and when you try to compare what is missing, you find barely one or two things. To be able to see what was present a few generations ago, you would need to adopt a paradigm shift approach, but that is a lot to ask of anyone.

The signs are visible

To prescribe a solution, the first step is to conduct a thorough investigation of the current state and identify the root cause. It's similar to your yearly physical check-up. You examine the body, check for any symptoms, and check your vitals to determine if you're doing fine or not. Once we have completed those steps, if necessary, a prescription can be written.

The visible signs mentioned earlier can be organized into a Top 10 list:

1. Structural racism.
2. Widening gaps in wealth and income inequality.
3. Public health crisis: Chronic diseases.
4. Drug and alcohol crisis.
5. Mental health epidemic.
6. Depletion of family values and loss of family bonds.
7. Long-standing injustice toward the black and poor in society.
8. Excessive materialism and resource waste.
9. Climate change and pollution.
10. Impact of pornography on family and society at large.

Why bother?

Now, one might ask, why all the fuss about searching for a solution? We could start answering that question, but I would counter with another: why not? In fact, the search has been ongoing in the political, social, and academic fields for some time, in fact, more than a decade, whether you've noticed or not. And there's a valid reason that I briefly alluded to in the opening of the book: the cost of losing this great civilization, which has brought so much good to humanity, is too high. I have been living in American society for more than a decade and a half, and I have witnessed the greatness of Americans. There are many positive traits that are prevalent within the majority of American society.

- America has built a civilization in just a few hundred years that is unparalleled in the history of mankind. The scale of American civilization, with its superior scientific and technological innovations, has created a superpower that benefits humanity in every aspect of life: education, healthcare, agriculture, military, computing technology, industrialization, etc. Just one statistic says it all: 954, or 40% of Nobel Prizes, have been awarded to Americans.[2]
- America welcomes immigrants from all backgrounds, colors, races, religions, and ethnicities more than any other nation on earth—it's a land of immigrants. By the way, America has also benefited enormously from this. Out of the 954 Nobel Prize winners who are Americans, 334 were immigrants to the USA.
- Americans respect talent regardless of race. If you are hardworking and talented, then you can rise to the top of a company or organization. Barack Obama, the child of a Kenyan father, made it to the White House—not once, but twice! I challenge any country to show a better example than America.
- Americans, in general, are honest and truthful. The reference to Pew Research supports this fact. However, if you travel through the

country, as I did, covering 35 states by driving, you will find that people are generally honest. Let me give you an example: we have been on many camping trips in many states. Over there, I have seen many homes leave firewood or eggs for sale with a box for payment through the honor system. It's an anecdotal story, but I am sure you've seen that across the country (yes, there are areas that are contrary to it, but I am talking about in general, not in entirety).

- Americans are among the most generous in terms of donating to humanitarian causes around the world.
- Americans are generally hardworking with a strong work ethic and personal discipline.
- Americans greatly value self-dignity and self-reliance. The U.S. Constitution's Bill of Rights is something you will not find in any contemporary nation. The Second Amendment right is a shining example of a freedom-loving nation's emphasis on self-dignity and self-reliance.
- Yes, I am ready to use this strong phrase: America "saved the world" during World War II from Nazi domination. It paid an enormous price to free the world from fascist powers.
- America defended the world from the ideologies of communism and atheism, which were proven wrong within just eighty years through the collapse of the Soviet Union.
- Even though this has changed in the last several decades, most Americans used to live a very healthy lifestyle. I would assert that many are still living that healthy lifestyle and, most importantly, many of them are desperately looking for ways to get back to that lifestyle. The concept of Shifting Baselines[3] is an obstacle in their path, which will be covered in detail in subsequent chapters.

If you don't have any solid opposition to the list I made above, you should already understand why we should bother. The positive influence this country has had on the world is undeniable; humanity would lose a great contributor to humane civilization without it. However, without addressing the issues plaguing the West, the civilization we know and observe is heading towards a catastrophic collapse. Every civilization undergoes a cycle of rise and fall, and while there's no single universal reason for a civilization's decline, a common theme across them is that injustice, corruption, and a lack of purpose in living undermine the very foundation of a civilization—essentially destroying the morality of the population who built and sustained it. Now, the question arises: why not wait for the institutions (political, social, economic) to come up with solutions? The answer is - haven't we waited long enough? Haven't we seen enough futile attempts leading to more chaos? These institutions concoct new solutions for one problem, only to create ten more in the process. Then, in attempting to solve those ten issues, they inadvertently generate ten more for each, leading to a hundred additional problems. Ten is a figurative number used to illustrate that it's creating more problems than it is solving. Do you want proof? Let's examine a few examples to understand how we got here:

1. Climate change presents us with an existential threat. According to the majority of climate scientists, if we don't cease burning fossil fuels NOW and switch to renewable energy sources like solar, wind, and electric, planet Earth, our only habitat, is doomed. Regardless of the debate on whether climate change is entirely human-made, it is certain that Earth has been contaminated and imbalanced by massive developmental endeavors since the twentieth century, all in the name of development and civilization. Scientists, in a good faith plea, are urging us to turn off all our combustion engines. Let's ask a simple question: who introduced the combustion engine that led to the Second Industrial Revolution? Who developed the scientific solutions and engineering technologies to extract fossil fuels from the Earth? Now, they propose new technology to "cool down" the Earth. Some ideas, such as spraying billions of tons of phosphorus into the

atmosphere to reflect sunlight or burying carbon deep within the Earth, are alarming. If this hasn't scared you yet, consider this: the same scientists who can't create a medication for the human body without side effects, and who have also developed "miracle" chemicals, thus contributing to the "cancer" treatment industry through the chemical revolution, are now proposing to throw phosphorus into Earth's atmospheric system to regulate sunlight and temperature. As someone who is not a biologist, shouldn't the obvious risks immediately halt these dangerous experiments on our Earth—the only accessible and habitable planet for the human species? The problem is not science itself but the materialistic societies profiting from every scientific research, patent, and invention, driving scientists to endanger humanity for material gains—be it money, fame, or something else. Renewable energy, like the Ivanpah Thermal Power Plant in California and the extensive solar panels in Nevada's desert, destroys natural wildlife habitats and kills thousands of birds, all in the name of clean energy. This solution to our endless power consumption, replacing it with alternate power generation methods, is flawed. Scientists, who once fed us endless power using fossil fuels, now urge us to stop because it's harmful to Earth and humanity. In 50 years, they might declare renewable energy sources like wind turbines, solar panels, and geothermal plants harmful for another reason. We're just moving from one evil to a lesser evil, but no one addresses the root cause of our problem, as it doesn't align with their interests in obtaining research funding or securing another patent to sell more products. They become wealthier, whether through fossil fuels or renewable, while humanity is paying the price in the end. Have you ever thought about what we are paying?

2. Social injustice and racism are two of the most dynamic experiments that have been undertaken since the formation of this country, and they are showing visible progress, at least outwardly. This is true at a macro level with the abolition of slavery in the Civil War, the end of

official segregation in the South through the civil rights movement, and the election of Barack Obama to the White House—milestones in American history that showcase the success of American exceptionalism. While this is true in broad strokes and also represents an outcome where society is attempting to take the country back to square one. Consider Donald Trump's election and the resurgence of white supremacy and racism as public setbacks. These are big-picture issues at the macro level, but true social justice and racism have almost never disappeared for the country's most marginalized minorities, including African Americans, Native Americans, and in many cases, Latinos. The systemic racism has created inner cities and suburbs where segregation is still visible throughout the country. The fundamental mindset of the country hasn't shifted towards viewing other non-White populations as equal on a human level. This change needs to occur at the level of belief rather than just within political discourse. We must fundamentally believe that all people are born equal, regardless of their ethnicity. The civil discourse has repeatedly tried to instill this belief in the American psyche, with the previously mentioned results. The fundamental change that is needed is not related to how Americans are doing in terms of the economy or world politics but at an "absolute" level on how we define equality that embraces the universality of humanity.

3. There were, and still are, legitimate concerns about men treating women unjustly in society. To solve this, we don't need to redefine men and women within society. We are being treated as if we're guinea pigs in a social lab, subject to constant experimentation. What started as ignoring the biology of the human species and forcing "biological equality" in the name of "social equality" has led us on a convoluted journey towards equality. For example, Iceland has been fighting for women's rights for decades, and on October 23, 1975, had a nationwide strike as part of its fight for equality. After 50 years, in 2023, women in Iceland organized another strike, the "Women's Day

Off," as equality remains elusive in one of the most progressive countries in the world. Gender-based wage gaps and violence are still pervasive. Awareness is a good step towards fighting injustice, but is it achievable solely through reducing the wage gap? I would argue that women should be paid even more than men for equal job responsibilities due to their significant contributions to the sustenance of humanity on this Earth. Even if they were to earn dollar-for-dollar, I would say that's unjust, and it should be two-dollars-for-a-dollar, or even more. We need to approach the problem holistically rather than just as a monetary issue. That was not the original point of this discussion, but it has become more about redefining the very definition of gender. Now, our natural biology is being questioned, and whether I am a man or woman is also under social experiment. A new term has been introduced to sideline natural men and women as "cis man" or "cis woman" to make space for new categorizations of men and women. The institution of marriage has already been experimented with and altered in most states and countries in the West, as if that were not enough.

4. Remember OxyContin, produced by the Purdue family? This "miracle" pain medication has now contributed to a prescription drug epidemic causing over 100,000 deaths each year in this country. Scientists' research aimed at fixing heart diseases has inadvertently triggered obesity and other related chronic diseases (refer to Dr. Robert Lustig of the University of California, San Francisco). Cancer research has become the most profitable industry because almost 9 million people die from cancer worldwide every year, and countless others receive treatment. This area of research and industry is immensely lucrative. Why is all the research focused on finding a cure and not on understanding why we have faced this pandemic for the last 50 years? PFAS, a chemical found in everyday items like paper plates and cups, plastic utensils, and dishwasher detergent, is consumed by us without a second thought. We use plastic for

everything and even microwave it, oblivious to its dangers. Have you noticed the labels on many chemical and plastic products cautioning that they can cause cancer? It's hypocritical when they're labeled with warnings like "known to the State of California to cause cancer." Really? So, is cancer now a disease based on California's geographic coordinates? Do these chemicals have GPS, activating to trigger cancer once they reach California? These industries and regulators are playing a deadly game with us. Another vivid disaster in healthcare is obesity. Research by a pharmaceutical company has led to FDA approval of a medication designed to suppress the urge to eat by altering the brain signals that have been working for millennia in our natural biological bodies. As if that weren't bad enough, they've created this medication to be taken for life – a boon for the company's shareholders if they can convince us to take it, making it a cash cow for the next few decades, much like OxyContin was for the Purdue family. I hope they won't be successful in infiltrating society with this drug, but if they are, the complications could be disastrous for our natural metabolic system. Later in the book, I discuss the metabolic system and how our biology is elegantly designed to maintain the balance between hunger and eating through leptin, so continue reading to understand why this is a big fat scam. A Harvard Medical School researcher proudly compares her medication to "chronic medication to solve chronic problems." If you need to eat vegetables every day to stay healthy, similarly, you would have to take this medication daily to curb your eating urge and maintain weight. She likened it to the vegetables we eat every day. The relentless profiteering economy knows no bounds in profiting from any research. They've lost all restraint, treating us like sheep and goats, and we, content to be their sheep and goats, accept their business model, helping them profit from our ignorance.

5. In the 1970s, there was a significant effort to reduce fat and increase carbohydrate intake to combat cardiovascular disease. However, this

approach, combined with factors such as the indiscriminate use of chemicals, led not only to a worsening of cardiovascular disease but also to the emergence of a range of metabolic dysfunctions and diseases, including Type 2 Diabetes, Hypertension, Dementia, and Cancer.

This list could go on and on. Therefore, the problem cannot be merely addressed on the surface; the root of the problem needs to be understood to devise a cure. In the next chapter, we will delve into the destruction that is visible and imminent to the naked eye.

Chapter II: Deep into the Destruction

It is known that understanding the problem itself constitutes fifty percent of the solution. We have touched upon the problems at a very high level, but it would not be fair to judge the depth of those problems based on a superficial analysis. Therefore, let's take a deeper dive into the problems first. Then, you will appreciate the search for a solution, especially if you genuinely care about preserving this great Western civilization.

Structural Racism

Even after hundreds of years have passed since the era of slavery and legal racism, the country has not been able to eradicate structural and societal racism. The country is divided into black and white neighborhoods. I have driven through the country and seen firsthand how zip codes are often associated with skin color and sometimes wealth. Suburbs are predominantly for whites and wealthy individuals, while cities are where many black and poor people live, although the wealthy reside in the suburbs. Harrisburg, PA; Memphis, TN; South Boston, MA; Detroit, MI; Columbus, OH; Baltimore, MD; St. Louis, MO; Baton Rouge, LA; Chicago, IL—the list goes on. The structural segregation is so prevalent that one must close their eyes to ignore it. I haven't even mentioned the plight of Native Americans: life in the Navajo Nation in Arizona, New Mexico, and Utah states. This represents a dark chapter in America's history of ethnic cleansing that we often gloss over. It may sound like ancient history to many Americans, but during a cross-country road trip in 2021, I saw a billboard announcing the hundred-year anniversary celebration while entering Arizona from New Mexico. This forced me to confront the reality of America's history and its indigenous population, who had lived here for thousands of years. This plight became more vivid as I drove through the Navajo Nation, Indian country. This plight has been recorded and documented by historians, and award-winning documentaries like "We Shall Remain," an American Experience series by the Public Broadcasting

Service (PBS)[4]. are available. Watching it will reveal the reality. Moving on to the focus of this section.

A few years ago, a study conducted in Boston, MA, examined the assets and net worth of different demographics. The median net worth for Black individuals was $8—yes, that's not a typo—it's eight dollars, compared to Whites, who had a median net worth of $247,000. While 80% of White individuals own a home, only 30% of Black individuals own a home.

Incarceration, police harassment, and brutality disproportionately harm the Black demographic. Blacks make up only 13% of the total US population, yet they constitute 38% of the incarcerated population.[5]

If this isn't a structural problem, then I'm sorry, but I have no way to wake you up. The issue with net worth isn't that they don't have wealth; it's that they can't earn wealth. They can't own a home, not because they don't want a home, but because they can't afford one. Do you remember the FHA—the Fair Housing Act? Do you know why it was enacted in the 1960s? It's because the suburbs created post-World War II, following the construction of the Interstate Highway systems, were exclusively for whites, and Blacks were systematically barred from buying houses. There was a legal tool to perpetuate the racial segregation in housing that's called "Restrictive Covenants". Using that legal tool, the sell agreement was constructed to limit the use or ownership of property for decades until the Supreme Court struck down that in 1948 and then the FHA in 1968 explicitly prohibited such discrimination in housing. Here's an excerpt. Below is an excerpt from the list of restrictions in the homeowner's association bylaws for Blue Ridge, one of several neighborhoods in northwest Seattle and Shoreline developed and restricted by airplane industrialist William Boeing.

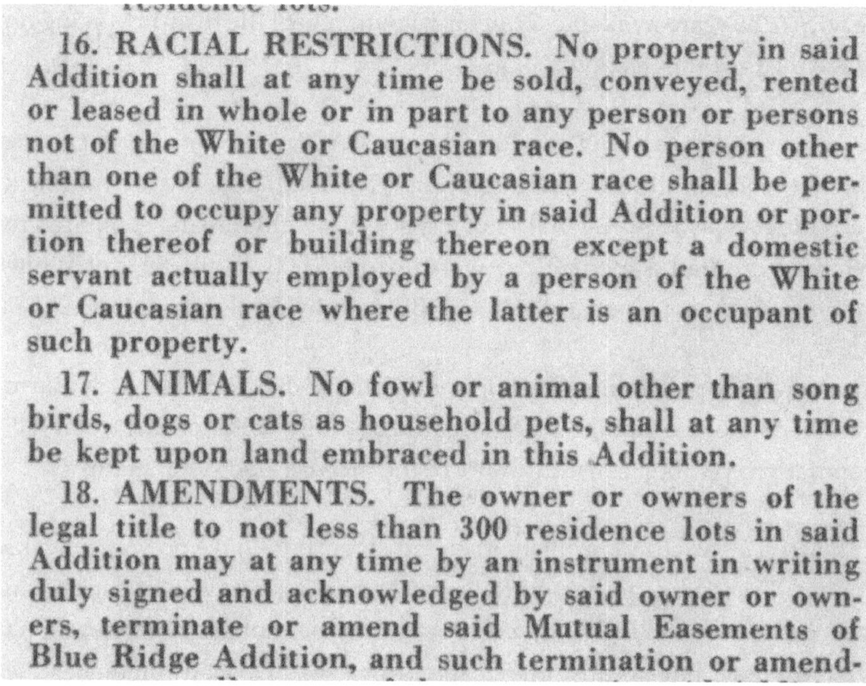

16. RACIAL RESTRICTIONS. No property in said Addition shall at any time be sold, conveyed, rented or leased in whole or in part to any person or persons not of the White or Caucasian race. No person other than one of the White or Caucasian race shall be permitted to occupy any property in said Addition or portion thereof or building thereon except a domestic servant actually employed by a person of the White or Caucasian race where the latter is an occupant of such property.

17. ANIMALS. No fowl or animal other than song birds, dogs or cats as household pets, shall at any time be kept upon land embraced in this Addition.

18. AMENDMENTS. The owner or owners of the legal title to not less than 300 residence lots in said Addition may at any time by an instrument in writing duly signed and acknowledged by said owner or owners, terminate or amend said Mutual Easements of Blue Ridge Addition, and such termination or amend-

Figure 1: List of restrictions in the HOA bylaws for Blue Ridge.[6]

According to HUD's history: "The deaths in Vietnam fell heaviest upon young, poor African-American and Hispanic infantrymen. However, on the home front, these men's families could not purchase or rent homes in certain residential developments because of their race or national origin."[7]

That's just few examples of structural racism. A similar story unfolded with the Farm Bills, where Blacks were systematically deprived of the opportunity to get loans from the government, leading to the loss of many farms they had owned.[8],[9]

“The end of slavery was followed by about 100 years of racial discrimination in the South that limited, although it did not entirely prevent, opportunities for black farmers to acquire land”[10]

Widening wealth gap and income inequality

The statistics showing the continuously widening gap in wealth and income would horrify you if you're interested in thinking a bit more long-term rather than just living for today. What would your answer be if you were asked how many people own 70% of the wealth in the USA? Here, read for yourself:

"By 2021, the top 10% of households by net worth owned 70% of the country's wealth. Between 2007 and 2019, household wealth declined for all but the top 20%, despite a historic period of GDP growth."[11]

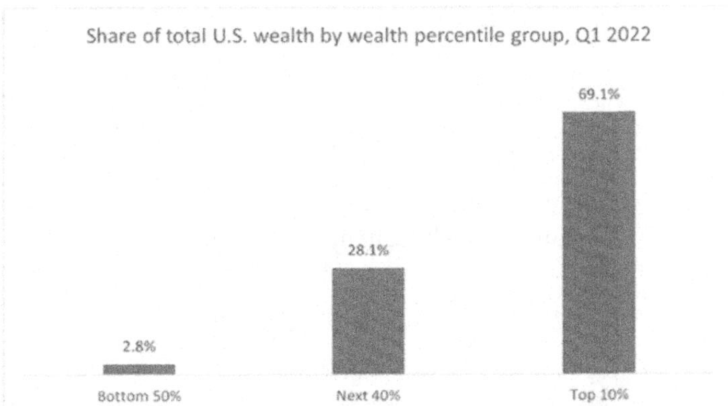

Figure 2: Share of total U.S. wealth by wealth percentile group in 2022

If the bottom 50% of a country's population owns less than 3% of the total wealth in that country, then something is seriously wrong—dead wrong! You might expect such dire statistics in a colonial empire where a small few rules over the majority of subjects. However, the US Constitution grants equal rights to all its citizens. Moreover, the life, liberty, and the pursuit of happiness are enshrined in the Declaration of Independence, which sounds hollow when the majority of the citizens are squeezed to almost nothing.

The percentage is good for academic conversations, but let's translate it into real numbers. The total net worth of the US is $149 trillion, and the population is 330 million in the year 2022. The top 10%, that is, 33 million people, own $104 trillion, and the bottom 50%, or 165 million US citizens, get only $4.4 trillion—almost 20 times less than what the top 10% of the population in the country owns. It's not just unfair; it's unsustainable. This is also reflected in wages. "The gap between the richest and the poorest in the U.S. more than doubled between 1982 and 2016."[12]

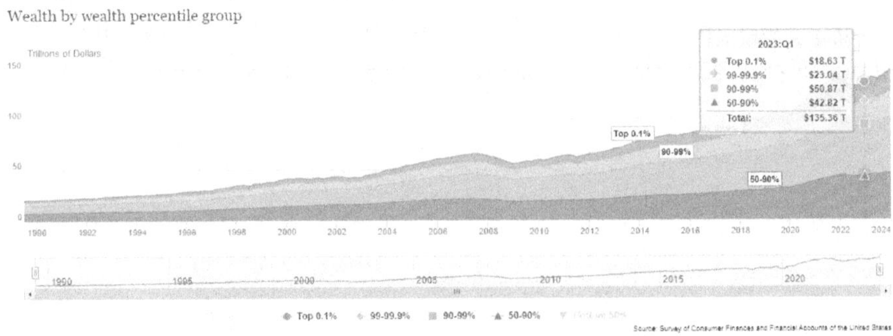

Figure 3: Wealth gap in the USA in 2023

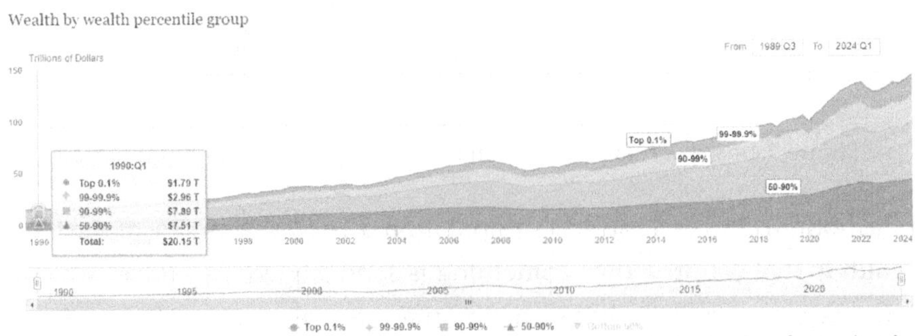

Figure 4: Wealth gap in the USA in 1990

The worst has yet to be said. It's getting worse every year. After a year, in Q1 2023, the top 0.1%, that is, 330,000 people, were holding $18 trillion (12% of total wealth), whereas 165,000,000 people held only $3.44 trillion

(2% of all total wealth). What was that 0.1% of the population owning in 1990, just 33 years ago? They owned $1.8 trillion, and the bottom 50% of the population owned $0.77 trillion. That means the top 0.1% had a little over double the net worth of the bottom 50% in 1990, whereas now it's almost five times more. So, the gap is clearly widening at an alarming rate.

It's only a matter of time before the people who "have not" will become fed up with the few at the top who "have." No civilization or nation (again, not an enslaving or colonizing empire) has ever survived with such a vast widening gap in wealth.

Enough has been said about the facts, but why is this happening? There can't be just one reason; there must be a handful, if not more. I would argue that the root cause is the form of capitalism currently dominating the world. Do you want proof? One simple piece of evidence is to look at the countries that have started embracing capitalism: China, India, Brazil, etc. Their statistics are almost mirroring ours in terms of economy and timeline. It's the same story with the healthcare crisis, where Western food and lifestyle are causing the same chronic diseases in those countries.

Capitalism, in its essence, is a pure economic system. Pure economics examines the production of goods and services through the lens of the demand-supply paradigm. From a pure economics perspective, the Ricardian "Iron Law" of wages suggests that any increase in wages above the subsistence level would lead to population growth, which in turn would increase the labor supply and drive wages back down. Conversely, if wages fall below the subsistence level, the mortality rate among workers would increase, leading to a reduced labor supply and pushing wages back up. This cycle implies that workers' wages naturally gravitate towards the minimum required for survival, thus maintaining a low wage level within the economic system.

On the other hand, a socio-economic system, which Capitalism is not, would investigate the rationale of whether or not a production should be undertaken from a higher moral aim, i.e., to benefit human society as a whole. In essence, Capitalism enshrines these attributes: private ownership over public or State ownership, and profit maximization through upholding an individual's personal interest. However, what we see in the current Capitalistic system, like in the USA, is a mix of Capitalism and Socialism. Public utilities, universal school systems up to high school, infrastructure like roads and bridges, Social Security and Medicare, etc., are a few examples of exceptions. This includes regulations such as anti-monopoly law (Antitrust law) that were implemented within our Capitalistic economy to keep it functioning.

However, don't think that a Marxist economy was even worth considering because this hypothesis has been proven to be an abject failure in the Soviet experiment for eighty years until it collapsed. Just to highlight the flawed nature of the Marxist economic model: it's a government-enforced system based solely on public ownership and denies the intrinsic human desire for private ownership. China, for example, survived by creating a new hybrid economic model that combines Socialist and Capitalist elements. Otherwise, their fate would have been similar to that of the Soviet Union. There must be a more moral socio-economic policy than just an economic policy that doesn't regard people as mere "numbers" in their economic theorems and hypotheses, as well as a system that doesn't deny inherent human nature and dispositions towards love of wealth and family, individual ownership of property and business, and finally, a balance in terms of societal and individual needs.

Drug and Alcohol Crisis

More than 200,000 thousand Americans die from drug overdose and alcohol related deaths.

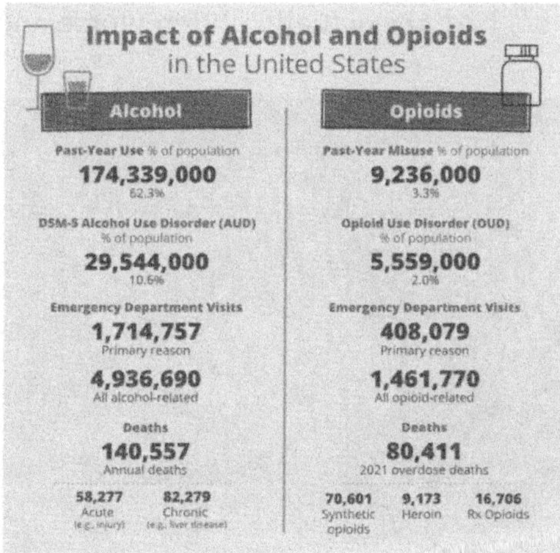

Figure 5: Alcohol related emergencies and deaths in the United States[13]

Alcohol contributes to approximately 18.5% of emergency department visits and 22.1% of overdose deaths related to prescription opioids. Alcohol related diseases were liver diseases (e.g., alcohol-associated liver diseases and unspecified liver cirrhosis), cardiovascular diseases, cancers of various types (e.g., organs of the upper respiratory and digestive tracts, liver, colon, and breast), and alcohol use disorder (AUD). Close to 30 million (29,544,000) people are suffering from AUD out of 174 million (174,339,000) alcohol users i.e. more than 60% population are consumers of alcohols. The Substance Abuse and Mental Health Services Administration (SAMHSA) reports that approximately 7.7 million young Americans aged 12 to 20 reported drinking alcohol in the past month, and 4.9 million reported engaging in binge drinking.[14]

Between 2015 and 2019, it is estimated that more than 140,000 people (approximately 97,000 men and 43,000 women) die from alcohol-related causes annually, making alcohol the fourth-leading preventable cause of death in the United States behind tobacco, poor diet and physical inactivity, and illegal drugs.

If you're thinking it's bad, it's actually gotten worse and worsening year over year.

Figure 6: Number death in the US from excessive alcohol use

"Excessive alcohol use was responsible for about 178,000 deaths in the United States each year during 2020–2021, or 488 deaths per day. This was a 29% increase from 2016–2017, when there were an estimated 138,000 deaths per year."[15]

Let's see the full picture and the impact of it on the American society. The United States is currently facing a severe and multifaceted crisis: the escalating issues of drug and alcohol abuse. This crisis permeates every corner of society, affecting individuals, families, and communities nationwide. Here we delve into the most impactful statistics surrounding the drug and alcohol crisis in the United States, supported by credible sources, shedding light on the gravity of this situation and emphasizing the urgent need for comprehensive solutions.

The opioid epidemic has become one of the most pressing public health crises in the United States. According to the Centers for Disease Control and Prevention (CDC), opioids were involved in over 70% of all drug overdose deaths in 2019. The CDC also reports that approximately 500,000 people died from opioid overdoses between 1999 and 2019.

The drug and alcohol crisis tears families apart. The National Council on Alcoholism and Drug Dependence (NCADD) states that substance abuse is a factor in 40-60% of all cases of domestic violence. Moreover, children in households where substance abuse occurs are at a higher risk of neglect and abuse. The economic impact of drug and alcohol abuse is also staggering. The National Institute on Drug Abuse (NIDA) estimates that the total economic cost of substance abuse in the United States, including healthcare, crime, and lost productivity, exceeds $740 billion annually.

The drug and alcohol crisis in the United States is multifaceted and deeply concerning, affecting millions of lives and costing billions of dollars. It is imperative that comprehensive, evidence-based strategies are implemented to address this crisis, including improving access to treatment, providing education and prevention programs, and reforming drug policies. By understanding the gravity of the situation through these impactful statistics, society can work collectively to mitigate the devastating effects of drug and alcohol abuse, offering support and hope to those struggling and creating a healthier future for all.

Public Health Pandemic: Chronic Diseases and Metabolic syndromes

According to the British Medical Journal (BMJ): "Researchers examined data from 204 countries between 1990 and 2019. They found that there were more than 3.26 million early-onset cancer cases reported in those countries in 2019, up from 1.82 million in 1990, an increase of 79.1%." It has concluded that, "Encouraging a healthy lifestyle could reduce the early-onset cancer disease burden." This warning sign couldn't be more vivid and clearer. Let's begin by examining some interesting facts related to our understanding of lifestyle:

Is the yolk of an egg bad for your heart?

Is all sugary food bad for your health?

If you have a normal weight within the range of normal BMI, do you not need to worry?

Is olive oil always a better choice than all other oils or lard (solid, typically from cow fat), including when used for frying food?

If you're answering "yes" to all the above questions, then you must continue reading this section. The answers to all of the above questions are - no. Surprised? Yes, I was surprised when I first discovered that too. Let's first address the egg question.

Many of you might answer the egg question with, "Egg yolks are good for health when we're young." Some might say, "It depends." And a few of you might assert, "They're bad, and eating them will give you a heart attack." Instead of providing a straightforward answer, let's take a quick tour of the fiasco of the American Heart Association (AHA) regarding egg consumption recommendation. It's akin to something from a thriller movie.

Back in 1968, the AHA issued a grave warning to all Americans: eggs are the enemy of your heart, so if you want to live longer, reduce your egg consumption! They even set a limit on what was considered a safe amount of egg intake, advising us not to consume more than 3-4 eggs per week.[16] Fast forward to 2015, and the AHA made a global announcement that the recommendation, which had lasted for 47 years, was simply discarded. They cleared the warning, and we were all free to add eggs back into our diets without any restrictions. It's almost as if they had a change of heart about eggs (pun intended).

The AHA started to realize its debacle in 2002, but it took another 13 years for them to publicly accept their mistake and announce that there's no need to restrict egg consumption anymore. What changed in eggs that made them not harmful anymore? Did the chickens start laying "healthier" eggs? Or did our hearts become stronger to withstand the dreaded egg attack? Absolutely not! It was the shortsightedness of the AHA that led them to incorrectly label eggs as the enemy.

Now researchers prove without any doubt that eggs bring enormous benefits to our health. It is widely recognized that eggs are a highly nutritious food based on their high-quality protein and complement of vitamins and minerals[17]. Egg protein, especially egg yolk protein, has a significantly greater satiety effect than other protein sources.[18] Eggs provide highly bioavailable forms of the xanthophylls lutein and zeaxanthin which are related to lower risks for age-related macular degeneration and cataracts. Eggs are an excellent source of choline, an essential nutrient which has been shown to be inadequate in the diets of 9 out of 10 adults in the U.S. Choline plays an important role in fetal and neonatal brain development.[19,20]

Let's pause for a moment and consider the collective impact of the American Heart Association's (AHA) erroneous research over the past 47 years. I bring this up because I personally experienced a significant transformation during my 30-pound weight loss journey that I had started in 2020, precisely on February 23rd. I didn't embark on this journey for fun; it was a necessary step to save myself from a health crisis and regain a normal life, steering clear of a downward spiral.

During this weight loss journey, I made a change in my diet by consuming 2-3 whole eggs every day, despite the previous advice from doctors and others to avoid egg yolks due to concerns about hypertension and cardiovascular disease. It's worth noting that I also eliminated all added sugars and limited my carbohydrate intake, mostly deriving them from fruits and vegetables. Do you know how my body reacted to those eggs?

The results of this dietary adjustment were clearly reflected in my lab report done afterward, which even surprised my primary care physician, who asked me, "What did you do to get here?"

It's a personal experiment on eggs and proved myself. Yes, it was a little nerve wracking when I had started but I was checking my blood pressure and did the Lipid profile immediately after going through that journey. Also, this was done after the warning on egg consumption was taken out by AHA. This experience proved the "egg-fiasco" and highlights the importance of critically evaluating health recommendations. While my personal journey saw positive outcomes with regular egg consumption, it's crucial to remember that individual responses to dietary changes may vary. What works for one person might not be suitable for another, and it's essential to consult with healthcare professionals to make informed decisions about our health and dietary choices. The journey taught me to be vigilant about the information we receive and to prioritize evidence-based practices when it comes to our well-being

Is that all? Hell no! This is the history where general mass people were always manipulated by powerful interest groups. The sugar disaster that the society is suffering from is another example of such misinformation. This is actually worse than the "egg fiasco". The Sugar Association secretly paid two professors and the chairman of the Department of Nutrition at the Harvard School of Public Health. This is not a criticism of Harvard itself, but I feel ashamed because it is my alma mater. They published a review paper on the prestigious New England Journal of Medicine and "...downplayed evidence that sucrose consumption was also a risk factor[21]" and "...concluded there was "no doubt" that the only dietary intervention required to prevent Coronary Heart Disease (CHD) was to reduce dietary cholesterol and substitute polyunsaturated fat for saturated fat in the American diet."

"Industry and non-industry funding of the review authors' experimental research was disclosed, but the SRF's funding and participation in the review was not. Evidence reported in the review was relevant to 2 questions: (1) Does the high sucrose content of the American diet cause CHD? and (2) What is the comparative effectiveness of interventions modifying the sucrose or saturated fat content of the diet for the prevention of CHD? The review concluded there was "no doubt" that the only dietary intervention required to prevent CHD was to reduce dietary cholesterol and substitute polyunsaturated fat for saturated fat in the American diet."[22]

Call it dishonesty or ignorance of the top researchers of the top most university in the world, but the world has paid the price for the last half century by increased metabolic dysfunction related diseases, such as, obesity, type 2 diabetes, hypertension, heart diseases, cancer, and dementia. The biggest industry and corporations are behind that. The American Sugar Associations, Coca Cola, McDonalds, and other large corporations placed their thumbs in the scale and directly or indirectly influenced people to continue their profiteering. Remember Coca Cola's campaign "Calorie is a calorie, from wherever it comes from " and McDonald's Happy Meal toys for kids? They let society crumble to continue their profiteering. The horrifying stats of the crumbling society are crying out loud.

Around 124 million out of 330 million Americans are now suffering from these diseases (i.e., obesity, type 2 diabetes, hypertension, heart diseases, cancer, and dementia) known as "Metabolic Syndrome" which will continue to rise.

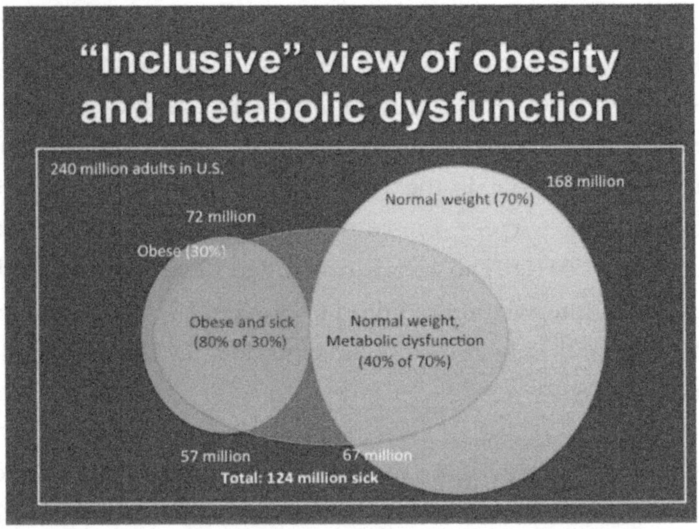

Figure 7: Inclusive view of obesity and metabolic dysfunction[23]

If you take a look at the above carefully, you will find that 80% of obese people are sick with metabolic dysfunction. Surprisingly, 40% of normal weight people are also sick with the same metabolic dysfunction, such as Type 2 diabetes, hypertension, cardiovascular disease, dementia, etc. They are called TOFI - Thin Outside and Fat Inside. This should be the "aha" moment for us, as Dr. Robert Lustig mentioned in his presentations, highlighting how our lifestyle is eating us alive from within. How do you know if a normal weight person is a victim of metabolic syndrome? An indication of metabolic dysfunction in a person with normal weight is fatty liver. Insulin resistance is another diagnosis that can determine if you fall into that category.

Around the world, 537 million people are suffering from diabetes. It's projected that 634 million people will be diabetic in 2030.[24] Here are the nerve-wracking statistics of Hypertension, Coronary Heart Disease, Cancer, Dementia, etc.

- 1.28 billion people around the world are suffering from hypertension.[25]
- 610 thousand deaths in the USA and 19.1 million deaths worldwide. 244 million people are living with CHD.[26, 27]
- 18.1 million people in the world are suffering from cancer.[28]

It's a global pandemic and we are all ignoring it.

The aftermath of this pandemic is causing the health care cost in this country to skyrocket year over year. This is now so unaffordable that even Obama's "Affordable Care Act" couldn't make it affordable for the middle-class population. In 2021, Americans spent $4.3 trillion (18.3% of total GDP) or $12,914 individually on average for health care and yet America is spiraling into a health care disaster with Hypertension, Type 2 Diabetes, Heart Disease, and Cancer.[29]

Let's see what other developed countries are per capita spending on health care? Way above all other developed countries.[30]

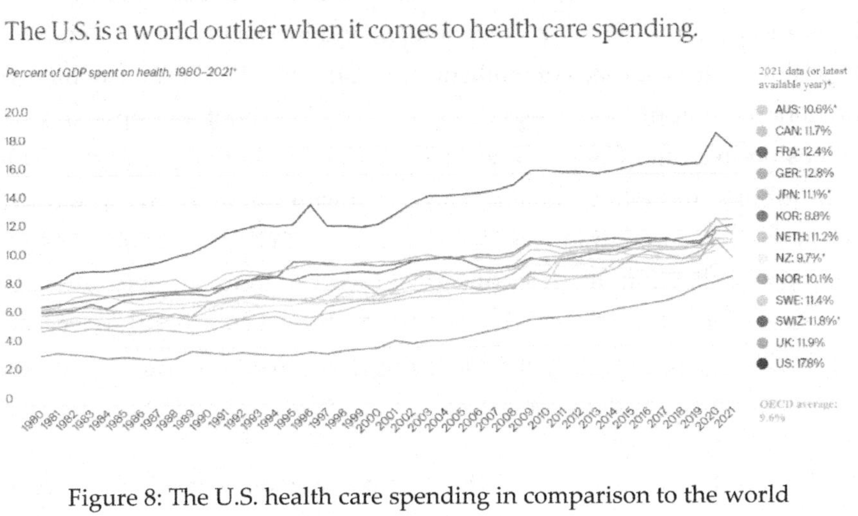

Figure 8: The U.S. health care spending in comparison to the world

And yet, U.S. life expectancy is much lower than other developed countries and in sharp decline.

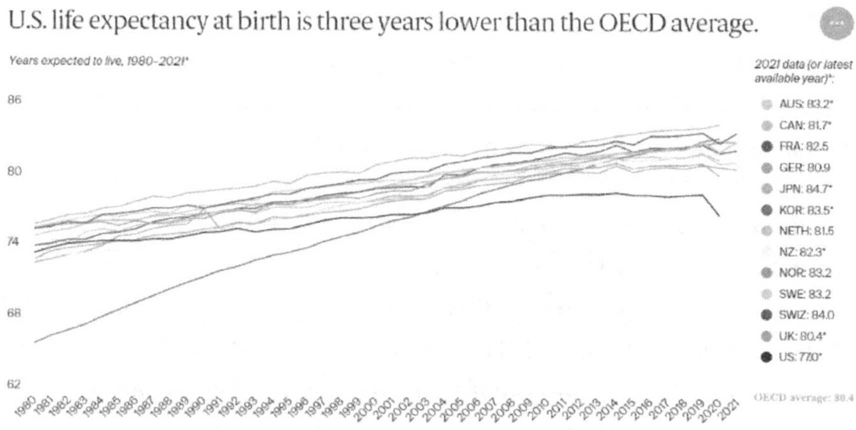

Figure 9: The U.S. life expectancy in comparison to the world

If it continues at this pace and we don't reverse the direction, America and whatever countries are blindly following this diet and lifestyle wouldn't be able to sustain for long. The civilization that brought so much good to the world in terms of science, technology, and medicine (I am leaving the dark side of it, such as, colonialism, transatlantic slave trade, wiping of indigenous population, segregation, etc. for another episode), is collapsing in front of our own eyes, if not for anything else but only due to crumbling and ailing citizens. Never in history a nation with so much sick and weak population was able to maintain their civilization, let alone leading a civilization. If we let this great civilization to crumble, it will be a disservice and a great loss to humanity. We have a choice: either we steer the civilization to the good or let it crumble and wait for another to come in another few hundred years.

Dr. Robert Lustig and others have done a wonderful job to create awareness about this impending disaster (read his book *Metabolical*[31] if you haven't - this is a gem). He has explained very nicely how sugar and processed food affect our health. Yes, he strongly emphasizes the need to create awareness of the sugar disaster and the processed food apocalypse. He said it nicely: it's not just what food you eat but what you do to the food, i.e., how you process it. A quick example is: oranges are full of fructose, but they are good and healthy for us. However, when you process them to make juice, you drastically reduce their nutritional value by removing the fibers (both soluble and insoluble fibers). This causes the liver to process the fructose into VLDL (the worst part of LDL), uric acid, and other harmful substances.

Take a quick tour of the biochemistry of Glucose vs. Fructose metabolism:

- 80% of Glucose is metabolized by the body cells - any cells can metabolize glucose. Only 20% of Glucose is metabolized by the Liver.
- Even that 20% of glucose, most of it can be stored as glycogen which is the storage format.
- If we don't use it immediately, a small portion of that glucose is turned into VLDL i.e., the bad protein which causes clot in the artery and causes heart diseases.
- Insulin is increased in the blood to metabolize the glucose which triggers as we get more food. Two hormones play a vital role: Ghrelin and Leptin. It suppresses Ghrelin so that we don't feel hungry after eating and it releases Leptin to trigger the brain that we got enough food for now and stop eating further.
- 100% of the fructose has to be processed by Liver. No other body parts can process it.

Here're the diagrams that shows in detail the complete metabolism of Glucose and Fructose. If you want to learn from Dr. Robert Lustig, watch it from his presentation.[32]

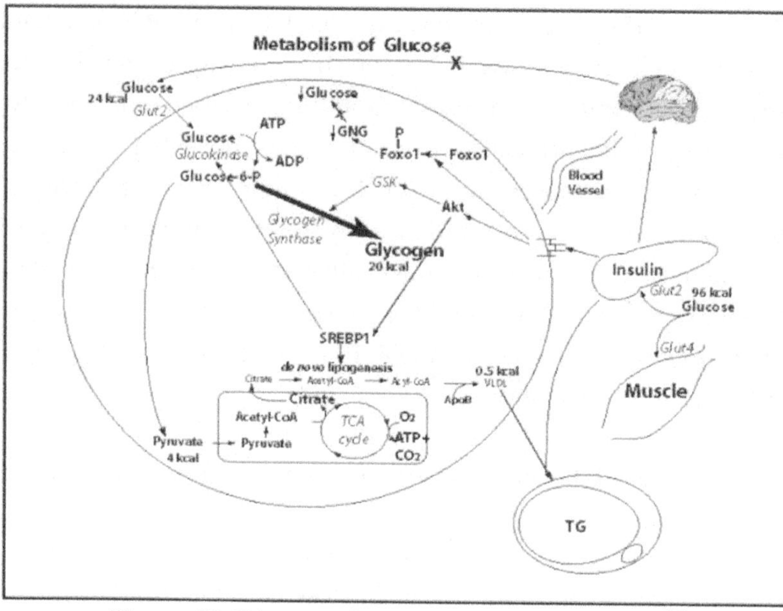

Figure 10: Diagram for Metabolism of Glucose[33]

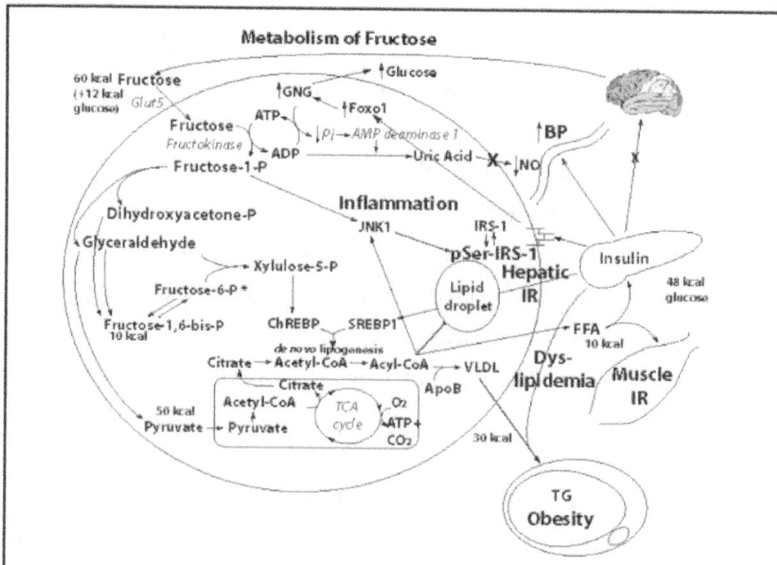

Figure 11: Diagram for Metabolism of Fructose

By the way, we're talking about a regular diet and not for patients who need such fiberless juices. It's just one simple example, but processing applies to almost all our food. The more you process it, the less beneficial and more harmful it becomes. Rice and wheat are real foods and naturally good for us, but the more we refine them, the more harmful they become.

However, I would like to take it further from their warnings of imminent disaster. If you read Dr. Lustig's books and watch his interviews, he is clearly raising much-warranted awareness on added sugar and eating minimally processed, i.e., "real food," which is definitely a big issue and doing so rightly. However, he's missing it again by not focusing on the holistic environment and the Western lifestyle (which is copied by the world as a de facto "modern lifestyle") outside of the food that caused this food style. He briefly touched on one aspect (the profiteering by the food and pharma industry) but didn't go further on it. Maybe he doesn't want to dilute his effort and prefers to concentrate on the single biggest cause to save Americans. I respect his approach. However, if we embark on fixing the lifestyle without even asking why the West ended up with this lifestyle, then we will just chase the shadow and not the true problem. The culprits of this healthcare pandemic will change the direction of the light on the "object," the true problem, and present the problem differently through a new shadow. We will then chase that shadow for another 50 years. We may feel complacent by doing something, but the root cause would not be addressed. What's the root cause? It's not actually one but many causes. The root of the root causes is the mindless materialistic rat race and profiteering without any bounds, where we are taught to stop asking questions but to believe from the authority—in the form of government, corporations, cultural influence, or scientific short-sighted research. Whatever we are told by the "experts" from corporations, TV, newspapers, journals, etc., we take at face value. You have seen the research and publications by the biggest names such as Coca-Cola, Harvard University, and the New England Journal of Medicine, and how that shaped our lifestyle. How can we be certain that we won't encounter a similar situation of partial truth with our current "aha" moment based on the latest findings?

I would like to add a disclaimer before I go further. Modern medicine has brought tremendous good to human society. I consider medicine a blessing. Think about the success of modern medicine:

- Smallpox has been eradicated from the face of the earth.
- Antibiotics are miracle medicines that save millions of lives.
- Modern surgeries are so advanced that people's lives are saved from complicated heart and brain diseases almost every day.
- Maternal and infant mortality rates have drastically reduced.
- Many vaccinations have helped protect children from devastating diseases like polio, tuberculosis, mumps, etc.
- Antiviral drugs are saving lives every day.
- Organ transplants are saving critical lives.
- Life expectancy has steadily risen, except for a few exceptions.

That list can go on. So, I am in no way saying that modern medicine is the culprit, but it's how we started to use it as "the solution" for everything. If I ask, are combustion engines and fossil fuels inherently evil? Of course not. If we didn't have engines to run our trains, cars, and airplanes, then our lives would have remained at the speed of a horse. Is industrial production inherently evil? Of course not! Otherwise, we wouldn't have the basic standards of living that we take for granted. The problem is when we started excessive consumption of every material surrounding us and pushed everything to the brink of collapse. Our air, water, and land are being polluted by excessive consumption. Our use of plastics, chemicals, and clothing is wreaking havoc on the world's natural climates and polluting beyond repair in the short run. While some parts of the world are not only deprived of basic necessities but also suffering the impacts of pollution and climate change due to our excessive consumption. So, we have to think holistically to find the solution.

If you lived through the 1960s to 1980s, you likely remember how sugary soft drinks and fast foods became a part of our daily lives. I have vivid memories of my first taste of a soft drink in the early eighties—it was 7-Up, and I was fascinated by the carbonated water. However, because I couldn't afford to buy it frequently, I used to drink it on special occasions like large gatherings of guests or marriage ceremonies. When I was in 6th grade, my father started a side business of a convenience store. Coca-Cola was sold in that store. I used to get a "token" from my mother, and when I showed that, I got one Coca-Cola—maybe once a week.

How about sugary food? Yes, we used to have sugary food cooked at home and sometimes bought snacks from the store. It was not a problem at all in my childhood because those sugary foods were sporadically consumed, and almost everything else was home-cooked "real food"—fish from the nearby ponds, fresh vegetables, and fresh foods—because we didn't have refrigerators, so we had to do daily shopping for fresh foods. Things started to go in the wrong direction when we started to get fast food often—a few times a week. The metabolic syndrome started slowly. The older we grow, the weaker the metabolism becomes, and the "ultra-processed food" lifestyle ruins the whole metabolism. Inevitably, I started to see the metabolic syndromes.

I am not going into much detail, but I had no option but to take drastic measures. I kept searching for the root cause of the problems since 2010 but couldn't pinpoint the root cause. Like many of you, I embarked on a two-pronged plan: eat less and exercise more. I would eat less for a month and exercise for a few months and then lapse into old habits. I wasn't able to identify why I couldn't continue to eat less or feel energetic enough to get up for exercise every day to burn off my extra body fat. I always felt hungry, so I ended up eating snacks (mostly ultra-processed and sugary) between my regular meals. I talked to my doctors, read many articles, but couldn't solve the problem for good. Among other things, the most beneficial was a month of daily fasting during Ramadan when I usually lose 10 pounds, but immediately after that, I gained the weight back. So, it was a see-saw of losing and gaining fat.

Through that journey, I intuitively realized that food was one of the key causes of my overweight and metabolic syndromes, but I didn't know that ultra-processed, low-fiber, and high-sugar foods were the primary causes of my inability to maintain a sustainable state. Other issues like a stressful life and bad sleep habits were also present. Long story short, in 2020, I came across Dr. Jahangir Kabir, who had extensive educational resources on a healthy lifestyle. That was accidental. I had heard about him for years, but as soon as I heard he advocated Keto as part of a lifestyle change, I didn't feel comfortable. My reasoning was very simple: we grew up on a diet where carbs were the key ingredient. We were never overweight and never sick with such metabolic syndromes. As a matter of fact, I was never sick during my entire childhood. It's not just me; people around me were also all "normal" at that time. If carbs are bad, then why didn't we have all this overweight, obesity, type 2 diabetes, high blood pressure, obstructive sleep apnea, cancer, dementia, etc.? So, a carb diet alone can't be the cause.

Long story short, my elder sister called me on a Saturday morning, and she almost begged me to try the approach from that doctor. With no other solution in my hand, I decided to give it a shot. I started learning extensively from his educational videos, and I read other resources. Officially, I started the journey on February 23rd, and in 8 weeks, I was able to lose 30 pounds. I did 5 weeks of Keto and then stopped. I still believe Keto isn't the solution, but it is like getting into the ICU to recover as I had messed up my health. I methodically recorded and put the details on a blog (and live on Facebook) in June 2020. Anyway, a lot has been said about my personal story. Let's get back to the point: what we collectively can do to live a healthy life.

To do this, we must look back at least 50 years. If you have the means to travel the world, you can still find answers today in parts of the world that haven't been "modernized" through the Western lifestyle. Yes, I'm referring to the so-called "backward" countries. The COVID-19 pandemic served as a vivid and costly laboratory experiment for two years, exposing the underlying health conditions of nations that adopted the Western lifestyle. This was captured on July 22, 2023, from Worldometer.com.[34]

All Europe North America Asia South Ame

#	Country, Other	Total Cases	New Cases	Total Deaths
	World	691,795,048	+442	6,901,825
1	USA	107,435,531		1,169,144
2	India	44,995,055		531,915
3	France	40,138,560		167,642
4	Germany	38,428,685		174,352
5	Brazil	37,704,598		704,488
6	Japan	33,803,572		74,694
7	S. Korea	32,611,509		35,159
8	Italy	25,908,353		190,987
9	UK	24,641,596		228,144
10	Russia	22,971,107		399,772
11	Turkey	17,232,066		102,174
12	Spain	13,914,811		121,760

#	Country, Other	Total Cases	New Cases	Total Deaths
82	Guinea	38,563		468
83	Barbados	109,276		612
84	French Polynesia	78,615		649
85	Papua New Guinea	46,864		670
86	Belize	70,782		688
87	Qatar	514,524		690
88	Lesotho	34,790		723
89	Mali	33,151		743
90	Laos	218,700	+5	758
91	Ivory Coast	88,338		835
92	Bahamas	38,084		844
93	Tanzania	43,078		846
94	Malta	119,225		848
95	Haiti	34,306		860

Figure 12: COVID-19 Cases and Deaths - Top and Bottom 10

Mental health epidemic

How bad is the mental health of the American population? The numbers paint a grim picture of the current situation: in 2021, 57.8 million adults were experiencing some form of mental disorder, i.e., 22.8% of all US adults, out of which only 26.5 million received mental health treatment. Furthermore, 14.1 million adults (5.5% of all US adults) were diagnosed with serious mental illness, i.e., they are substantially impaired and unable to live a normal life without medication.

In 2023, "The percentage of U.S. adults who report having been diagnosed with depression at some point in their lifetime reached 29.0%, nearly 10 percentage points higher than in 2015. The percentage of Americans who currently have or are being treated for depression has also increased to 17.8%, up about seven points over the same period. Both rates are the highest recorded by Gallup since it began measuring depression using the current form of data collection in 2015."[35]

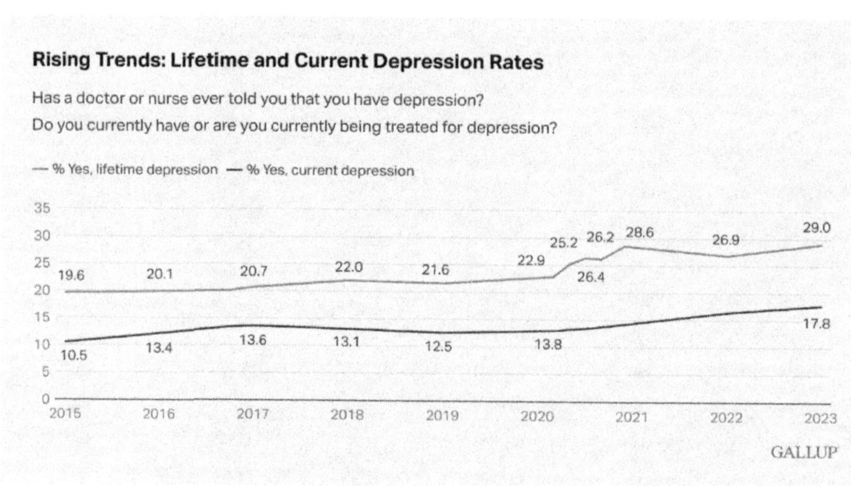

Figure 13: Rising Trends of Depression Rates in the USA

"From year 2005–2050, the total number of US adults with depressive disorder will increase from 33.9 million to 45.8 million, a 35% increase"[36]

Last year (in 2022), more than 49,000 Americans killed themselves, marking the highest number in history. This number is staggering, and it has not even plateaued but continues to rise. Since 2000, the suicide rates in the country have gone up by more than 36%. Suicide is now among the top 10 causes of death in America. "Although there is no single cause of suicide, the Centers for Disease Control and Prevention, using data from the National Violent Death Reporting System, estimates that 46% of people who die by suicide had a known mental health condition. However, this statistic is likely an undercount because of the inherent limitations of the database, which does not account for undiagnosed or untreated mental illness. In fact, other research shows much higher numbers."[37]

Depleted family values and loss of family bonds

"About 40% to 50% of married couples in the United States divorce, according to the American Psychological Association. The divorce rate among those who remarry is even higher."[38]

Do you think there are no consequences? You see the effects all around you every day and read about the aftermath. What consequences are we observing in the society?

- The family is the fundamental unit of society. Some may argue that a functional society can exist without the family structure. While theoretically, anything can be built from anything, let's be realistic. Consider a society where even two men and women cannot coexist with their children under a formal structure; how can we then expect such a society to function on a larger scale? The family demonstrates how we create a structure within our home, which we then extend into the wider world. Human society has operated this way since the dawn of civilization. Thus, the notion that we could survive without the family structure is unrealistic. To understand this, consider the following analogy: most atoms form molecules, which make up everything around us. Atoms, with few exceptions, are more stable as molecules. Similarly, if individuals are atoms, then men and women bond into a family, enjoying natural stability.

- Divorce as a process in itself isn't forbidden or bad. Without this exit-procedure, a perpetual suffering between a misfit-marriage, for whatever reasons that may be, would do more harm than benefit of marriage. However, divorce is the most traumatic and costly event in life (after death) that most of man or women would through regardless of their social circumstances. This becomes more traumatic and unrecoverable loss when it comes to a family with children. And the highest price is paid by the kids who go through that trauma and unrest before, during and after the divorce takes place. Ask any man or woman who went through the divorce, and the high majority of them will tell you that it was the most difficult time in their life. Here's what this NIH paper has concluded about the negative consequence about divorce: "There are clearly negative long-term consequences of divorce—children, parents, and society all suffer. Wallerstein's long-term study shows that many children never have full "recovery" as each special event, holiday, or celebration reminds the child of his/her loss."[39] So, less the number of divorces a society goes through lower the price it pays and stronger the social fabric remains.
- The collapse of traditional values such as marriage and family, inevitably impacts the birth rate. A 2.1% fertility rate is considered the replacement level for a nation's population; below this threshold, a nation will naturally begin to decline. Currently, the USA's fertility rate is hovering at 1.64%, which is significantly below the replacement level. It's worth noting that this rate is buoyed by immigrant families who typically have higher birth rates and contribute to the population statistics in the United States.
- Another consequence mentioned earlier is the epidemic of mental health issues. Not surprisingly, since society operates as a system with

intertwined causes and effects. Forty-four million adults in the U.S., or 17% of the population, have experienced some form of loneliness in their life.[40] The US Surgeon General's office refers to this loneliness as a lack of "Social Connection," which encompasses the number, variety, and quality of interactions necessary for humans as social beings. Loneliness has been equated to the health risks of smoking 15 cigarettes a day. The office has also issued a dire warning about the devastating physical consequences of poor social connections, including a 29% increased risk of heart disease, a 32% increased risk of stroke, and a 50% increased risk of developing dementia for older adults.[41] Loneliness is not solely caused by the absence of family; there are other factors, but it is not difficult to understand that individuals living alone are more prone to loneliness. In fact, the root word of "loneliness" is "lone," which implies being alone or solitary. Remaining alone without feeling lonely often requires a range of "gymnastic" activities that not everyone is capable of managing.

As mentioned above, the health of a society is a complex function of the well-being of all its individuals. When the foundational building block of society—the family—is weakened, the very structure of civilization is inevitably compromised. Therefore, it is imperative to preserve this civilization by protecting the family structure before it is too late.

Long Injustice to the Black and Poor

The United States of America was founded on the principle that "all men are created equal," with the intention of enshrining freedom and equality. However, it bears the heavy burden of a history marred by prolonged injustices toward its Indigenous peoples, Africans, and other non-European ethnicities. The systematic injustice against the Indigenous population was so severe that their numbers have dwindled to around 1%, approximately 3 to 5 million people. The largest recipient of systemic injustice has been African Americans, who were forcibly brought to the USA through the trans-Atlantic slave trade, primarily to sustain the plantation economy. Although slavery was abolished following the American Civil War, segregation persisted in the South for nearly another century. The echoes of these dark chapters in American history continue to reverberate, shaping the experiences and opportunities of Black and impoverished individuals. Sometimes, we are reluctant to confront the horrific nature of the history of slavery in this country. To highlight the gravity of the issue, consider the states of the slaves: "All slave codes made slavery a permanent condition, inherited through the mother, and defined slaves as property, often in the same terms as those applied to real estate. Being property, slaves could neither own property nor be party to a contract. Since marriage is a form of contract, no slave marriage had any legal standing. All codes also had sections regulating free blacks, who were still subject to controls on their movements and employment and were often required to leave the state after emancipation."[42] This should be sufficient to understand what slavery did to the African-Americans and its lingering effects of injustice that are still prevalent in American society till today. However, it would not do justice if I were to leave you to ponder this without first going back a few hundred years to understand the historical context that triggered and perpetuated this inequality and injustice into the present time. So, let's take a walkthrough of the slavery and its effect to the society.

The Trans-Atlantic Slave Trade: lasting from the 16th to the 19th century, forcibly transported millions of Africans to the Americas. Stripped of their freedom and dignity, enslaved individuals endured unimaginable hardships on plantations, contributing significantly to the economic prosperity of the Southern states. The legacy of this barbaric trade lives on, as the descendants of those enslaved continue to grapple with the social and economic ramifications of their ancestors' suffering.

Plantation Economy and Slavery: The plantation economy, driven by slave labor, significantly contributed to the economic prosperity of the Southern states. However, this wealth came at an immense human cost. I don't need to mention it that enslavement in the plantation stripped off the most basic human rights, ironically enshrined into the declaration of independence of this country, "Life, liberty and the pursuit of happiness". Slaves were denied education, family stability, and the opportunity to own property and wealth, perpetuating a cycle of poverty that persisted long after the abolition of slavery. The lack of access to resources and education left generations of Black and poor individuals disadvantaged, hindering their ability to break free from the chains of poverty.

Institutionalized Discrimination through Segregation: Following the abolition of slavery, the enactment of segregation laws, commonly known as Jim Crow laws, institutionalized discrimination against Black Americans. These laws enforced racial segregation in public facilities, education, housing, and employment, further marginalizing Black communities. The impact of segregation was profound, creating separate and unequal societies that persistently denied opportunities and resources to Black individuals.

The segregation ended in 1964 however, the unfair systemic practices in the housing sector continued till 1968. The suburbs across America were rapidly expanding since 1950s but the Federal Housing Administration (FHA) had policies till 1968 that reinforced racial segregation. This practice, known as redlining, where minority neighborhoods were marked in red on maps, indicating areas considered too risky for loans, involved the denial of loans or insurance to people in specific geographic areas based on their racial composition. Minority communities, especially African Americans, were often redlined, leading to limited housing opportunities, and reinforcing racial disparities.

Additionally, developers and real estate agents employed tactics such as blockbusting and steering to maintain segregation. Blockbusting involved persuading white homeowners to sell their properties at low prices, claiming that minorities moving into the neighborhood would decrease property values. Steering involved guiding minority homebuyers towards specific neighborhoods while discouraging them from considering predominantly white areas, further perpetuating segregation.

These unfair practices created lasting divides in housing opportunities and wealth accumulation. The FHA Act, while instrumental in expanding homeownership, was tainted by discriminatory policies and practices, which have had enduring consequences on American society. That practice continued openly until the passing of the Title VIII of the Civil Rights Act aka, the Fair Housing Act (FHA) that stands as a landmark legislation in the United States aimed at combating housing discrimination. The Act provided legal protections, ensuring that everyone had equal access to housing opportunities. It was a significant step toward dismantling the deeply entrenched racial segregation that persisted in American communities.

Not so distant past, the "war on drug", the government-led initiative that aims to stop illegal drug use, distribution, and trade by increasing and enforcing penalties for offenders. It was a "zero tolerance" era on not only drug dealer but even a small amount of marijuana consumption was considered a criminal act that carried minimum incarceration. That had started in 19th century and has continued for decades with various strategies and levels of intensity. Just a few years ago, in most states, possession of marijuana started to become legal, even though it is still a crime at the federal level. This seemed like a step towards a more logical approach to treat it as an addiction rather than a criminal act, except that it had already devastated Black communities across the country. You may argue that treating marijuana as a crime was necessary due to its pervasive nature, but then consider what is happening now with the opioid pandemic. The opioid crisis has been declared a social crisis in America, and instead of treating it as a crime, billions of dollars are being invested to combat this social problem, which is the right approach. Why the discriminatory treatment of these two drugs? I will leave it up to you to guess why marijuana and the opioid pandemic are treated differently. In the meantime, the black Americans are disproportionately impacted due to the drugs and the harsher drug laws, dubbed as "war on drug". Harsher treatments of Black population created higher incarceration rate, broken family structure, and huge crisis in public health. Despite similar rates of drug use and sales as other racial groups, Black people have been significantly more likely to be arrested and receive harsher sentences. This has contributed to the United States having one of the highest incarceration rates in the world, with a large percentage being Black Americans. Which had significant effects on the family structure within Black communities where many families are left without a parent or primary breadwinner, contributing to higher rates of poverty and single-parent households. Not only that, the stigma of a criminal record can make finding employment difficult, and the loss of voting rights for felons can reduce political representation. These factors combine to hinder economic and social mobility. Finally, the diversion of resources towards enforcement and incarceration rather than education and community development has also had a long-term impact on opportunities for younger generations in these communities.

Pollution and Climate change

In recent decades, we have been experiencing unprecedented pollution and environmental crises due to our excessive consumption and pursuit of "economic development." We are burning all the fossil fuels we can extract, not only from underground but also deep beneath the Earth's shale, known as "shale oil & gas", using hydraulic fracking technique. We are destroying forests, natural animal habitats, and water bodies such as wetlands, rivers, lakes, and oceans. Among the worst impacts is the release of toxic chemicals. Additionally, the climate is changing rapidly. While Earth's climate has always undergone changes over thousands and millions of years, the rate of these changes has become either more severe or more catastrophic due to our pervasive impact on every corner of the Earth. Climate change is also having significant effects. These interconnected issues are wreaking havoc on Earth's ecosystems, weather patterns, and human societies. Here are few aspects to this crisis:

Global Temperature Rise: According to NASA and the National Oceanic and Atmospheric Administration (NOAA), the Earth's average temperature has risen approximately 1.18°C (2.12°F) since the late 19th century.[43] This warming trend is accelerating, with the past few decades being the warmest on record.

Melting Ice and Rising Sea Levels: The polar ice caps are melting at an alarming rate. "The last 17 years, from 2007 to 2023, are the lowest 17 sea ice extents in the satellite record."[44] The Intergovernmental Panel on Climate Change (IPCC) predicts that global sea levels could rise by up to 1.1 meters (3.6 feet) by 2100, displacing millions of people.[45]

Extreme Weather Events: The frequency and intensity of extreme weather events, including hurricanes, heatwaves, droughts, and wildfires, have surged. The World Meteorological Organization (WMO) reported a significant increase in the occurrence of extreme weather events globally, attributing these changes to climate change.

Air Pollution: Air pollution, primarily driven by emissions from vehicles, industrial processes, and deforestation, leads to approximately 7 million premature deaths worldwide each year, as per the World Health Organization (WHO).[46] Particulate matter (PM2.5) and ground-level ozone are major contributors to respiratory diseases and cardiovascular problems. Cities in the developing countries are seeing it firsthand but American cities aren't immune either.

Plastic Pollution: The world produces over 300 million tons of plastic annually, and a significant portion ends up in our oceans. According to the Ocean Conservancy, there are about 150 million tons of plastic circulating in marine environments, endangering marine life and entering the human food chain.

Water Pollution: Water pollution, caused by industrial runoff, agricultural pesticides, and untreated sewage, affects both marine and freshwater ecosystems. The United Nations Environment Programme (UNEP) states that over 80% of the world's wastewater is released back into the environment without adequate treatment, contaminating water sources and aquatic life.[47]

Loss of Biodiversity & Human Health Crisis: Climate change and pollution have contributed to a devastating loss of biodiversity. The World Wildlife Fund (WWF) estimates that the Earth is currently experiencing a mass extinction event, with species disappearing at a rate 1,000 to 10,000 times higher than the natural extinction rate.[48] Pollution and climate change have severe implications for human health. The Lancet Countdown on Health and Climate Change reported that climate change is already harming people's health by increasing the frequency and intensity of heatwaves, exacerbating air pollution, and spreading diseases such as malaria and dengue fever.

The statistics and facts presented here are not mere numbers; they represent the suffering of our planet and its inhabitants. Urgent and comprehensive action is essential to mitigate climate change and curb pollution. Governments, industries, and individuals must collaborate to transition to renewable energy sources, implement stringent pollution control measures, and promote sustainable practices.

Excessive materialism and waste of resources

The excessiveness of our consumption is causing anxiety in our lives and creating significant pollution on Earth. The development of countries has become synonymous with excessive consumption, a concept deeply ingrained in capitalism. For example, in the USA—and similar stories can be found in many other countries—excessive consumption is evident everywhere. Examples include the massive solar thermal power plant in California's Mojave Desert, which has destroyed miles of desert ecosystem; the leveling of mountains in Utah for mineral extraction; and the extensive farms in Oklahoma and Kansas. Moreover, we consume more food than necessary, discarding 40% of it. [49] We build large houses for a few people, which occupy more land, require more building materials, and consume more energy. While scientists and environmentalists advocate for reducing our carbon footprint to save the Earth, we should also focus on curbing our excessive consumption and waste. By reducing our consumption, we would decrease production, thereby creating less pollution, fewer toxic products (such as plastics and chemicals), and less overall waste. Driven by greed and consumption, our actions are wreaking havoc on the Earth. Then comes the rat race to create the ability for unlimited consumption. Many of us may not even realize that we are living lives where our success is defined by our profession, job title, income, the size of our house, the car we drive, or the achievements of our children following in our footsteps. Essentially, it boils down to what social status we hold in comparison to others.

Success in our lives is defined by someone else, and we race to achieve it without questioning their background or motives. Someone else dictates how we should live, and we immediately start conforming to that lifestyle. We are told to work like slaves during the week and wait for the weekend to recharge, to go on vacation a few times a year to escape the nightmare we create for ourselves, to enjoy each summer repeatedly as if stuck in an endless loop. We are supposed to earn a fortune working for 67 years before retiring, leaving little of our youth for doing anything meaningful or fulfilling the purpose of our lives. We think material possessions will bring us happiness, until we discover they do not. It's like being thirsty and only being given salty water to drink; it only makes you thirstier until you collapse emotionally, psychologically, or physically.

Why don't these "happiness-inducing" materials bring us tranquility? Because we weren't created for that. As soon as we reach one height of success, we see the next one to conquer, and then the next. But to what end? As soon as you start to question this, you find no answer. This materialistic system doesn't even want you to ask that question—it keeps you perpetually busy, with no time alone to reflect, lest you fully realize the truth. Once you understand that you will leave all your worldly success behind, whether in 40, 60, or 80 years, in comparison to the eternity of life, you realize that you are merely collecting the things that others have left behind in this world. Then what? This realization can make you anxious about what you are truly striving for. Some of us can't bear it any longer and declare that there is no life after death, simply wishing it would all end. They then question why they are racing for material success and begin to seek new, innovative thoughts. The rest of us, who aren't rash enough to declare such nonsense, become frightened as we realize we aren't gathering anything for the journey ahead, and we start hopelessly hoping for nothing.

Then, we start taking drugs to continue living for material things: some of us consume alcohol to forget reality; some of us take psychiatric drugs to ward off stress and depression; some rely on medication for blood pressure or cholesterol to keep our bodies running in the rat race; some resort to 'vacation pills' every season, every month, or every weekend to escape the madness; some take the "materialistic success" drug to show off to others that they are doing better than everyone else around them. In one way or another, all of us are on some kind of drug.

Here are few alarming statistics:

- "In the United States, food waste is estimated at between 30-40 percent of the food supply. This estimate, based on estimates from USDA's Economic Research Service of 31 percent food loss at the retail and consumer levels, corresponded to approximately 133 billion pounds and $161 billion worth of food in 2010."

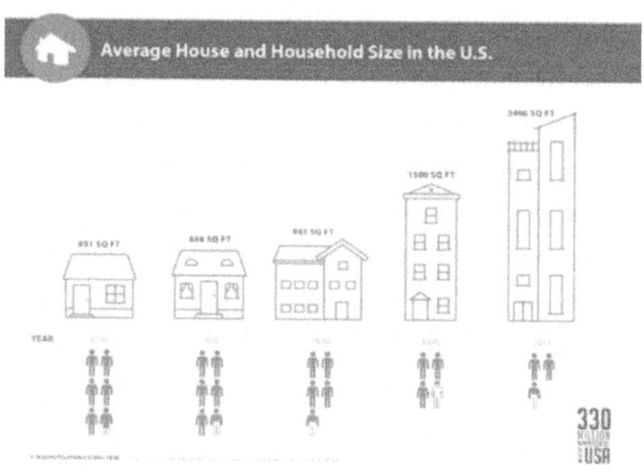

Figure 14: Average House and Household Size in the U.S.

- "The average size of houses in the United States has increased from 831 square feet in 1790, to 945 square feet in 1910, to 2,496 square feet in 2019. Over the same time range, the number of people living within each house as decreased. The average number of people per house in 1790 was nearly six, but by 2019 the average number of people per house had dropped to less than 2.5." [50]
- This excessive consumption goes on in all other areas proportionate to the size of the house. The size of the house is an indicator that is like the thermometer of our excessiveness in consumption. Think for a moment how it impacts our lifestyle, if it's not obvious already to you. We heat up or cool down the 2400 square foot space for just 2-3 family members. Materials used for the additional space requires more production in the factory or more cut in trees. We pay more mortgage and more insurance every month and need to earn that money – often sacrificing the own family. The maintenance of the interior and exterior of the house cost is proportionate to the size of the house keep us busy chasing for more material.

Gun violence and mass killing

The first time I encountered the issue of gun violence and mass killings was in 2007 when the Virginia Tech shooting unfolded before my eyes. I was watching the news live on CNN. At that time, I didn't have a deep understanding of the complex political and sociological dynamics involved. I found myself wondering what could trigger a student to indiscriminately shoot at fellow students and kill 22 of them. My innocent mind was searching for a motive, but I couldn't fathom it—how could that person be offended by random students to the point of going on a mass killing spree? I didn't know much about the Columbine school shooting at the time, so it intrigued me to learn more about the issue. However, life pulled me into the materialistic rat race, and I forgot about it until the Sandy Hook Elementary School shooting in 2012. That incident was shocking. Those were little kids. How could a grown man go to an elementary school and shoot children? Adam Lanza killed 21 little kids and their teacher. That event shook me to the core. My two children were in elementary school at the time, and I could feel the anguish of the parents who lost their children.

Let's see the statistics of mass shooting and school shootings.

- After the Sandy Hook school shooting, there are 239 more school shooting till 2018 – in just 6 years. Total 438 were shot out of that 138 were shot dead.[51]
- Since 1970, 2057 school shooting incidents occurred, 680 were fatally shot and 1,926 were injured.[52]
- Gun violence is in the steady rise. Last year, 48,830 Americans died in gun shot. Out of that more than 26 thousand were suicidal case. [53]

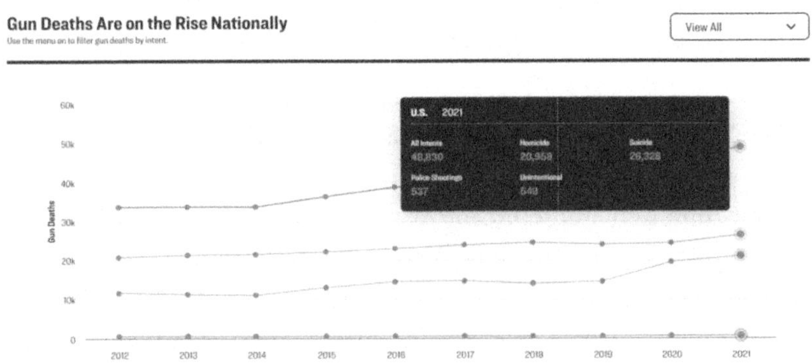

Figure 15: Gun Deaths trend in the USA

The left and liberals blame the unrestricted access to guns by mentally ill individuals and demand stricter gun control laws. In contrast, the right and conservatives argue that the lack of guns in the hands of every citizen is the problem and call for more guns in the country. Who is right? Left, or right? That debate continues, and mass shootings still wreak havoc in this country. My question to both groups is: have you asked these basic questions?

- Adam Lanza used an AR-15 rifle to kill 21 innocent, angelic children. This semi-automatic rifle has been the weapon of choice for countless mass shooters. There is no doubt that the AR-15 is a favored weapon among mass shooters. When was the AR-15 first marketed? It was in 1959. Why did it take more than 50 years for this gun to be used in widespread killing sprees? Last year, a shooter in Tennessee used an AK-47 assault rifle to kill elementary school children. When was the AK-47 manufactured? It was in 1947. Why wasn't this assault rifle used in mass school shootings until recently? What has changed?
- The U.S. Constitution has recognized gun rights since its inception in 1776. How many mass shootings in American schools were recorded until 1999? None! Why is that? What caused Americans to engage in school shooting sprees? If gun laws are the problem, then why weren't these issues evident from 1947 and 1959 when the AK-47 and AR-15 rifles were made available to the American public?

It's akin to "not asking" an obvious question about cancer. Currently, up to 10 million people are dying from cancer each year. It's one of the leading causes of death worldwide. How many people were dying from cancer in the 1950s? It wouldn't have even been close to the top 10 causes of death. What caused the epidemic of cancer? If you don't ask the right questions, how can you expect to find the right answers? The issue likely resides not just with the guns themselves but with the people behind them. The answer lies in lifestyles, the same root causes that are contributing to the potential collapse of American civilization: health epidemics, mental health crises, the materialistic rat race, lack of purpose in life, depleted family values, and the breakdown of social structures, among others.

Pornography

In recent years, the proliferation of pornography in the United States has reached unprecedented levels, thanks to the internet and technological advancements. While pornography has always been a part of human culture, the digital age has given it new dimensions and raised concerns about its negative impact on individuals and society as a whole. It's just like sugar disaster: you don't need to go for sugar but added sugar comes to you in every food you buy, be it milk, juice, bread, ketchup…you name it. Similarly, now pornography or like that doesn't need to be sought but it comes to you with anything – you open any web page or YouTube or Internet gaming sites – you get baits or even a sample of it. It's a pandemic that the materialistic society has learned to ignore, or I would say deceitfully believed that we can ignore it. I don't want to go any details to it as that only add the spreading of it so I would like to mention some of the facts and its affect to this society. By the way, this problem isn't the problem of USA but almost everywhere in the world.

Let's check out the alarming statistics and consequences of the pornography industry in the USA.

The pornography industry in the United States is a multi-billion-dollar behemoth, overshadowing the revenues of even some mainstream entertainment sectors. According to a 2020 report of one of the world's largest adult content websites, they received a staggering 42 billion visits throughout the year, averaging over 115 million visits per day. This not only underscores the ubiquity of pornography but also highlights its immense influence on the digital landscape.

One of the most significant concerns surrounding pornography is its impact on personal relationships. A study published in the Journal of Sex Research found that high pornography consumption is associated with decreased sexual satisfaction among couples.[54] The unrealistic and often degrading depictions of sexual encounters can create unrealistic expectations, leading to dissatisfaction and conflict in real-world relationships. Pornography has been cited as a contributing factor in numerous divorces and breakups, further emphasizing the corrosive effects it can have on personal connections.

The addictive nature of pornography is another aspect of concern. A survey conducted by the American Psychological Association (APA) in 2016 reported that an estimated 8-9% of adults in the United States struggle with compulsive sexual behavior, which often involves excessive pornography consumption. The ease of access to an ever-expanding array of explicit content online can contribute to the development of addiction, leading to detrimental consequences for individuals and families.

Perhaps one of the most alarming statistics pertains to the exposure of children to pornography. According to a report by the National Center for Missing and Exploited Children, 42% of unwanted online pornography exposure cases in 2019 involved minors.[55] Exposure to explicit content at a young age can have profound and lasting effects on a child's emotional and psychological development, distorting their understanding of healthy relationships and sexuality.

The pornography industry has been widely criticized for its connections to sex trafficking. While it's important to clarify that not all pornography is linked to trafficking, there is evidence to suggest that some individuals in the industry are coerced or exploited. The dark side of the industry fuels an underground market where vulnerable individuals are at risk, creating a troubling cycle of abuse and exploitation.[56]

Numerous studies have indicated a strong link between pornography consumption and negative mental health outcomes. Excessive exposure to explicit content has been associated with increased feelings of depression, anxiety, and loneliness.[57] A 2017 review of studies published in JAMA Pediatrics also found that adolescents who consume pornography are more likely to engage in risky sexual behaviors and develop sexual health problems.[58]

The statistics surrounding pornography in the United States paint an alarming picture of its impact on individuals and society. From strained relationships and addiction to the exposure of children and links to sex trafficking, the negative consequences of pornography cannot be ignored. It is crucial for society to address this issue by promoting awareness, providing education, and offering support to individuals who may be struggling with pornography-related problems. In doing so, we can hope to mitigate the detrimental effects of this widespread issue on our communities and our well-being.

Chapter III: Searching for Solution

"Do not seek for the truth by means of men; find first the truth and then you will recognize those who follow it." – Ali Ibn Abi-Talib

The issues mentioned earlier are significant and, in some cases, interconnected. Continuing to chronicle these problems might not be beneficial for either of us. We need to search for a solution—a solution grounded in truth. I would like to make a bold offer: Are you ready to explore the truth, regardless of its source, or are you still seeking truth through the interpretations of others rather than discovering it firsthand? Have you ever explored Islam on your own, without intermediaries or constant exposure to 24/7 media channels? If not, are you brave enough to undertake this exploration through your own efforts? If you are ready, you can form your own opinions after conducting your research. You might be surprised by this suggestion and wonder: What's in Islam? Haven't we observed Islam around the world? What about the people who follow it? As previously mentioned, we should seek the truth directly, not through others, to address the widespread challenges and potentially preserve Western civilization. So, why might Islam be the solution to both the explicit and the more subtle, unlisted problems that Western civilization faces? If a religion could be the solution, why not revisit the religion with which the West is so familiar? Christianity was the religion, in various forms and shapes, followed in the West for over a thousand years until the European Renaissance. After all, isn't Western civilization fundamentally built on Christianity? Understanding this is not straightforward. To grasp it fully, one must recognize the role of religion, specifically Christianity, in Western civilization.

Role of Christianity

This may sound contradictory or confusing when stated—European civilization was not built because of Christianity, but rather when

Christianity was isolated from public life and the role of religion was confined to the four walls of churches. Allow me to explain.

European civilization is a product of Western civilization. If you take a Western Civ course from any European or American university, it will explain that Western civilization began with Mesopotamia and Egypt around 4000 BCE and continued through Greek and Roman civilizations until the first decline in 476 AD. This leads to the dark age, i.e., the Medieval period, which lasted for almost a millennium. Here's a formal definition of the medieval or dark age:

"In the history of Europe, the Middle Ages or medieval period (also spelled mediaeval or mediaeval) lasted approximately from the late 5th to the late 15th centuries, aligning with the post-classical period of global history. It began with the fall of the Western Roman Empire in 476 AD and ended with the fall of Constantinople in 1453 AD before transitioning into the Renaissance and then the Age of Discovery."[59]

And then came a period that brought Europe out of that darkness into the light, known as the Renaissance, which "is a period in history and a cultural movement marking the transition from the Middle Ages to modernity, covering the 15th and 16th centuries and characterized by an effort to revive and surpass the ideas and achievements of classical antiquity; "[60]

Disclaimer: I am using the word 'Christianity' to cover both Protestantism and Catholicism. Where I need to compare the roles of one individually, I will explicitly mention it as 'Protestant' or 'Catholic'.

Europe has experienced a renaissance by separating church from the state, which is fundamental to the belief that underpins secularism. America didn't go through secularism like Europe did but ensured that Christianity could not enter the life of society, at least publicly. The government, education system, scientific exploration, invention, intellectuals, etc., completely expelled Christianity from the buildup of civilization. Even the US Constitution ensures through the First Amendment that the government cannot be influenced by, nor can it influence, any religion. The separation of church and state that triggered the renaissance in Europe has done similarly in the rise of civilization in America as well. Had Europe and America held onto the Bible, it could not have become the civilization that we see today. The Bible, the holy scripture of Christianity, and science are incompatible with each other. Though we will cover this more in-depth in subsequent chapters, I would like to present a sharp contrast of the role of Christianity, in comparison to Islam, in building civilization. This phenomenon can be summarized as follows: Muslims, starting from no civilization at all in the desert of the Arabian Peninsula, went on to build their Golden Age of civilization and knowledge in astronomy, mathematics, medicine, philosophy, and many other academic fields when they embraced Islam. Europe came out of the medieval dark age into its Golden Age of civilization after it isolated Christianity and separated from the Bible.

If this sounds like a grand statement, you need to read the Bible for yourself. The most basic scientific facts are in clear contradiction to the Bible: The Sun rotates around the Earth, the Earth is a flat planet, humans came into this Earth six thousand years ago, the sky is placed on pillars and the Earth is also standing on some pillars, the blood of a slaughtered bird mixed with fresh water can be sprinkled as medication for leprosy, and Christianity can be tested by you drinking poison. This list goes on and on. Am I exaggerating? I have covered that in detail, fully based on the Bible. So, I am going to defer those contradictions, fabrications, and authenticity issues on any theological basis, but there are so glaring contradictions that are just plain numbers and scientific facts that cannot even be reconciled. I have put a short list from the Bible in the Appendix for your easy reference, but there are many scholars who have researched and put those in books if you're willing to spend more time to learn in detail. We'll dive deep in subsequent chapters.

By the way, you may also blame my ignorance on how modern Christians use the Bible in their lives. You may remind me, rightly so, that most Christians today don't use the Bible as the word of God but as an inspiration and historical book that's not to be followed word for word; rather, you use it metaphorically or in any way but following the words. I agree with you. And that's the point that I made above: that you can't use the Bible's words in this modern life. It's not a matter of choice; you can't, even if you want to!

So, if you can't use the holy scripture for your daily life, how can you claim that you follow that book? It's like claiming that I am an American at heart but decline to use the country's constitution, instead picking up bits here and there from the constitutions of Canada, France, Russia, India, China, and whatever someone else convinces me of on that day. You can continue to shout out loud that you're an American citizen while putting your fingers in your ears, but, sorry, I have to wake you up: you are not following that book.

So, Europe did what it needed to enter the realm of basic logic and scientific facts—it expelled religion from the public realm and confined it to the church, keeping the Bible as reading material for anything but practical purposes. It rightly did so in the medieval age in Europe, which was officially labeled as the dark age, until the renaissance, by creating that clear separation. Now, the Bible is considered by most Christians as a masterpiece of literature and food for the soul, and not for the intellect. Because if you turn on the "intellect switch" of your brain, then you would be forced to stop reading it because of those unscientific, mathematical errors, and lack of authenticity to the original sources. So, what would happen if you decide to turn off the "intellect switch" of your brain? You essentially shut down the current civilization. The civilization of our time is entirely knowledge-based, and without the millions of intellectuals, you don't have a civilization. In that case, how can we even say that Christianity can be the solution for modern Western civilization? After all, Christians only became scientific when they left the Bible. Either you roll back civilization to roll out Christianity again, or you keep spiraling down the civilization crisis that was mentioned in earlier chapters.

Role of knowledge and sciences in the early Christianity:

According to Dr. Roy Casagranda of The Austin School, "...Rome switched to being Christian and dumped its pagan roots. It also started to slowly move away from this idea that it needed to be advanced technologically and in 391 A.D it took that to the maximum level when Emperor Theodosius issued a decree declaring that (the Roman Empire was not) it wasn't just that Christianity was the official religion, it wasn't just that Christianity was the state's religion, it was also the only religion. Non-Christians were no longer welcome in the Empire. Jews and pagans needed to convert or leave and when that happened the Archbishop of Alexandria, Archbishop Theophilus, issued his own decree asking the Christian population of Alexandria to go ahead and get rid of the pagans and the Jews. They went to the Jewish quarter. Alexandria was the largest Jewish City on the planet....The mob goes to the Jewish quarter and just begins massacring the Jews. When they're done destroying the Jewish quarter which won't be inhabited again for another 1500 years. They then go and try to find the pagans. The problem with the pagans is they were intermingled with the Christians. So, you just literally had to knock on doors and go - 'you pagan?'. ...They then go to The Great Library. The Great Library was run by a woman named Hypatia, wasn't actually technically a pagan. She was a theist so she did believe that there was an entity that created the universe a single entity but she didn't think that anybody could know its nature so she rejected Christianity and but the majority of the students at The Great Library, the majority of the professors of The Great Library were in fact pagan and so the mob decides to get rid of The Great Library and they destroy it."[61]

On the contrary, Islam had the Golden Age when the Muslims at that time held the Quran. In fact, the very definition of modern science was defined by Hassan Ibn Al-Haytham, who seeks the knowledge and established the experimentation-based Science, has done so because he was inspired by the religion of Islam: "I constantly sought knowledge and truth, and it became my belief that for gaining access to the effulgence and closeness to God, there is no better way than that of searching for truth and knowledge."[62]

It's no wonder that the Muslims had to leave the basic teaching of the Quran i.e. use of intellect and reasoning; to initiate the dark age to begin. You don't need to take my word on a face value. For that you have to read the Quran to appreciate it. Here is a short summary of the Quran's insistences stressing on the use of intellect and reasoning:

Islam has given the highest status to the people who are of intellect and who use reason. On the contrary, labeled the people as the worst of God's creatures who don't use reason.

"Those who remember Allah standing, sitting, and lying on their side and ponder on the creation of the Heavens and the Earth: "our lord, you didn't create these without any purpose…" - Surah Al-Imran (3:191)

Allah has also commanded us not to pursue without first acquiring knowledge. Check the below verses from the Quran:

"And pursue not that of which thou hast no knowledge; for every act of hearing, or of seeing or of (feeling in) will be enquired into (on the Day of Reckoning)." - Surah Al-Isra (17:36)

Moreover, Allah has repeated stories after stories, with metaphor, with the analogy, and asks us to ponder on it.

"(Here is) a Book which We have sent down unto thee, full of blessings, that they may meditate on its Signs, and that men of understanding may receive admonition." - Surah Saad (38:29)

Finally, here's the list of verses that I have taken from the Quran that unequivocally asks us to use our reason and intellect. As a matter of fact, Allah admonishes those who don't use intellect or reasoning and refers to them as the lowest form of life.

"Indeed, the worst of living creatures in the sight of Allah are the deaf and dumb who do not use reason." - Surah Al-Anfal (8:22).

Mentioning all the verses would make the book longer so I am just giving the references with a summary so that you can read on your own from the Quran. The theme of all these verses is asking for the same thing- think and use your intellect:

Surah Yunus (10:5): "...No wise did Allah create this but in truth and righteousness. (Thus) doth He explains His Signs in detail, for those who understand."

Surah Yunus (10:24): "...Thus do We explain the Signs in detail for those who reflect."

Surah Yunus (10:16): "…A whole lifetime before this have, I tarried amongst you: will ye not then understand?"

Surah Al-Hijr (15:75): "indeed there's a sign for the people of intellect."

Surah Al-Noor (24:44): Allah changes days and nights. It has a lesson for people who are keen on observing.

Surah Al-Furqan (25:55): Allah made humans from water.

Surah Yunus (10:100): Allah imposes filth on those who don't use intellect.

Surah Al-Jasiyah (45:3-5): There are signs for believers – on earth and sky, our creation and animals spreading. Day and night, bringing rain from the sky, flow of air- there are signs for the people of intellect.

Surah Al-A'raf (7:185): Don't they ponder on the skies and earth's management and what Allah has created?

Surah Al-Imran (3:190-191): Heavens and earth day and night – there are signs for those who are knowledgeable. They ponder and say you didn't create us without any reason.

Surah Al-Mu'minun (23:80): Allah creates, gives life, gives death- will you not use reason?

Surah Al-Hadid (57:17): Perhaps you will understand.

Surah Al-Rum (30:28): This do we detail for who use their reason.

Surah Al-Baqarah (2:170-171): Following blindly, ignoring reason, like deaf, dumb, and blind"

Surah Al-Baqarah (2:44): Will you not reason?

Surah Al-Ankubat (29:43): But none will understand except who use reason.

Surah Yusuf (12:2): Quran in Arabic so that you understand.

Surah Al-An'am (6:151): So that you may use reasons.

Surah Al-Nisa (3:118): So, you may use reason.

Surah Ya-Sin (36:62): So, did you not use reason.

Surah Al-An'am (6:32): So, will you not reason?

Surah Al-Qasas (28:60): Will you not reason?

Surah Al-Hajj (22:46): Travel through the earth and use reason.

Surah Al-Mulk (67:10): If they used reason, they wouldn't be the companion of the blaze.

Science *ain't* the Problem!

While going through these examples, do not fall into the trap of renouncing science itself. Let's clearly understand the distinction between science and scientists. Science is the faculty of human pursuit of understanding natural phenomena and creation in this universe. It systematically looks through observation to find patterns and answer questions objectively about how things work in nature. On the other hand, scientists and scientific journalists are in the business of using science to achieve their professional goals. Their purposes fall within the spectrum of, for instance, being dedicated to learning and exploring; using intellect to make a living; persuading people/humanity towards good and away from bad. However, scientists and journalists are human in the end, and some are influenced by their materialistic desires: profiteering from inventions and interests; gaining authority or power over others, etc. So, if you blame science because someone used science for their profiteering purpose, it would be like discounting religion because of a few large groups of ignorant or selfish people who use religion for their profiteering business. Hence, I blame those scientists who created those issues, and science has nothing to do with it, for or against its original purpose whatsoever, i.e., to seek knowledge of the universe. For example: it is scientists who invented the antibiotic to cure many diseases; vaccines to eradicate polio and smallpox. On the other hand, scientists have invented fossil-fuel mass production, combustion engines, pesticides, plastic products, toxic chemicals, and massive industrialization that is now destroying the climate and human health. It's not science that's the problem, just like a knife, it's what you do with science as a tool.

Ibn al-Haytham (965–1039), a polymath of the Golden Age of Islamic civilization, was the first to define the very definition of modern science and considered to be the father of modern scientific methodology, due to his emphasis on experimental data and reproducibility of its results. The Greeks had tremendous advancements from the science of the Egyptians and Babylonians. Then, Muslims advanced the science of the Greeks' achievements from being heavily philosophy-based to pure experimentation (that's the controlled experiments in modern science), trusting in natural disposition. Controls eliminate alternate explanations of experimental results, especially experimental errors and experimenter bias.[63] Here's what *Ibn al-Haytham* said on the premise of science:

"Therefore, the seeker after the truth is not one who studies the writings of the ancients and, following his natural disposition, puts his trust in them, but rather the one who suspects his faith in them and questions what he gathers from them, the one who submits to argument and demonstration, and not to the sayings of a human being whose nature is fraught with all kinds of imperfection and deficiency. The duty of the man who investigates the writings of scientists, if learning the truth is his goal, is to make himself an enemy of all that he reads, and ... attack it from every side. He should also suspect himself as he performs his critical examination of it, so that he may avoid falling into either prejudice or leniency."[64]

"The Greeks had great success in the areas of mathematics, particularly geometry, borrowing heavily from the Egyptians (who were concerned primarily with practical applications) while raising the theoretical and intellectual bar to new heights…While the Egyptians and Babylonians had made great advances in astronomy, their work was based heavily on centuries of observation. It was the Greeks who introduced mathematics into astronomy greatly expanding the range of questions that could be asked and answered about the solar system."[65]

Science isn't a matter of belief; rather, it's the tool to seek the truth about materials and anything else. Even though some people define science with an alternate definition for their benefit, do not fall into that trap. Science is always evolving and will continue to do so. That is science. It has given us huge advancements in our human civilization, which are abundant around us, so it doesn't need to be retold. However, I will just recap a few foundational advancements that science has provided to prime us for further discussion:

The modern *farming* is a product of science: hybrid seeds, irrigations, fertilizers, insect repellant, irrigation, farming machineries, weather forecasting, etc. Without the science and technology, we couldn't imagine such production of agricultural produces in the world.

Industrial Revolution had changed the speed of human civilization. Steam engine, combustion engine, and then electricity, the industrial revolution is the direct product of scientific revolution. Railroad, road transportation, Airplane, and rockets are the wonders of science of technologies. Then came digital revolution that changed the world through digital computers and Internet. Now, we're seeing the fourth Industrial Revolution (4IR) through Artificial Intelligence, that will take us to place that we aren't sure about the outcome of it.

The invention of *modern medicine* has made a tremendous impact on the quality of human life. Humanity has invented medicines for many causes of death such as antibiotic, polio vaccines, smallpox vaccines, and the list goes on and on. The modern surgeries are no less than wonder and miracle of modern medical science. We would fool ourselves to not seeing the wonder of the scientific revolution in our time.

I quickly touched on it from a hundred thousand feet just to show that if someone is talking about going back and trashing science, they aren't in their right mind. This book isn't for them.

A fair question needs answering first

You may ask: If the current Western civilization needs Islam to solve its problems, then why many of the Muslim majority countries in such a deep hole? Aren't the poorest, most corrupt, and most helpless countries on Earth from Muslim countries? Aren't most Muslim countries looking to the West to solve their problems? Why are Muslims leaving their "heaven" countries and flocking to the European and American continents?

That's an absolutely honest and trillion-dollar question that needs to be answered before we go any further.

If you raise this question and move on, then you're not being honest with yourself but just trying to avoid the truth. I hope that you're not of that kind and that you will continue to read through. The problems or issues affecting Muslim majority countries aren't so different from those of Western countries. Though that may sound weird at first glance, current

Muslim majority countries are either the product or extensions of the West and are not following the teachings of Islam, nor are they fully in the Western model. A vivid example is modern-day Türkiye. It not only tried to become just like another European secular country, but they also bent over backward to prove themselves more secular than any other EU countries and went one step further. They changed the written script from Arabic to Latin, banned the hijab and headscarf in public, banned the Quran in public, and so on. After 50 years or so, that experiment fell apart. Another example is Albania, a Muslim majority country, that became the first and only constitutionally atheist country in 1967, a status that lasted until 1990. The borders of modern nation-states in most Muslim majority countries are the product of Western experimentation over the last couple of hundred years.

Secondly, all other Muslim majority countries were colonized by either Britain or France (with some exceptions by Portugal and the Dutch). When those colonized countries left the Muslim countries, they completely collapsed in terms of economy, political systems, and religious structures. They were almost forced to be heavily influenced by Western-trained bureaucrats/elites to mimic Western ideology. They are still struggling to come out of that colonial trauma amid the constant influence and interference by those colonial powers. Britain and France are still exerting political, economic, and military power in their former colonial countries. Post-WWII, the USA has influenced most global events, and many times they have not gone well for those countries or for itself. A few examples are India-Pakistan-Bangladesh, Vietnam, Cuba, Panama, Afghanistan, Iraq, Libya, Syria, and Palestine, where they are struggling to this day. You may have started to doubt how this is possible. If that feels too unreal or illusory to you, look at these two examples of British messes that the world is still suffering from: Palestine was divided into Israel and Palestine by the British Balfour Declaration, and India was split into India and Pakistan by the same British authority. The creation of Israel has kept the Middle East in turmoil for over 70 years, and India and Pakistan, two nuclear-armed countries, have already fought four wars in the last 70 years. Setting that aside, those Muslim majority countries have either abandoned Islam or, in a few cases, tried to adopt extreme forms of Islam to find solutions to their broken systems. Nothing has worked, and none has been the right solution. The true Islam that ushered in the Golden Age has yet to be seen. An example of not following the basics of Islam is Bangladesh, a country where 90% of the population is Muslim. Islam is very strict and clear about extramarital relationships, yet the country has legal brothels. Alcohol is forbidden, yet people can drink alcohol legally and pseudo-legally. Pakistan, the second largest Muslim-populated country, was second in the world in streaming pornography. These are just glimpses and barely scratch the surface. The problems are deep-rooted.

Bottom line - they also need the same solutions that the West would benefit from. Islam isn't the property of any ethnic group but a universal religion for humanity. I will cover that in a subsequent chapter.

So, if we can solve the problems of the West, then those countries will readily follow the lead from the West because they have gotten used to mimicking the West for so long.

One may put forth a follow-up assertion: the West, and especially America, should wait to see if the current Muslim countries can prove that Islam would bring the solution to the mess. That's a fair question. As a matter of fact, I am not proposing solutions for either the West or Muslim countries. However, as mentioned above, those countries need many basic civil institutions to be rebuilt that the West already has. So, if the West wants to take the shot, it may even lead those countries out of their current situation. Another point is that Western countries, especially the USA, Britain, and France, influence and to some extent control the policies of those countries. So, to maintain the current status quo, however unethical it may be, the current political powers do everything possible to prevent them from changing independently. You see this every day where we instigate social unrest, political crises, and even military coups when we see countries in the world trying to operate outside of Western sphere. So, the bottom line is, there is a better chance that we fix both the West and the other countries simultaneously. Let the Muslim countries fix themselves without interference, and better yet, help them to fix their problems.

America has a long history of unimaginable success that not many nations have been able to accomplish in such a short period of time. In just a matter of several hundred years, the USA expanded to 50 states, became the unquestioned sole superpower of the world with the top economic, scientific, and most importantly, military power. Albeit the price was paid by the indigenous native population as well as the millions of Africans through the Transatlantic slave trade.

By the way, I have written another book on what the Muslim countries should do to get out of their current mess, and you can read it if you're interested. However, if you're in a rush, I have added a summary in the Appendix for you to get a quick tour of that book.

America was built by Christians and with mostly Christian moral values, but now Christians are leaving their faith in droves. There's no way a person can be faithful to both the Bible and fully embrace science and other moral issues (e.g., slavery, racial segregation, indignity towards women) without experiencing a constant inner conflict of conscience. These concepts have become irreconcilable and have diverged so much that there's no way to return to Christianity, which was the root of America's foundation. The alternate option is constant experimenting with the society to see find what works – like we do in a lab with guineapig. The alternative option is constant experimentation with society to find what works—like we do in a lab with guinea pigs. Making everything subject to experimentation and social engineering, up to the definition of the biology of our bodies—the building blocks of Homo sapiens for hundreds of thousands of years—is not just an endless distraction but is spiraling down into the destruction of society. Moreover, humanity, ingrained in its biology, can't live without a higher purpose. Love it or hate it—that's how we were created. Through the course of civilization, we've lost the purpose of life in the West and have thus made materialism the purpose of life, which is not compatible with human needs—a direct result of losing faith in Christianity. We're falsely led to believe that just having a good job, a house, occasional vacations, and a retirement plan will keep humans satisfied. We are created to ask the obvious questions: where did we come from, and where are we going? The West is struggling to find a divine belief system that is rational and compatible with the scientific minds of human intellect. What are the choices, viable and fit for purpose, that will not only sustain but also rejuvenate the civilization of this great country in particular, and the West in general?

Chapter IV: What are our choices?

"Two roads diverged in a yellow wood,
And sorry I could not travel both
And be one traveler, long I stood
And looked down one as far as I could
To where it bent in the undergrowth;
Then took the other, as just as fair,
And having perhaps the better claim,
Because it was grassy and wanted wear;
Though as for that the passing there
Had worn them really about the same,
And both that morning equally lay
In leaves no step had trodden black.
Oh, I kept the first for another day!
Yet knowing how way leads on to way,
I doubted if I should ever come back.
I shall be telling this with a sigh
Somewhere ages and ages hence:
Two roads diverged in a wood, and I—
I took the one less traveled by,
And that has made all the difference."

- The Road Not Taken by Robert Frost

I barely scratched the surface in previous chapters on why Islam could be a viable choice for the West, especially for America. However, it deserves a deep dive into other choices that the West has at hand. This is especially true for America as the leader of the West, which is in serious soul-searching to save this current civilization. There are a few apparent choices available in front of America. As a matter of fact, America has tried those solutions on a small or large scale, but let's analyze them again.

Christianity

If Islam could be a solution, then why not Christianity? After all, isn't Christianity from the same God as well?

This is a legitimate question if we believe that Christianity and Islam both come from the same God. Yes, all Muslims believe that both Christianity and Islam (and all monotheistic religions in the world) originate from the same God. That's fundamental to Islam. Therefore, God cannot send the incorrect solution to Jesus (peace be upon him) while Muhammad (peace be upon him) receives the correct one. Indeed, both received the right messages; however, the message known as the Gospel of Jesus has not been preserved. Consequently, what we see today as the Bible was essentially written by others, not by Jesus. The teachings of Jesus are scattered throughout the Gospels in the Bible, leading to the discrepancies observed within. The primary challenge remains that you will not find the preserved teachings of Jesus. This was the endeavor of many scholars of theology and even historians to find the origin of the Bible. There has been much research on this, and I will draw from one of the respected scholars of our time: Richard Elliott Friedman, an American biblical scholar and theologian who currently serves as the Professor at the University of Georgia. He began with the following opening in his famous book, 'Who Wrote the Bible?':

"It is a strange fact that we have never known with certainty who produced the book that has played such a central role in our civilization. There are traditions concerning who wrote each of the biblical books – the Five Books of Moses are supposed to be by Moses, the book of Lamentations by the prophet Jeremiah, half of the Psalms by King David – but how is one to know if these traditional ascriptions are correct?"

He concluded his book with:

"Simply put, the question all along was not "Who inspired the Bible?" or "Who revealed the Bible?" The question was only which human beings actually composed it. Whether they did so at divine direction, dictation, or inspiration was always a matter of faith. Joseph ben Eliezer Bonfils, perhaps the first Jewish scholar to say outright about a verse of the Torah, "Moses did not write this," made this point six hundred years ago.

...Now we can study and appreciate the artistry that went into forming each part of the book. We can appreciate the variety of human experience over centuries that made it so complex and so rich. We can learn how responsive the parts of the book were to the real needs and real situations of life. If we say that the book is great, we can better understand what made it great.

Reading the Bible will never be quite the same. Aware of the Bible's extraordinary history and its resulting complexity, we can – and probably must – read the book with a new depth of appreciation. We can read a page of the Bible and know that three or even four persons, all artists, all writing from their own experience, in their own historical moments, separated by centuries, contributed to composing that page. And, at the same time, we can read the page as it is, to enjoy the story, to learn from it, to find out how others interpreted it over millennia....The question, after all, is not only who wrote the Bible, but who reads it."

Allow me to offer a simple analogy, and you will appreciate why the concept of preservation is so important. Imagine a chef who is perfect at preparing food that satisfies hunger and is perfectly balanced with all the nutrients needed by humans. He cooks this food for us and sends it through couriers from time to time. As the food is delivered to us through many intermediaries, these well-intentioned middlemen try to preserve the food's quality to fulfill its purpose. However, the original food was lost, but they memorized the recipe as it was passed down to them. Therefore, they compile this recipe and prepare the food for us with the best intentions to serve and assist. However, since the original recipe was not preserved, as time passed by, common cultural norms, without any malicious intent, are injected into the food preparation, thus altering the food despite good intentions. Most of these alterations are benign, but some deviate from the original. The original recipe was intended for eternity, covering all-time needs, but the addition of local cultural norms compromises its omnipotence and timeless essence. And so, we receive this food. It may work for a time and in certain places, but as time passes, it becomes less useful and, at times, harmful. For example, food that is beneficial for a healthy individual (e.g., sugary or fatty ingredients) can be harmful to those with diabetes or high cholesterol. This is merely an analogy; do not dwell too much on the metabolic details. This analogy represents the Bible: well-intentioned but deviating from the original recipe of God through Jesus (peace be upon him), given in the Aramaic language and lost, then written by subsequent wise and pious men in Koine Greek, and translated into many languages.

Today, it contains many original and useful elements, but also additions and modifications that can do more harm than good if followed literally. Many scholars have worked on this and written numerous books, so I will keep this minimal and you can check out those references. Thus, I will cover the bare minimum: all prophets are referred to as gods or sons of God. What is the Greek word for 'god'? '*Theos,*' and '*Ho Theos*' or '*Ton Theon*' in Greek mean 'god' and 'the God,' respectively. Greek does not use capitalization in the same way as some languages (including Arabic, Bangla, and many others). 'Ho' and 'Ton' are definite articles used for nouns to specify them. In Greek, this is expressed as '*En arche en ho logos, kai ho logos en pros ton theon, kai theos en ho logos*.' Focus on the phrase *'kai theos en ho logos'* ('and the Word was god'). We are concerned here with the Greek noun *'theos'* ('god') written without the definite article, contrasting with the first mention of this noun as '*ton theon,*' the accusative case of *'ho theos'* ('the God'), i.e., the noun *'theos'* preceded by the definite article *'ho.'*

Here are two English translations side by side: 'In the beginning was the Word, and the Word was with God, and the Word was a **god**.'—John 1:1, **New World Translation**.

'In the beginning was the Word, and the Word was with God, and the Word was **God**.'—John 1:1, **New International Version**.

The capitalization of 'G' made all the difference, which is an interpretation by Christian scholars, and they themselves differ. We're talking about Greek vs. English, not even the original language of Jesus (a.s.), which wasn't even Greek. Anyway, I mentioned this to give a flavor of what I was referring to: the effect of intermediaries, all well-intentioned but not preserved for eternity. I will discuss the Quran in the next chapter, and you will see the contrast for yourself.

Then you may ask the question, why was Christianity able to get by for so many centuries with that Bible? I will cover this in detail below, but in a nutshell: Christianity provided many spiritual and social benefits in personal life, but Europe and then America had to abandon the Bible for the most part in aspects of life like governing the state, the economy, legislation, and most specifically, the scientific endeavor, to trigger the current civilization that is based on science. Essentially, the Bible was confined to a part of the private life only. You will see below that Europe and America couldn't progress without the separation of Church and State. So, you can go back to Christianity, and I would say that some of the current catastrophes would be resolved, but for that, you would have to roll back the current civilization to pre-Renaissance times. Want to see what that would look like? Visit Amish Country. They have avoided much of civilization's side effects but they couldn't progress, especially in science and engineering because they are holding the Bible dearly in everyday life. Essentially, they have avoided Western civilization altogether. Don't get me wrong. I personally praise their living a healthy and happy life in Amish country, but I also see what opportunities they are leaving on the table to utilize the potential of human ingenuity and scientific exploration.

At first, let's clear up a misconception that Western civilization is based on Christianity. Western civilization started in Mesopotamia and Egypt five thousand years ago. The Greek and Roman empires are considered to be the foundation of later Western civilization. Europe and America are now claiming the succession of that civilization. However, that's far from the full story. Muslims also claimed the Roman Empire as they ruled Egypt and Syria in the early sixth century and then Constantinople in the year 1453 AD by the Ottomans. According to Professor Paul Freedman of Yale, "There are four heirs to the Roman Empire. One is the Byzantine Empire, the Eastern Roman Empire, which calls itself the Roman Empire. It doesn't call itself the Eastern, doesn't call itself the Byzantine, it calls itself the Roman Empire, even though it does so in Greek. The second heir are the barbarian kings…They are attempting to prop up the remnants of Roman culture, civilization, and material society. The third heir in some ways, is Islam, which we meet in the seventh century, the century of its invasion. And the fourth heir is the Church. Even though the church grew up in opposition to Roman."[66]

The Ottomans had embraced and claimed to rejuvenate the Roman Empire. By the way, you may say that the Ottomans conquered the Byzantine Empire, which is a historical lie that was fabricated by a German historian a thousand years later. It was a move to position Germany as the inheritor of the Roman Empire and to downplay the Ottomans' claim to the Roman Empire. The Roman Empire was divided into two administrative divisions, known as the Tetrarchy[67], by Diocletian in 293 AD: the Western Roman Empire and the Eastern Roman Empire. Constantinople was the capital of the Eastern Roman Empire, and the empire always referred to itself as the Roman Empire. As a matter of fact, if you had told the emperor and people of Constantinople in 1453 that they were part of the Byzantine Empire, they would have looked at you as if you were an alien coming from Mars. Coming back to the point: the Roman Empire was at its peak in the late 1st century when it was a pagan empire and a staunch opponent of Christianity. Professor Paul Freedman mentioned as follows: "But they (Roman empire) found Christianity alien. They didn't like that fact that Christianity was intolerant. Every other religion of the Roman Empire, with one exception, accepted other gods. If you worshipped Isis, you had nothing against other people worshipping Jupiter. If you worshipped Cybele, you had nothing against other people worshipping Mitra. But Christianity, of course, ridiculed all of these gods. The only other religion that was like this was Judaism. But Judaism made some accommodations with the Roman Empire, recognized the authority of the Roman emperor, and did not defy the state in the way that Christianity at least appeared to. And Christianity was not a Roman religion in many of the ways that it rejected worldliness, rejected engagement in or enjoyment of the material world: the pleasure of the theater, the circus, the celebrations of civic paganism, emperor worship, law courts. Well, law courts may not be pleasurable. But this sort of civic involvement of the emperor and the Empire are rejected by Christianity. Christianity, when you see what Roman pagans write about it, is a kind of killjoy religion. It's a religion of people who seem to have their eyes focused on anything but the actual process of getting ahead in Roman society."

Constantinople's conversion to Christianity occurred in 312 AD, and then Emperor Theodosius I (379 – 395) made Christianity the state religion and banned all forms of paganism from the Roman Empire. So, as a matter of fact, the medieval age, or the dark age in Europe, coincided with the time of the Roman Empire's conversion to Christianity. Emperor Theodosius I (with another opinion held by some historians: it was Theodosius II) discontinued the Olympic Games as they were held in honor of Zeus, the ancient Greek god of sky and thunder. So, if you are under the impression that the current Western civilization is a product of Christianity, then I would suggest the lecture from Professor Paul Freedman at Yale, depicting that time: "as you may guess, the catastrophists think the fall of the Roman Empire, whether we date it 476 or there's some reasons to date it, really 550…Between 450 and 550, a catastrophe happened. A civilization was wiped out. And really, if not literally a Dark Ages, a more primitive, more war-like, more illiterate, and more rural period was ushered in. The disappearance of ancient texts, things that the Roman knew from that lost Hortensius dialogue of Cicero…I can't remember exactly how many plays Aeschylus wrote, but it's something on the order of 60, and we have three. So, the disappearance of text. The end of literacy, except for a very small portion of the Christian clergy. A more primitive architecture. The end of grand civic projects like aqueducts, coliseums, theaters, baths. A more isolated society without these urban centers. A diminished population spread across the countryside, mostly engaged in subsistence. Hence, if not end of trade, the radical diminution of trade."[68]

Here's another account of the same event and the consequences of the Roman Empire embracing Christianity. Dr. Roy Casagranda of The Austin School summarizes the transition to Christianity and how it took the Roman civilization from a knowledge-based society backwards: "So, they

(*Roman Empire*) had steam they just hadn't made trains yet if they had a little bit more time, they might have but they run out of time. They run out of time because Rome converts to Christianity… as Rome switched to being Christian and dumped its pagan roots. It also started to slowly move away from this idea that it needed to be advanced technologically…"[69]

Now let's come back to our modern time. By design, the USA is not an atheist or secular country but is built on the notion of freedom to practice any religion, with a strong base in Christianity. However, the founding fathers of this country and all future leaders kept the church strictly out when creating laws. They mostly kept religion out of the public sphere, except for some forms of showmanship for election purposes. This was a success story where religion wasn't pushed too much into public policy. The reason I call it a success is that otherwise, the progress of this nation could not have been realized in America. I would claim that the founders made the right choice in keeping it such. Moreover, Americans were essentially the product of the European Renaissance, the protestant movement, where they saw how the church-state separation produced a great civilization in Europe. But as I mentioned, the choices were limited. Because Christianity provides a great base for a sense of purpose, morality (with the exceptions of certain stories of prophets and treatment towards women, etc.), community building, and a spiritual tool for public psyches. And why would it not provide such? After all, Christianity is the outcome of the prophet Jesus, who came to Earth through a miraculous virgin birth and with glad tidings from God. However, the Bible did suffer from human interjection, thus many contradictory facts were injected into it.

After all, the original message that the prophet Jesus brought isn't even found intact in the Bible but is scattered throughout the Gospels. And then various councils throughout the early history of Christianity added to or subtracted from the fundamental creed. For example, the Trinity was added to a version of the Bible and then later removed from it. The division of the Bible into two editions, Catholic vs. Protestant, and many denominations including Jehovah's Witnesses, made it more fragmented. Regardless of all these, Christianity largely held because the Bible was pushed to the sidelines of public and, in many cases, even private life. This is because the Bible cannot withstand the basic facts of reality around us and goes against something that almost all Christians today don't believe. For example, the Bible's claims of a flat earth, the origin of Homo sapiens being only six thousand years old, the sequence of creation of the Earth, the Sun, vegetation, and lights, the Earth and Sky standing on pillars, treatment of diseases with blood, drinking poison to prove faith, etc., are just a few mismatches that left no choice but to keep it sidelined from day-to-day life. On a related note, "Bishop Usher deduced that the first day of Creation began at nightfall on Sunday, October 27, 4004 BC. Refinements by others further pinpointed this to 9 a.m. London time, or midnight in the Garden of Eden." When a scientifically-minded person comes across such "profound" claims, pun intended, how can you blame them if they leave the religion? Without that, you couldn't avoid the existential clash between Christianity and human civilizations through the sciences. So, it remained strictly as a great literature book of (partial) moral content and full of stories. I said "partial" because the question arises about the moral stories in the book, which I won't copy but just referenced as they aren't befitting for young minds to read (e.g., the stories of Lot and his daughters), then the literal, mathematical, historical, and intellectual contradictions start to surface if you try to pull it into the mainstream. Thus, Christendom is left to handle all the issues by some other authority as the Bible has lost its place due to corruption in the text. Consequently, science took the place of authority to define many fundamental aspects of life as well as the purpose of life. As we know, science itself is a tool for humanity to explore, experiment, and benefit from materials that have nothing to do with the soul - life and afterlife. But scientists and scientifically-minded people began to fill that gap and introduced 'materialism,' which is a fundamental of atheism: we descend from matter and dissolve into matter, and that's all. Christianity couldn't propose an alternative because it lacked the rational and logical basis needed to counter that. Thus, you see various ideologies popping up to fill the void. Here are a few big-ticket items that are hard to swallow for almost any civilized and rational mind.

Treatment of women

"And I will put enmity between you and the woman, and between your offspring and hers; he will crush your head, and you will strike his heel...To the woman he said, 'I will make your pains in childbearing very severe; with painful labor you will give birth to children. Your desire will be for your husband, and he will rule over you." - Genesis (3: 5-16)

Women are cursed by God due to the act of eating the forbidden fruit and are made subservient to men. This is according to the Bible. I don't know how many of you are ready to accept that daughters, mothers, sisters, and wives are to suffer painful labor and be subservient to their husbands. How can you reconcile this with a civilization where human dignity is based on piety and actions, regardless of gender? There are biological differences between men and women, which only a fool would ignore, but attributing their biology to a curse is not something this civilization or any future civilization can accept and flourish under.

Human Evolution and the Age of Homo Sapiens

Scientific consensus, based on extensive fossil records and genetic data, supports the theory of evolution, which details a gradual process of change in the characteristics of species over billions of years. Modern humans, or Homo sapiens, are believed to have evolved approximately 300,000 years ago. This contrasts sharply with the biblical timeline, which some interpretations suggest places the creation of the Earth and humans at only about 6,000 years ago. This figure is derived from genealogies found in Genesis and other parts of the Bible, leading to a Young Earth creationist view that contradicts the timeline established by radiometric dating and other scientific methods.

The Flat Earth and Earth's Pillars

The shape of the Earth as described in the Bible also presents a contradiction. Verses such as Isaiah 11:12 and Revelation 7:1 refer to "the four corners of the earth," which has historically been interpreted by some to suggest a flat Earth. Furthermore, 1 Samuel 2:8 and Job 9:6 mention the Earth being set on pillars, an image that aligns more with ancient cosmological views than with the modern understanding of Earth as a spherical planet orbiting the sun in space. These descriptions are poetic and metaphorical, reflecting the contemporary understanding of the universe at the time they were written.

The Pillars of Heaven

Similarly, the concept of "pillars of heaven" found in Job 26:11 portrays a vision of the cosmos where the heavens themselves are supported by physical pillars; a notion not aligned with current astronomical observations. This depiction likely served as a literary device to emphasize the strength and permanence of God's creation from the perspective of an ancient culture.

Lapresi treatment with blood

In the Book of Leviticus, chapters 13 and 14, the Bible provides detailed instructions on how to handle leprosy (now more accurately known as Hansen's disease). These chapters describe not only how to identify the disease through a series of inspections by priests but also elaborate on the rituals for cleansing a leper who is deemed to be healed. The purification process described in Leviticus 14 involves the use of sacrificial animals, including birds, lambs, and the application of their blood in a ritualistic manner.

One of the most striking elements of this ritual is the use of blood from a sacrificed bird. The priest was to take some of the blood of a bird killed over fresh water in a clay pot and sprinkle it on the person being cleansed from leprosy seven times. After this, the individual is pronounced clean. This act of sprinkling blood is symbolic and carries a spiritual meaning, reflecting purification and the restoration of community relationships rather than having any medicinal effect.

Cognitive consistency

Now many argue that the Bible is one of the best pieces of literature and read it as literature rather than as the word of God. That may sound intellectual at first, but if you think rationally, you will see the inconsistency in it. If you are to use the Bible as literature, then you would be in a cognitive dilemma all the time. Which one would you accept for your life - what's in the Bible or what you are seeing in the reality of your day-to-day life? If someone argues that they would accept both the Bible and science, then your statement isn't much different than if someone claims that they accept the sky is blue but also believe the sky is green.

Moreover, if you take the Bible as a literature book, then why the Bible? Why not Shakespeare or Dostoevsky to form your faith? Why not the 'Ramayana,' the Hindu mythology? To be more realistic, why not go back to Greek or Roman mythology, which is very close to Western civilization? You didn't choose those books to shape your moral boundaries, so you must believe those stories; otherwise, you would choose any. Because even though you say that you read it as a storybook, you must believe it to adhere to it. If you say I am just lazy to find any alternative, then I would challenge you that either you are not honest with yourself, or you are essentially an atheist, sticking to Christianity as a culture to just go along with the crowd by giving your brain a complete rest. Because if you believe that there is a God and you will have an eternal afterlife, then you can't be relaxed without finding the path that will take you to your destination.

Judaism

Judaism is the second-largest religion in the USA, following Christianity. Could it be an alternative? It's important to note that Judaism does not actively encourage conversion nor enthusiastically accepts other ethnic population. Although there is a path to becoming Jewish, it is not only cumbersome but also lengthy, potentially taking several months to years. Furthermore, Orthodox Jews may not accept conversions performed by more liberal Jewish communities. This is covered concisely in this article in University of Birmingham:

"Curiously you will not find Rabbis trying to convince people to convert to Judaism. In fact, even if someone approaches the Rabbi asking about conversion, Jewish law demands that he tries to dissuade the person from becoming a Jew.

Of course, Judaism is not an exclusive "club" and it is possible for one who is not born Jewish to become Jewish. However, Judaism teaches that there are different paths to G-d therefore a Gentile can have a full and meaningful relationship with G-d, without becoming Jewish. To quote the Talmud, "The righteous amongst the Gentiles have a place in the world to come"."[70] So, it's like saying, "Of course, you're welcome to my party, but are you sure you want to be at this party? I am certainly okay with inviting you, but I don't see any reason for you to leave your party and join ours. Just a reminder that your party is as good as mine."

Finally, Judaism is not a universal religion; it is primarily an ethnic religion followed by the Jewish population, which primarily traces back to Judah, the son of Jacob. Therefore, the solution we are looking for must be universal and not ethnocentric, which Judaism largely is not. So, for all practical purpose, this is not also a choice for the West to turn towards.

Atheism (and Agnosticism)

What about not looking towards any religion at all? After all, an ever-growing number of people in the West are convinced that religion is not the solution. To be more specific, they think that religion is actually the problem rather than a solution. Thus, people are leaving religion in general and Christianity in particular, in droves. The idea is religion is something of the past and we can solve anything and everything just following scientific exploration. This is the prevalent idea to solve every problem of our civilization because it is "kind of" based on the science that created this civilization in the first place and solved most of the "visible" problems like, medications, infrastructure, technology, governance, etc. So, by virtue of solving those "visible" needs, it has claimed that position. I said "kind of" because atheists actually don't believe in science either. If they did, they could no longer deny God based on their demand for "proof in the real world," after quantum mechanics proved that the reality, we see around us is not real anymore. Superposition and Quantum Entanglement are now given the highest acceptance in science by the Nobel Prize in 2022, adding more nails to the coffin of atheism. Thus, atheists should wake up from their plain egocentric arrogance rather than any rational reasoning whatsoever. The "superdeterminism[71]" theory, developed from the discovery of the quantum entanglement state, claims that the universe is predestined and predetermined. Although this theory is still in its early stages, it is so intriguing that a variation of it has been present in the Quran and in other monotheistic religion, for millennia, where God is omnipotent and knows not just the past and present but also controls what is yet to come. However, the Quran goes further than "superdeterminism"; it says that God knows and predetermines the future but also changes it as He wills and according to the actions of His creation. This theory surely will go through further experimentation and will take a long time before it can be considered for our conversation, but I was watching a discussion at Richard Dawkins and Khalil Al-Jibran's Humane Society where they were saying that if that theory is true, then all their actions were preordained. It was kind of funny but also sad how top atheists were losing hope that they aren't even in control of their own statements, let alone their actions. Here's Professor Richard Dawkins' statements on free will: "...Yes, free will is an illusion. Everything that I do is determined. However, it's such a powerful illusion that you might as well forget about that; we all of us behave as if and believe." Professor Jim al-Khalili further explained it more scientifically: "...we live in a deterministic universe where, you know, the laws of physics will determine cause and effect into the future and therefore we don't have free will. If everything's preordained, but we are unable to predict what the future will be, that's because we can't step out of space-time." Richard Dawkins tried desperately to find a way out of the "deterministic" world: "...but I want to ask you a question: even in the quantum world, does that make any difference to the deterministic universe?" Jim al-Khalili responded: "My view is no. Because the Quantum Indeterminism, the true randomness in the quantum world, is constrained to the quantum world and that once you get to large macroscopic objects, that Quantumness decreases…"[72] It's amazing to see how they accept the defeat while pretending no-defeat.

Setting aside poking fun, let's get back to serious conversation. Before we go if it's can be a solution or not, let's understand the fundamentals of Atheism. Atheism is disbelief or lack of belief in the existence of God or gods. But if you ask a "regular Joe" atheist, you would probably be more surprised than you wanted to be. You would find three categories of Atheists:

- First Category: Atheists who are brought up in a religious family but as they started to go through education and finds the science, the foundation of the civilization that we live in today, contradicts with the sacred texts they are taught to read and believe. So obviously, instead of renouncing science that is visibly encompass our everyday life, they renounce those sacred books and then religion. In the west, this group comprises the largest group. Many from this group also fall under the third category.
- Second Category: Atheists who have seen theists in their surroundings and distaste them so much due to their behaviors or level of intellect that they deem religion must have caused it. So, they don't just renounce those theists but also altogether renounce religion itself. They form the second largest share of atheists in the world.
- Third Category: Finally, you will find the rest of the atheists who are "second-hand" atheists. Let me explain. They look at the "smartest" people in their lives, such as professors, intellectuals, entrepreneurs, celebrities, etc., and see them publicly living an atheist belief. These atheists are often the most sought-after people, even by the theist population. They derive from this that if there were a God, these smart, "successful" people in our society must have exhausted all avenues to find God and concluded without any doubt that God doesn't exist. So, by outsourcing their intellectual quest to these celebrities, they blindly follow their "idols." Examples include Isaac Asimov, Carl Sagan, Neil deGrasse Tyson, Christopher Hitchens, Salman Rushdie, Mark Zuckerberg, Brad Pitt, Larry King, Bill Gates, Bill Maher, Richard Dawkins, Sam Harris, and so on. By looking at these big names, it's pretty obvious why most atheists are in this group.
- Now you can ask, what about the high-profile intellectuals like Christopher Hitchens or Richard Dawkins? Why they became atheists? Didn't they study all the religious scriptures? You may be surprised to hear that; they grew up with the Bible and in Christianity

and got so fed-up that they read excerpts here and there as well as others commentary about Islam to make up their mind on Islam. Their reading of the Quran is conjectural at best. Because they have heard so much that Judaism, Christianity and Islam are all Abrahamic religion, they didn't "waste" time read the third, and final revelation cover to cover. I read it many times and I laugh at their quote of Quranic verses taken out of context. They also fall mostly under the first two categories.

Regardless of your reason to be atheist, or to sound smarter, an agnostic, most of the logic behind atheism are pretty empty. I am not going to defend it through the Bible as even the Christians have accepted that the Bible is either a book to read like a literature or a book that has errors written by men (through divine inspiration). So, I am going to use the lens of the Quran to unravel the atheism. See for yourself.

Emptiness of Atheism

Most of the beliefs in atheism originated from identifying the shortcomings and incoherence in the Bible's claims about things that aren't founded on substance. One such example is the claim that the Earth was created six thousand years ago. There is more such misinformation that fueled the atheistic movement in Europe and America. You would find that most atheists, including their de facto leader in the twenty-first century, Richard Dawkins, know very little about Islam as fundamental knowledge. They bring up a few popular questions about the Quran and Sunnah without having an understanding of the Quran. This makes it easier for a Muslim to counter them but also falls into the same trap that Christians fell into for years, i.e., trying to explain everything with the certainty of knowledge of the Divine book. Another mistake Muslims make is that they counter them without acquiring much knowledge in science and not reading the Quran in light of that. For example, in *Surah Al-Mulk,* Allah asks Muslims to "look at the creation and if you see any fault? Look again and your vision will tire and you will be humbled in awe - you won't find any defects." So, we have to look at it through the lens of reasoning. However, before diving deep into it, let's first debunk the concept of "believing in science" that many scientifically-minded people, especially in the media and public sphere, preach to the commoners. The discipline of astronomy and its history have always fascinated me, which is why I have read "The Brief History of Time" at least three times. Each time I read it, I find myself in a clearer state of understanding than the last. By the history of astrophysics, I mean examining how the knowledge of astronomy has evolved over thousands of years of human civilization, from Aristotle to Stephen Hawking. By the way, I am not a scientist by profession but a student of science and an engineer by trade. I am a curious reader who enjoys reading about astronomy to get the context of what we are, where we are now, why we are here, and finally where we are heading. Now let's get to the point. Aristotle believed in the geocentric universe, which essentially claims that the Earth is the center of the universe and all the heavenly bodies circle around the Earth. Here's an analogy for the people who claim that they believe what they see and only accept what's rational and can be reasoned. Think about a scenario where someone is telling you that there's a giant purple spherical object behind a wall larger than the giant wall and asking you to believe in it without seeing it. You can see the giant wall to the extent that you can with your eyes, and using your knowledge, you can assume that the wall is almost infinitely tall and wide. Rational people would certainly not accept that without seeing or reasoning about that giant sphere because they don't see the spherical object. Now, some very intelligent people have discovered a way to poke a hole in that wall, and through which you can have a peek. Then you see, there's a purple object, and it's not spherical but flat. Now you argue with the people who believe in that spherical object by showing them through the hole. And after that, another intelligent person created a bigger hole in another part of that wall, and now you can see that purple object in a better way and you still see that the purple object isn't spherical but flat. By showing through those two and maybe more holes, you prove that the believers of spherical objects are fools and you show everyone that you're smarter than them. Now the point is, if you could rumble down that giant wall and managed to see that purple object, you would see that it is, in fact, a spherical object but as you have a limited number of small holes in that wall, your ability to envision it is also limited to see a very small portion of it which would be evident as flat - just like people hundreds of years ago believed that the earth is flat. Isn't it very naive to dismiss those people by saying that they're wrong just by poking a few holes in that infinitely large wall? If you agree with that, how can you dismiss the creation of this universe (or multiverse) without even knowing how big this universe is and just making a few laws of nature which you prove later as incorrect or insufficient? Isn't it like declaring that the purple object behind the wall is flat just by creating a few holes? Before you declare the object flat, first tear down the wall and see it with your eyes of reasoning, and until you can do that, don't make yourself a fool every few years by poking a new hole in that wall and declaring that as a flat purple object. Similarly, the way Aristotle declared that the universe is in an eternal state and has no beginning and no end but later on, you prove yourselves that actually the universe has a beginning and it will certainly end. Think about how many, so-called, science believers in the past thousands of years, until the Big Bang theory was accepted as the de facto theory, died with their false belief in science believing in the eternal state of the universe. It's okay to declare that you came to a new understanding of the universe but don't declare that you have determined that you have full knowledge of the universe (or multiverse) until you reveal it completely; otherwise, you would be proved wrong, just like Aristotle. Aristotle or other great scientists might not have had the intention to declare that they have absolute truth (in science, by definition, no one has absolute knowledge or truth). But some followers of those great scientists claim that they have absolute truth by rejecting other notions that aren't proved to be right or wrong yet. By doing that, those people would be responsible for fooling other people who have limited capability to discern false from truth. Imam Al-Ghazzali has said very nicely about those blind followers of scientific scholars in his book, "The Confessions of Al-Ghazzali." When we see a person is very smart and intellectual in an area, like in Physics, Engineering, or Medical Science and has done great intellectual works in their professional life and later on claims something about religion or God, then others get convinced by not doing any research but just believing in those scholars. They think that there is nothing to be found out that can't escape their intellectual minds. Those followers don't understand that one person can be super smart in one branch of knowledge and be completely flawed in other areas.

Atheism is essentially believing in science in disguise. The basis of modern atheism or agnosticism essentially is: if you can't prove it through observation and experimentation, then it's not worth believing. In other words, if science should prove the existence of God, otherwise, they won't believe. So, they believe in science as if it can provide any answer, including about God. Is it rational to believe in science while disbelieving in God? No, if you believe in science, you can't disbelieve in God. Let's unravel this thought by looking at it from three angles. It's such a vast topic, I don't think I can cover it in this short section, but to provide at least some explanation of the title, I am making an attempt, Insha'Allah.

Believing in Science

"Believe" is a state of mind where someone holds an opinion or has a firm conviction about something. This can be aided by evidence, but it's more of a psychological state where a person holds something as true with or without explicit reasoning. That's why you might see a person holding two beliefs at the same time that contradict each other. By definition, "believing in something" is not truly "scientific"—as per the Scientific

Method, which involves systematic observation, measurement, and experimentation, and the formulation, testing, and modification of hypotheses. Because even science can be proven wrong through the scientific method, and at that point, you have to accept that. So, believing in science is a kind of "oxymoron." Thus, if someone says they believe in science but don't want to believe in God because they can't prove the existence of God, it's like saying they can believe one thing in their mind with or without proof but can't believe something else without proof. This is inherently contradictory because, by definition, belief doesn't need firm proof to begin with, and science is all about "observation, experiment, and proving hypotheses." Disbelief in God—if you're of a scientific mind—to prove or disprove anything, you would have to prove a hypothesis through experiment in a repeatable manner. If you believe (hypothesize) that God doesn't exist, then the next step is to prove your hypothesis in a repeatable manner. I have never seen such a hypothesis proven so far by any atheists, for or against God's existence. So, until you can prove or disprove it, you should be quietly working on that experimentation using the scientific method. To clarify a common misconception: most atheists waste their time proving the idiotic arguments of some religious people. When you prove certain religious people to be idiots, you are only proving those individuals as such, but that's not advancing your hypothesis on God's existence or nonexistence. I know it's very hard, or at this point, perhaps not even possible, to conduct experiments on this hypothesis because there are so many basic fundamental things, for instance in physics, but in general in science, that even science can't prove or disprove; they just know that it happens. I am just taking one example of God's attribute—if it can be proved or disproved: God is omnipresent, i.e., God can be everywhere at the same time. How can that be possible? This is a concept even a theist has a hard time comprehending (no wonder, as we try to explain things based on our knowledge of classical physics where we know nothing can travel faster than the speed of light, at which point time becomes constant or irrelevant, thus causing all theories of classical physics to fail). On the contrary, if you delve into the world of quantum mechanics, you would see that our traditional understanding doesn't apply (such as quantum superpositions, which state that a quantum particle can be in multiple states at the same time until it's measured). Though physicists still don't fully understand how it works, it's evident that it works and is now being used in real-world applications. I am not saying that this is proof of the "God's Omnipresence" attribute, but I am just pointing out that the "night is still young"—science has a long way to go to even understand creation before it can begin to prove the Creator.

The scientific mind can't disbelieve God

This may seem the opposite of what you experience in a real-world situation. Most atheists claim that they are students of science or at least have an affinity for science. But this is actually far from the truth. It is like someone's proclamation that "I am the least racist person there is anywhere in the world." Would you buy into his claim and agree with that person without verifying that claim with their actions? No, you wouldn't. Because you would check this statement against the actions he has taken or what he has said on other occasions. In the same sense, even though most atheists would claim that they are the most science-minded persons you would find anywhere in this world, you would judge their actions and other statements to justify that claim. Let's see what science tells us to do. Science never claims that it knows everything; rather, it is the process of discovering the truth through observation and experiments. Through that discovery process, you find new truths and dismantle old truths—even the truths that science had asserted as "truth" in the past through scientific experimentation. Do you want evidence of it? I am giving you a few as headlines (otherwise it would be a few pages long for each of them).

- Aristotle's eternal state was shattered in the early nineteenth century by the Big Bang theory, which is now recognized as the widely accepted theory (until the next big theory shatters it).
- Einstein's cosmological constant was introduced to adhere to the static universe model.
- Lord Kelvin's claims that "No balloon and no airplane will ever be practically successful" and predictions of running out of oxygen's supply in 400 years (in 1898 when the world's population was just around a billion).
- Newton was absolutely wrong about the cause of gravitational force, which was then superseded by Einstein's theory of general relativity. Spoiler alert: Einstein was also dead wrong about quantum mechanics (see below).
- Quantum physics and classical computing do not agree with each other on many things. Quantum entanglement is one area where Einstein denied the existence of such behavior, but it is now not only accepted, but also one of the founding principles behind quantum computing.
- Opioids, once hailed as a "miracle painkiller," are now proven to be the root cause of America's opioid epidemic, where almost 50 thousand Americans die every year due to the addictive nature of this prescription medication. In just 50 years, the miracle drug has led to a deadly opioid epidemic.[73]
- The list goes on...

By going through the evolution of scientific discovery, you would see with certainty that science doesn't stand still on anything for long, but is an eternal journey to find new discoveries and truths while shattering its own past truths. Given such a state of science, how would you rely on science to decide whether there is a God or not? For science to reach the point where you can have a candid discussion about God, you would probably need to wait hundreds or thousands of years. Until then, what should a science-minded person do? If honest, they could hide behind the tent of Agnosticism, which is another hypocritical stance that needs thorough discussion as well. The Oxford Dictionary defines an agnostic as "a person who believes that nothing is known or can be known of the existence or nature of God, or of anything beyond material phenomena; a person who claims neither faith nor disbelief in God." This sounds intellectual at the outset, but if you peel off the first layer, it sounds rather dumb. First of all, it starts with "who believes," words that kill it all. When the word "belief" comes in, it just takes them to the level of a religious person, which they so despise. This may end the discussion on the hypocrisy of agnosticism, but if you really want to ignore that glaring red light, let's dive deeper. If you are agnostic and think of yourself as inquisitive, why do you stop there and feel complacent? Isn't it true that you have a limited time in this life to know the answer before you start the journey to the next life? Either you are sure, with proof, that there is no God, like an atheist, or you should find the truth of the existence of God and follow His instructions for your own salvation. If you don't know the truth and still cruise through this life while indulging in this extremely temporary life, you are nothing but ignorant. You're fooling yourself but not others. The parable is like a person aboard a cruise ship on the Niagara River, heading towards Niagara Falls, knowing that he will reach there in a short time and doing nothing because he hasn't discovered the physics of falling from the top of the fall to the bottom, but decided that "I would rather enjoy this time on the cruise ship than waste my time knowing what will happen once I reach the edge of the fall." Just remember, there's no return. Why would you take the chance, if you're not truly ignorant? "If you could but see when the criminals are hanging their heads before their Lord, [saying], "Our Lord, we have seen and heard, so return us [to the world]; we will work righteousness. Indeed, we are [now] certain" - Surah As-Sajdah (32:12)

Having said that, I would like to delve deeper into why atheism isn't, and cannot be, the solution for America or the West in general.

Atheism essentially tells you that there's no objective morality and everything is up for experience. That's because there's no higher being who created this universe and no one created you with any sense of purpose. So, just find your own baseline and recreate it every day. This essentially is happening in the West and all-over secular countries. The result is that you don't have any objective baseline to fall back on, and you end up in constant experimentation with life. The outcomes of that are many, and here are a few examples:

- Use as much material as society needs. Society will somehow maintain the balance of material usage through the "demand-supply" pull-push. How much would be needed by a person? It's not for anybody else to decide, but it would be solely based on the society you live in. The rules are created by society. Look around you. What are we consuming and how much are we consuming? We ended up in a world that is frying the planet with fossil fuels, flooding the world with plastics and chemicals, and creating a world of healthcare disasters: Type 2 diabetes, cardiovascular diseases, blood pressure issues, cancer, and a mental health pandemic, etc.
- Created a world where income inequality is rooted in the design of the economic system.
- No stopping of defining and redefining through experimentation: redefining marriage from a basic biological construct, denying the biology of sex and creating a spectrum of genders, and the absence of objective morality are a few to highlight.
- At times the science is used as if it's "eternal truth" of every problem. Remember Eugenics taken from Greek words to selectively breed to transform for best human race. Charles B. Davenport written the book named "Heredity in Relation to Eugenics"[74] with the intent to create

the best human. Thanks God that with Nazi ideology, this is also gone – almost – from the mainstream.

Pick your own choice

These are groups of people who are either indifferent to any religion or are not convinced that atheism or agnosticism is a viable option. Their indifference is not because they believe all religions are true, but nonetheless, religious rituals attract them due to social norms and their upbringing. However, they consider all religions equally unreasonable. The sad part is that they do not spend time discerning the truth, instead opting to lazily pick whatever they experience around them. Most importantly, their choices have to be easy—they won't adopt any serious rituals but will choose whatever fits into their leisure time. Although this might seem like moderation, which is true in a social sense, it is essentially another form of atheism by denying anything divine. This may sound harsh, but to be more accurate, they are worshippers of their own selves. They create a new religion from the menu of available religions, crafting a hodgepodge lifestyle. This approach may work for some time in some places, but it is sure to fail for the same reasons atheism fails: this new "religion," or way of life, is designed by a person constrained by time, space, and other human limitations. The biggest risk with this approach is that it is hard to determine whether it works because they constantly change their menu, akin to moving the goalposts, making it impossible to prove its long-term ineffectiveness. I could go on and add more facts and factors to prove it, but those would be redundant to some extent after the coverage of atheism above. Therefore, the reason why atheism isn't a viable solution applies equally to this customized "hodgepodge"—it also isn't a long-term solution for the West.

"None" affiliated

These are the fastest-growing groups in the United States of America. I just created this section to recognize them explicitly, but they are nothing more than a medley of "Pick your own religion" and atheistic or agnostic ideology. They detach themselves from any religion and live their lives materialistically, moment by moment. So, why isn't this also a viable solution? For the same reason the above two ideologies won't work as viable solutions.

Then what?

After looking into those choices, if you think something is missing from that list, you're spot on. The other religions or dogmas mentioned above didn't satisfy your thirst. I won't blame you for that. How could you be satisfied with a religion that doesn't fit with the natural life surrounding you, which you can't deny? Also, how could you be living your "life" without being certain about what's next after this "life"? Welcome to the truth![75]

Let's talk about Islam. Can Islam be a choice for the West? Especially for America? Let's check that out.

If you've received education on Islam or Muslims from general media like Fox, or from "Islam Experts" such as Brigitte Gabriel, Robert Spencer, or Ayaan Hirsi Ali, then I doubt you would be interested at all in Islam. I wouldn't say that they were successful in convincing you, but I would suggest that you have failed to pick your "scholar". I can't spend much time on them, as this book is not intended to discuss their purpose, intent, or lack of wisdom. However, I will just mention one fiery speech by Brigitte Gabriel in which she passionately warned Westerners about Islam. Many Westerners have received this history lesson from her as she attempted to convey the history of Islam's 1400 years in just five minutes. Here's what she had said on the FRCAction platform:

"In order for you to understand why **Western civilization is very different than the Islamic world** you need to understand the history of Islam when prophet Muhammad supposedly revealed his revelation from the angel Gabriel that he is supposed to be the last of the prophets in the early six hundreds. He started preaching in his own City Mecca he tried to recruit friends and followers to be able to spread his religion and he tried for 12 years and failed. And after 12 years he was only able to recruit his immediate family and friends **so he decided if I go to Medina** which was the Jewish hub of Arabia, **the business hub** where the Jews lived, if I go there and **preach my religion to them** if they **accept me** that will buy me a respect and stature in between my own people and they will accept me. So, Prophet Muhammad started borrowing a lot from the Old Testament to make his religion more palatable to the Jews to make it a lot similar this is why you see a lot of similarities between Judaism and Islam. For example, Jews don't eat pigs Muslims don't eat pigs, Jews pray a few times a day **Muslims pray few times a day,** jews fast on Yom Kippur Muslims fast on Ramadan and this is why when you started seeing a lot of good writing and the beginning of the Quran when Prophet Muhammad was saying all the good things about the people of the book. He took his message and went to Medina **trying to recruit the Jews** talking about the people of the book talking about how similar the two religions are. When they refused to accept him and follow him as the last of the Prophet that's when he turned against them and **started killing them** and **started expelling them** that's one is went from a spiritual movement for the first 12 years of Islam into a political movement cloaked in religion after the year of the Hegira after Mohammed went to Medina and the Jews did not accept him. He became a military warrior and **declared war on them** and **started expelling them Jews** and **Christians became dimmie** or second-class citizens they were only allowed to stay alive **and not be**

killed only by paying vision or the production tax so they had a choice convert to Islam or if you want to **stay alive you have to pay the jizya** or protection tax living as Dimmie in the Islamic nation. Christians and Jews could not ring a church about Jews could not blow the shofar. Christians could not ring church bells **they could not pray publicly.** Christians and Jews could not gather together and build a new churches or new temples and the way they paid the jizya or the protection tax was a monthly ceremony where they would get together downtown and the **Jew would kneel on his knee and hand his goods to the mullah** who would take the goods as the as the price for buying the protection and in many areas **Jews and Christians were given necklaces to wail** as a receipt that they paid their jizya or their protection tax. Jews considered najasa under Islam. Najasa is bodily fluid, …as garbage …as dogs, najasa is dirty so **Christians and Jews were treated as second-class citizens**. Islam continued to grow as Islam grew more people became Dimmie second-class citizens till Jews and **Christians were given identifiable clothing the yellow star which was given to the Jews** that most people think is a German invention it was actually an **Islamic invention in the 9th century** in Iraq by the second Holly and motivic you love Iraq who invented the yellow star for the Jews to be identified as they walked down the street because **Jews were considered najasa if a Muslim man or a Jew walked on the same side of the street that you had to cross the other side so the Muslim man also he's not dirtied by the filth of the Jew. Christians were given the zunar the belt which most of you men are wearing right now that was an Islamic invention for the Christians.** Islam continued to grow. They went all the way to Jerusalem they conquered Jerusalem. **Christians couldn't ring their church bells in Jerusalem.** The Pope in Rome in 1090 told the Christians how could you sit idly by and allow your brethren to be suffered to suffer like this in the Holy Land you need to go liberate the Christians you need to go help the Christians. That's why the Crusaders were launched. The Crusaders were not launched because they just felt like waking up in the morning and going and converting a bunch of

Muslims or beheading them. The Crusaders were launched to liberate Jerusalem and they were able to liberate Jerusalem for less than 100 years before Salahuddin Ayyubi, Saladin took it back and Jerusalem remained under Islamic control until 1967 when the State of Israel liberated Jerusalem **where Christians Jews and Muslims to pray under the same sky.** The Crusaders continue fighting Islam, expansion of Islam and for 300 years they tried and failed and by the 1300s the Crusaders disappeared because they could not win against Islam. Islam continued to expand. They went all the way to Central Europe. They went all the way to China. They went to India. They conquered Spain. They changed the name of Spain from Spain to Andalusia and they started as as they advanced as they conquered more nations more people pay the jizya or the protection tax and this is how the Islamic empire grew. It went all the way until they were stuck at the gates of Vienna on 9/11. 911 is not a date that the Osama bin Laden just picked out of that. **9/11 is a symbolic date in the Islamic calendar.** Between the 1600 by the 1600s Islam had covered more of the Earth's surface than the Roman Empire did at its peak between the 1600s and the 1800s the Europeans were experiencing the repeal Industrial Revolution where the Europeans were to invent products on factory lines where they are able to make money and sell products which gave them the money to build the strong army in order to fight the Muslims and that's how they were able to stop them at the gates of Vienna on 9/11. The Europeans started the pushback against Islam. They pushed them out of Europe. They pushed them out of all the way to the Middle East and North Africa. By 1924 the Islamic empire ended. In 1924 the Islamic caliphate ended in Turkey by President Ataturk who was a secularist. He ended the Islamic empire and he gave women rights to vote he gave women a right to an education a right to work. **A right to choose a husband.** He forbids women from wearing the hijab. He forbids men from wearing the beard. The Muslim hate him so much that **they consider him a Jewish agent because they believe that his mother and her bloodline was Jewish** and that was the influence on Ataturk. By the time the Islamic empire or the Islamic caliphate or the Islamic state ended in 1924. **The Islamic caliphate had existed for 1400 years and it ended less than 100 years ago. By the time the Islamic caliphate ended in 1924, 270 million people around the world were killed by Islam.** 270 million and we didn't have weapons of mass destruction and there were nuclear weapons. **All of these people were killed butchered by the sword**. The people in the world less than a hundred years ago. How many people knew this history please raise your hand. We in America have failed to educate our children about history. We in America failed to educate our population about history. Wur children in high school you take any 17-16-year-old kids 18-year-old kid and asked them about World War II. They can't even tell you what happened that World War II. For them it's ancient history and we still have our World War II veteran walking among us. That's how little we know of history of Islam and in the 1924 the Caliphate people felt Islam when the caliphate will never be resurrected the caliphate will never come back but two things happened in the Middle East in the last century that made the Islamists be able to resurrect the caliphate. **Number one is the discovery of oil in Saudi Arabia which we were able to discover and were stupid enough to allow them to nationalize it** and the number two that happened was Ayatollah Khomeini coming to power in 1979 that gave the Islamists the money and also the spiritual covering in order to explode on the world stage. And people say over the Wahhabis exported there were Wahhabi radical religion. The Wahhabis are the name of Wahab they're not a different sect of Islam. **They follow the authentic preaching of Prophet Muhammad**. The way Prophet Muhammad lived and practiced his religion. This is why neither you or me or any infidel can step of foot in Mecca because **as far as they're concerned, we are filth and as infidels**. We're not allowed to step foot not President Obama and not anybody else as a matter of fact. **Al-qaeda used to use Saudi Arabia and its success as an excuse to recruit members as the example to show them how Allah has blessed Saudi Arabia because of the way they adhered to the tenets of Islam** and today we thought about Isis. **Isis is not a new invention. Isis resurrected that Caliphate** that ended less than a hundred years ago except we are too ignorant and too uninformed to understand why. What Isis is doing and **why Isis is succeeding** do things you need to understand about Islam and the principles of war in Islam. **One is the law of Taqiyya which means lying and deception it means that a Muslim man can lay his hand on the Koran and swear that he is telling the truth knowing that he is lying but also knowing that the Koran will forgive him because he is advancing the cause of Islam.** The second thing you need to know about is that the treaty of *hudaibiya* which is an Islamic principle of war and **a model on how to deceive your enemy** when you have to sign peace treaties with your enemy and it is based on an example by Prophet Mohammed. Prophet Muhammed was attacking the Meccans and their caravans when he was living in Medina. **One day he attacked them because this is how he got the duties. He would attack them robbed them** and **spread the goodies among his men and this is how he was able to recruit because this is how people made money without working and so he attacked the Macan caravans. When he realized he is not able to defeat the Meccans in that city of hudaibiya in that place he signed a ten-year treaty with them.** Does that sound familiar? A ten-year treaty with them **that says he will not attack them**. He will have peace with them. **He will not declare war on them. Muhammad used the treaty for two years to build his military. Strengthened his army and when he realized he was strong enough to attack his enemies when they least expected it because they said they thought they had a peace treaty with Muhammad he broke the treaty attacked** them two years later and **Mecca fell within 24 hours because they were not expecting the attack** and that became **a principle of war in Islam** and to give you an example of how that is practiced…"

Forget about you; even I, being a Muslim, would be horrified about Islam if she were right. If you're convinced that Brigitte Gabriel is the best historian about Islam and you are completely convinced that she's honest and right, then maybe this book isn't for you. However, if you are not convinced that she had the whole truth in just 5 minutes or maybe you haven't heard about her at all but want to learn about what Islam is and how it's relevant to the context of this book, please continue reading. Also, you may have noticed that I have made sentences that are complete fabrications bold and underlined those that are dishonest. Once you finish reading this book and read the sources in the references from scholars and academics, please come back and read again to see for yourself. There are many recent scholars in this country who have done extensive writing and teaching about Islam, but if you are in a rush to know that before completing this book, just check out these three professors' books and lectures, and you will be shocked at how dishonest or ignorant she was. These were such blatant lies that even I could debunk them, but I don't want you to take my words for it, as I am not a historian by profession but most importantly, you would be suspecting me as biased towards Islam due to my faith. These are lies and fraudulent claims, but in history, there were people who even made more outrageously insane propositions than her that Prophet Muhammad (pbuh) didn't even exist and that it was all made up. Here's an anecdote from Columbia University professor Richard Bulliet: "Other people in your field handle the history and you don't want to be such an outlier that it doesn't sound like Islamic history...after the third edition of the second edition one of the reviewers, a user I think in a small college in California, wrote and said he thought the entire chapter should be scrapped because the new scholarly view maintained that Muhammad never existed. That the Quran was composed by a gaggle of rabbis in Iraq two hundred years after the alleged date of Muhammad's life and that it arose as a Jewish heresy and had blah blah blah. Well now, that's a completely different view of Islam and it is one that has some distinguished if profoundly mistaken scholars who support it, and I could see that someone who is not a specialist might say, oh well maybe I should look into it and maybe I should lean in that direction so I leaned in that direction for about one paragraph just to acknowledge that there was this view out there and I thought that's fine you had a basic story of the rise of Islam..." He was referring to the book: Crossroads to Islam: The Origins of the Arab Religion and the Arab State is a book by archaeologist Yehuda D. Nevo and researcher Judith Koren. So, the misrepresentation isn't just Brigitte Gabriel or Robert Spencer, but there are also "scholars" who created similar outrageous dumb claims. There is so much proof lying out there that you don't always need written papers to find proof of things that happened. Just for example: how do you know that the Universe was created 14 billion years or so ago? How do you know that Earth is 4 billion years or so old? How do you know that glaciers in North America created all the landscapes? You don't look for written history but you use the evidence that fits the events and cause. Just an example: I went to Maine in a summer in the Acadia National Park for camping. We stayed for a little less than a week and was fascinated by the Bubble Rock hanging on top of a hill, Jordan ponds and Bubble ponds. The round huge rocks lying on the ground scattered miles apart on the meadows at the road side. I had no clue who did those. Until I read the history of the landscape of that area and it became so clear why those large sphere-shaped rocks were scattered and hanging on top of hills. Those were the work of glaciers as they moved and slid into the ocean, they brought those boulders and became sphere-shaped by the rolling of those boulders under the pressure of glaciers. Similarly, the Spectacular Island in the Boston Harbor was created by similar glacier movements. The landscapes of those areas told the story of glacier movement millions of years ago. If you had been looking for written and eyewitnesses who saw the glaciers move, then it will not change the history but it will make you ignorant. So, use all the evidence that was done by thousands of Arabs and the transformation of the surrounding empires (Byzantine i.e. Eastern Roman and Sassanid) and others – you can't just wash it away. Even there were written stuff if you're so adamant about that. However, that book was written in 2003. I hope the authors had lived through 2014 to see their "hard work" wasted by "just another" evidence i.e., The Birmingham Qur'an Manuscript that

"...contains parts of surahs 18-20 of the Islamic holy book, written on parchment in an early form of Arabic script known as Hijazi. The result of radiocarbon dating of the parchment on which the text is written places the manuscript in the period between 568 and 645 with 95.4% probability. The testing was commissioned from the University of Oxford and carried out in 2014. This result suggests that the manuscript dates back to the first century of Islam, close to the lifetime of the Prophet Muhammad (about 570–632) and the rule of the first three Caliphs."[76] It would also be hyper willful ignorance to overlook the fact that Prophet Muhammad (pbuh) came just 1,400 years ago. In the light of history, you can't pretend that we're looking back to the Stone Age. Take it from a historian: Ernest Renan (1823-1892), the famous French historian of religions, had confidently pronounced that "Islam was born in the full light of history."[77]

Take the words of the real scholars who have no vested interest in Islam.

- Professor Richard Bulleit: professor of history at Columbia University
- Professor Paul Freedman: professor of History at Yale University
- Professor Roy Casagranda: professor of History and Political Science at Austin School

By the way, I am not claiming that Islam is the only choice for America; however, I am asserting that, for many reasons which we'll explore in the subsequent chapter, Islam is currently the most plausible choice. I would like to state at the outset that Islam isn't a new framework for living, but rather claims the complete opposite: it represents the natural disposition of life, starting from Prophet Adam and passed through every prophet and nation in the world, including those of whom we are still fully aware: Noah, Abraham, Moses, David, and Jesus. It encompasses all the religions of the one and only God and believes that all nations were sent guidance, which may have changed, intentionally or unintentionally, to suit our purposes or out of ignorance, over the course of time. It is simply a continuation of the original message through a chain of prophets, culminating with Prophet Muhammad (pbuh). Yes, Christianity has highly influenced Western civilization; however, it cannot alone save the West for a simple reason: the foundation of this civilization is based on very basic scientific facts that directly contradict Christianity. Thus, the problem is not Christianity itself, since it was also guidance sent from God; however, as we do not have the original words of God preserved, it worked for a time but fails us in this different era. This is very natural for any man-made framework, proven throughout the history of humanity. If you are not ready to take that journey, just consider Communism, which took the world by storm just a century ago and now not only has it become historical and antiquated, but it has also proven itself absolutely unnatural for humanity. We have discussed this earlier in this chapter and will explore the contrast with Islam in the next chapter. Nevertheless, if you are determined to revert to Christianity, as mentioned earlier, you would have no choice but to roll back the scientific foundations and progressions made by this great civilization. Let's continue.

Chapter V: Why Islam is a Choice for the West?

"We have revealed to you the book with the truth for mankind. He who lets himself be guided does so to his own good; he who does astray does so to his own hurt" (39:41). This is selfishly for us to benefit from the choice we would make. We can take the guidance and benefit ourselves, or we can choose to ignore it and harm ourselves. We are given free will but with the ability to use our intellect to choose right from wrong. So, to see if Islam can be a choice, we must first be convinced that Islam is the truth and that it will offer benefits and save us from harm.

Let's see what Islam has to offer to the Western civilization.

You've come up to this point, which means you're at least convinced that you want to explore what other choices we may have, as Christianity, atheism, or any other alternatives mentioned above aren't viable choices for the future that the West needs to solve its current issues, as well as for the long-term viability of its civilization. Not only that, but you're also convinced that you need a solution not just for today but for the afterlife as well, and you would like to achieve success in both worlds: the life in this world and the hereafter. After all, this life is minuscule in comparison to the infinite life after we die.

What's the big deal of following Islam?

First, you have to be convinced that Islam is The Truth. If you just want to pick something from Islam, like many in the West do with everything else (yoga from Hinduism, charity from Christianity, intermittent fasting from Islam, a materialistic life from atheism, etc.), then you're going to miss the opportunity once again and irreversibly waste your valuable time. If you don't want to spiral down the rabbit hole, choose the path that will make a difference.

"Two roads diverged in a wood, and I—

I took the one less traveled by,

And that has made all the difference."

You may insist: if I can achieve materialistic success by doing a mix and match of the best from all the 'religions,' then why the big fuss about Islam? In fact, you may achieve a healthy body by following healthy living practices—be it from Islam or from your own ingenuity. Why rock the boat then?

As an example, in a materialistic sense, the best practices for a healthy lifestyle are:

- Go to bed and sleep early. The first part of the night's sleep repairs your body.
- Wake up at the crack of dawn. Sleeping during sunrise has a biologically toxic impact on your body.
- Be active - go for a walk every day for about an hour or so. Go out and earn a living.
- Eat less and do intermittent fasting twice a week.
- Live stress-free. Remember that, in the end, things will work out fine.

If you follow that lifestyle, you can be pretty sure that you will 'apparently' live a healthy life in this world; in fact, many healthy people already follow it. So, what's the difference if I follow Islam or not? What's the big deal about Islam claiming that you would live a healthy life by following exactly the same lifestyle?

There are two reasons why just following a healthy lifestyle isn't good enough for the long term of your life or for society.

First: Humans aren't just another animal, even though many "smart" biologists might tell you that by showing how similar our genes are to those of a banana, or how our biology and psychology are so similar to those of many other animals in this world. After stating that, they also "silently" accept that humans are actually totally different in terms of:

- Advanced Cognitive Abilities: Humans have highly developed brains capable of abstract reasoning, problem-solving, and complex planning. This cognitive capacity supports language use, complex decision-making, and the ability to project into the future or reflect on the past.
- Language and Communication: Humans use sophisticated languages involving syntax, grammar, and a vast vocabulary, allowing for the expression of abstract and complex ideas. Language is a crucial tool for communication, knowledge sharing, and cultural transmission across generations.
- Use of Tools and Technology: While some animals use basic tools, humans excel in their ability to create and utilize complex tools and technology. From simple stone tools to advanced digital technologies, human history is marked by continual technological innovation.
- Culture: Humans create and live within multifaceted cultural systems. Culture encompasses art, religion, customs, traditions, and knowledge that are passed down through learning and can profoundly affect human behavior and beliefs.
- Social Structures: Humans form complex social structures which include defined roles, social norms, and institutions. These structures facilitate large-scale cooperative behaviors, including forming nations, economic systems, and organized religions.
- Ethics and Morals: Humans have developed systems of ethics and morals, often guided by philosophical, cultural, or religious principles. These systems govern behavior and can influence lawmaking, personal interactions, and social justice issues.
- Artistic Expression: Humans uniquely create art for aesthetic, communicative, or symbolic purposes, including music, literature,

dance, and visual arts. Artistic expression is a fundamental aspect of human culture and emotional expression.

- Awareness of Mortality: Humans are uniquely aware of their mortality. This awareness influences many aspects of human thought and behavior, including values, goals, and existential pondering.
- Self-Consciousness: Humans have a complex sense of self and self-reflection. This self-awareness enables introspection, personal identity, and a conscious connection with one's environment.

If this life is the only life, you and I are living, then good luck with your 'only life.' Do not listen to any of the things I am going to cover next. However, if you're not sure if this is the only life, or you are sure that life has a bigger purpose and you will be resurrected for an eternal life hereafter, then do not be deceived by this mere healthy life devoid of a 'higher purpose.' The metaphor is like being in a trading business where you're selling your commodities as perishable items that are good for a day alone; if tomorrow comes, then your returns won't be of any use. Sell your commodities for hard currency that is good for 'today' as well as 'tomorrow' so that you're benefiting yourself today—i.e., in this life—and achieving the 'tomorrow,' i.e., the hereafter. By the way, what is the 'commodity' that we are sent with for that trade?

Time!

So, let's use that precious commodity wisely and trade it to purchase the Truth—the complete religion. For any religion to stand as the truth, it must be objectively true, able to pass the test of time with transcendent value, capable of building human civilization, and finally, it must substantiate its claim to be suitable for humanity in general, regardless of ethnicity, time, and geography.

For the example of healthy living, let's see what Islam has to say about that. It's the exact same thing, but connect your every step to a higher purpose in life:

- Pray the night prayer (in Arabic: *Isha*) and go to bed early. It's better if you wake up in the middle of the night for the midnight prayer (in Arabic: *tahajjud* and *Qiyamul-layil*).
- Wake up before sunrise (in Arabic: *Fajr*) and do not sleep afterward, especially during the sunrise. Read the Quran to get a reminder of the purpose of life. Once the sun rises, go out and seek the bounty of *Allah* in this world.
- Eat up to two-thirds full of your stomach – that's a highly recommended prophetic teaching, i.e. Sunnah.
- Fast for one month in the year – that's obligatory, and fast 11 days in a month, which is a highly recommended Sunnah.
- Do your part with your ability but live a stress-free life and believe in higher being that you are part of the bigger plan of this universe. (in Arabic: *tawakkul 'ala Allah*)

Why would you bother to adjust your healthy living, or your lifestyle in general, from a purely materialistic approach to an Islamic one? Let's check if Islam fits the bill.

Objective truth

This is the fundamental and very first claim that Islam must pass if it is to be considered as the solution for the West. Why is that so? Because, if Islam is from the omnipotent Almighty God who created this universe, life, and time, there can't be a single fact that contradicts the absolute truth. However, the question would be: How can we measure something if the measuring scale is not there? To simplify, how can we measure 'one foot' if there's no one-foot scale? After all, the universe where we live is relative in terms of space and time. For those who aren't well versed in physics, Albert Einstein discovered the relativity of time, which, until his discovery, was thought to be 'absolute.' In layman's terms: time slows down when things move faster and essentially stops for objects moving at light-speed. So, even if we're talking about absolute truth, we'd be looking at it in relation to this universe's space-time because there's no way we humans can place ourselves outside of those dimensions to assess those objectively. Thus, the term 'objective' is even relative but on a much larger scale – the universe scale rather than on a short scale like a few hundred years. Another approach is to take it from someone who is not bound by those limitations, i.e., space-time – the creator of the universe. As I will mention, we can't objectively prove the existence of the creator, so we use deductive reasoning to be convinced about the existence of the creator and then analyze the objective truth in light of our constrained capacity.

To tackle that challenge, we have to split the facts into two buckets: *Test the Testable* and *Test the Untestable.*

Test the Testable:

Test the truths that can be tested, for which we have a relatively stable measuring scale, such as facts that stand clearly before us without much room for doubt. Metaphorically speaking, if we can measure a large number of trees up to 100 feet using a 100-foot scale in such a way that no tree shorter than 100 feet is mistakenly measured as 100 feet, then we can be relatively confident that future measurements are highly likely to be accurate. This is why people have put their 'faith' in science, as we have seen science make the right predictions and outcomes repeatedly in a large number of cases. However, we must be careful when using science as a measuring scale. By definition, science is an evolving method of seeking the truth and continuously looks for new evidence.

For Islam, we can use the relative measuring scale, i.e., science, to measure the facts stated in the Quran to see to what extent it can stand. This is comparatively easy. We can find facts from either the Quran or science and see what the Quran says about them. The Quran has made many claims that have been independently worked on by scientists in various fields. These will be covered in the 'Scientific Truth' section. Here are a few such things:

Creation of universe; Origin of life; Creation of human; Lifestyles choices, such as, material life, charity, food and drinks that are forbidden or allowed, etc.; Predestination or deterministic nature of the creation; Religious rituals must have to be beneficial.

Let's see what Islam had to say about those clear facts and are they contradicting with Islam or not.

The creation of the Universe is mentioned repeatedly in the Quran and cannot be missed. The Quran mentions that the Universe was created in six 'days,' which, in a more accurate translation, means epochs. It is referred to as an epoch because the Quran clearly states that the 'days' created by God are equivalent to thousands of years in human terms. The Quran describes the Universe as having been initially compacted together and then separated through a massive explosion-like expansion, setting it in motion to expand continuously. Here are the references from the Quran that I have just mentioned.

"Indeed, your Lord is Allah, who created the heavens and earth in six days and then established Himself above the Throne…" – Surah Al-A'raf (7:54)

"And they urge you to hasten the punishment. But Allah will never fail in His promise. And indeed, a day with your Lord is like a thousand years of those which you count."- Surah Al-Hajj (22:47)

The origin of life is so astonishing that when I read the Quran's mention of the origin of life—stating unequivocally that 'all living things are created from water, and some move on their bellies, some on four legs, and some on two feet'—it seems as if I am reading a modern biology book on the origin and evolution of life.

Lifestyle choices like the forbidding of alcohol and drugs. The obligation of fasting for every adult Muslim includes at least 30 days of mandatory fasting and 130+ days of non-mandatory but highly recommended fasting. Prophetic teachings advise not to eat or drink to one's full stomach but to keep one-third empty.

Predestination or determinism in the Quran is uniquely direct. God knows and decides what will happen in the future, which is known as predestination. However, it goes one step further. God has predestined the future, but He also changes the future as He wishes, based on the actions of men and women. This may seem oxymoronic at first, but science is increasingly aligning with this concept every day.

Religious rituals in Islam are full of meditation; fasting, as mentioned earlier, and physical prostration occur multiple times every day. These are mandatory rituals where Muslims are obligated to take breaks five times a day for meditation that comprises spiritual and physical exercises.

Test the Untestable:

However, the harder parts are the facts that are 'not intuitive' or even counterintuitive to our senses and cannot be proved directly without any doubt. Nonetheless, they cannot be disproved with certainty either. So, what choices are left for these? Believe blindly without asking questions? Quite the contrary. A Muslim is not asked to blindly believe in God and those matters without using reason. This brings us to the unique proposition of Islam. In the Quran, God has repeatedly emphasized the use of intellect. Observe the creation of the Creator to develop an understanding of the Creation and thus understand the Creator. Many prophets have asked questions and used their reasoning to understand God. For example, Prophet Ibrahim (a.s.) used deductive reasoning to dismiss objects like sculptures, the Sun, and the Moon as deities and concluded with the existence of God. A similar story is told of Prophet Musa (a.s.), who wanted to see the Creator to comprehend the existence of God.

The approach to proving these can be deductive or involve a 'lingering effect' when we don't have direct measurements available at this time. Sometimes atheists use the term 'God of the Gaps' (inspired by Richard Dawkins's book) to mock religious people, but they themselves use those gaps in their everyday lives. I can provide many examples:

Astronomy, astrophysics, anthropology, archaeology, medicine, and other fields use deductive reasoning or the lingering effect technique to prove or disprove something. In fact, most scientific measurements utilize the 'lingering effect' technique.

- Consider a mercury thermometer: what does it do? It essentially expands the mercury in correlation to heat and thus calculates the temperature from the expansion.
- In astrophysics, the presence of gravitational waves, predicted by Albert Einstein, was measured by the length of light traveled in LIGO, proving its existence almost a century after the prediction.
- In quantum computing, the super positions of a particle is measured by the other particle that's entangled quantum to it.
- In medicine, various tests are conducted that could not be done otherwise. Tuberculosis (TB) is one such example. Scientists can't directly see the presence or absence of TB bacteria as they are either long gone or in a latent state. Instead, they check if a protein called

> interferon-gamma (IFN-γ) is released when mixed with TB antigens, or if the immune system is activated by a protein derivative of TB bacteria. They'll interpret your results as negative, positive, or indeterminate.[78]

Here are a few such phenomena that we can deduce by the presence or absence of their effects:

- Proving the existence of God through experimentation
- The creations of God that we do not observe in real life, such as Angels and Jinn
- How miracles were performed by the Prophets
- How the Quran was transmitted to Prophet Muhammad (pbuh)
- The resurrection after death
- The Day of Judgment
- Heaven and Hell, etc.

For these, we won't have the ability to use a measuring scale to prove them; instead, we can consider the possibility of their occurrence. If you begin with the first point, i.e., proving the existence of God through the use of the scientific method, you'll find it challenging. In fact, the Quran clearly mentions that there is nothing in this universe within our realm of comprehension that is like God. The only way to deduce reasoning for the existence of God is through the meticulous observation of His creation.

"[He is] Creator of the heavens and the earth. He has made for you from yourselves, mates, and among the cattle, mates; He multiplies you thereby. ***There is nothing like unto Him***, and He is the Hearing, the Seeing." – Surah Ash-Shura (42:11)

So, here I am going to show them through rational analogies and logically deduce, as it's not possible for me, and I would argue that for most of us, with the current level of knowledge, to 'prove' these with certainty through human 'observation.' To appreciate my reasoning, think about Quantum Entanglement and Superposition. Even Albert Einstein denounced the possibility of Quantum Entanglement, labeling it 'spooky behavior.' In his 1935 Einstein-Podolsky-Rosen (EPR) paper[79], known as the 'EPR Paradox,' Einstein suggested that Quantum Entanglement is not compatible with 'physical reality' because cause and effect cannot be predetermined. However, as we now know with 'certainty' and as is generally accepted through worldwide recognition (Aspen-Clauser-Zeilinger's 2022 Nobel Prize[80]), Quantum behavior is indeed a reality. With this newly discovered 'vocabulary,' we can think differently and explain many phenomena that were previously impossible to even grapple with. Having said that, let's quickly touch on those claims.

For example, consider the existence of Angels and Jinn as another creation that we cannot see. It's a simple possibility if we understand higher dimensionality. Since we live in four dimensions—Length, Width, Height, and Time—it would be impossible for us to experience the addition of another dimension. It's as if someone living in two dimensions would perceive a spherical object like a ball as merely a 2-D circle. Our current science, particularly physics, fully embraces the concept of higher dimensionality. It's not just a mere possibility; there are many scientific theories that suggest higher dimensionality (like String Theory, which is not that 'strong,' pun intended) is integral to our universe. We can't prove it today, and I'm not sure if we will in our lifetime, but it remains a possibility that we can explore through our scientific endeavors.

Coming back to proving the existence of God: the Quran never claims that we'll be able to experience that firsthand, but it teaches that they are to be appreciated through the creation of God. Consider the landscape created by glaciers on the East Coast (Massachusetts or Maine), which left imprints of glacial movement millions of years ago. You didn't see the glaciers, but you have undoubtedly seen the impact of that phenomenon (refer to Spectacle Island in Massachusetts, Bubble Rock in Acadia, and the entire formation of the landscape of Maine, just for you to read up and appreciate). The creator has shaped this universe and left all the imprints for us to appreciate. We witness the creator's power in the Universe, which is so magnificent that we often overlook it and live in a tiny locality. Let's just think for a moment: we are on Earth, spinning at 1,000 miles per hour, moving around the Sun at 67,000 miles per hour, and we're hurtling through the Galactic orbit with the Sun at 450,000 miles per hour, while our galaxy is moving at a whopping 1.3 million miles per hour. And we're a tiny planet in a mid-sized star's solar system. There are about 100 (possibly up to 400) billion stars in our galaxy, the Milky Way, and there are billions of galaxies in this universe, and we don't even know the full size of our universe. Let that sink in. How much power is behind that acceleration? A tiny SpaceX rocket uses 410 tonnes of propellant per launch to get the speed of 17,500 miles per hour. Can you imagine how much energy each object in the universe requires to achieve that speed? How powerful must the creator be to create that energy? That creator, God – Allah in the Quran – said that He just creates it out of nothing by merely commanding it to come into existence, and it does. That's true for every creation around us. I just provided a large-scale analogy. Similarly, you would be in awe if you delved into the smaller scale, from our biology to the atomic-subatomic level. Did you know that there are approximately 100 billion neurons in our brain? Does that ring any bell? It's comparable to the number of stars in the Milky Way galaxy. What a coincidence! The point I am trying to make is this: just observe the creation, and you have to be really arrogant to dismiss all these powers that arose from nothing as a mere coincidence.

I could go on and on with the rest of the issues at hand, but I think it would be better left to your own research and pondering in a similar approach that I have laid out above.

Transcendent truth - stand through time

We'll cover scientific and civilization aspects to show how Islam stands through time.

Scientific truth

Before we use the dimension of scale, i.e., science, let's make it very clear that science itself cannot be a measuring scale to test God because this represents a logical fallacy. You can't test the creator by the creation of the Creator. This isn't just my statement, but one echoed by many profound scientists and scientific minds. In the lecture titled 'The Unknown Universe Explained' by Neil DeGrasse Tyson, which is a more than three-hour-long fascinating presentation to explain 'the inexplicable universe from a time gone by that's now explained,' he made a profound statement. I am transcribing it from that lecture, while explaining Dark Matter and Dark Energy, he said, *'96% of all that is the universe is not anything we even remotely understand, and all of our laws of physics, everything we know, love, interact with, understand, and even can predict anything about the future, falls into the 4% that remains. Now, actually, it gets worse. Our most successful theory of the universe, Quantum Physics, allows you to calculate what you might expect to be the energy contained in the vacuum of space. We can do that calculation; it allows it. It predicts that there should be energy there. We do the calculation. Quantum Physics has never been wrong. It's our best understanding going. When you do that calculation, the answer you get does not match reality. The answer you get is off by a factor of 10 to the 120th power. That's a 1 followed by 120 zeros. That's just embarrassing, sorry. We put forth our best theory to our biggest problem, and it gets us nowhere. In fact, it is the biggest mismatch between theory and observation there ever was in the history of science. That's our state of science today. So, we're not only ignorant, but our best theories of the universe also can't guide us. So, I think that means we're driving blind.'*[81] So, I am not going to be so naïve as to use the 'scientific' yardstick as a blind driver to prove the Quran or Islam. However, by the same token, the religion, the way of life to live on this Earth, can't be full of contradictions with our day-to-day life. For example, if we say that both the Sun and Moon revolve around the Earth, or we say that the Earth is not floating but actually sitting on pillars, then you are certainly entitled to ask a simple question: what's going on here? That's true for Islam as well as any other divine religion, i.e., Christianity, Judaism, Hinduism, etc. So why should we use science to prove other religions are not the right solution for the future of the West and then say Islam can't be tested by science? We can't be hypocritical in our approach. So, what we're doing here is showing a comparison of the scientific facts of our time and presenting the candidate religions side by side so that you can see the wide gaps and contrasts with other religions in comparison to Islam.

So, what are the big-ticket scientific facts and theories generally accepted by the West that Christianity contradicts? What does Islam have to say about those facts?

The creation of the Universe and Origin of life:

The Quran makes astounding claims about the creation of the universe, the origin of life, and even evolution, that sometimes, if you weren't forewarned, you might mistake them for excerpts from a science book.

Spoiler alert: Just to give you a glimpse of the miraculous nature of the Quran, I would like to share a tidbit from an amazing lecture by Stephen Hawking. He delivered this lecture at the Hong Kong University of Science and Technology on June 11, 2006. The title of his talk was 'The Origin of the Universe.' You can watch the entire 1:07-hour talk, but if you're in a hurry, fast forward to the 20:35 minute mark, where he made this exact statement: *'To his surprise, Hubble found that nearly all the galaxies were moving away from us. Moreover, the further the galaxies were from us, the faster they were moving away. The universe was not unchanging with time as everyone had thought previously.* ***It was expanding. The distance between distant galaxies was increasing over time. The expansion of the universe was one of the most important intellectual discoveries of the 20th century, or of any century.*** *It transformed the debate about whether the universe had a beginning.*'[82] Now, read this Quranic verse:

"And the heaven We constructed with strength, and indeed, We are [its] expander" – Surah Al-Jariayat (51:47)

Another fascinating story: in the same 'The Unknown Universe Explained by Neil DeGrasse Tyson' lecture, he explained the concept of 'Zero Total Energy' (watch for 4 minutes from 2:26:52 to 2:31:41, if you're in a hurry). *'If you add together the three kinds of things that occupy the universe: the familiar matter, which is what we're made of and what our telescopes detect, the dark matter, which is the source of 85% of all the gravity we see in the universe and whose cause we do not know, and the dark energy, the stuff that's making us accelerate against the wishes of gravity, each one of these components affects the fabric of space and time, just as prescribed by Einstein's General Theory of Relativity. If you add those curvatures together, what you find is that they create a universe that is perfectly flat... If your space-time is flat, just as if your orbit were a parabola, it means the entire universe possesses zero net total energy. Think about that. If the shape of the universe were anything else, positively curved or negatively curved, it would not have zero energy. It would have negative or positive energy. We have* ***zero net total energy****. Is that good or bad? Actually, there's a silver lining to this. What it means is that you can create the universe out of nothing because nothing has no net energy associated with it. Had the universe been endowed with either negative or positive energy, we'd be forced to confront the question: What was the original source of energy that begat the universe? And if it had some amount of energy, why that amount and not some other amount? The fact that we live in a zero-energy universe bypasses that line of questioning. And does it leave us content in our emptiness? Perhaps. But we are no less enlightened by the ignorance that led to it.* [83]

"Originator of the heavens and the earth. When He decrees a matter, He only says to it, "Be," and it is."- Surah Al-Baqarah (2:117)

This has been mentioned many times in the Quran. He is the originator of the universe—nothing preceded it. The term 'originator' means someone who 'initiates' something. Before the initiation, there shouldn't be anything of that object. The concept of 'out of nothing' is more vividly illustrated in the second part of the verse where He decrees a matter by simply saying to it, 'Be,' and it is. If the Quran didn't include the second part, it wouldn't be that striking. However, I am sure that this isn't a full explanation of the verse because how can we explain, with our own knowledge or observation, that someone is creating something completely new by commanding the 'non-existent' object or thing to be created? If the 'thing' doesn't exist, how do you command it? In our laws of physics, that doesn't make sense. However, as Neil deGrasse Tyson mentioned, 'we're driving blind.' Thus, our science needs to go much further (the rest 96% of matter and energy to be explored) and hopefully, we will understand this verse better. By the way, science has made some progress since then. Quantum physics has proven without a doubt that 'cause' isn't a precursor of 'effect' but that they can occur in any order (the 2022 Nobel Prize in Physics is a testament to that recognition). So, I am hopeful that we may understand that verse a little better even in our lifetime.

There are many lectures and presentations from other scientists that, when listening to them, you might sometimes be confused as to whether they are quoting from the Quran. You can be sure they are not because most of them are atheists. Here are a couple more examples to inspire awe.

Take a look at the Circadian Rhythm and Biological Clock. Jeffrey C. Hall, Michael Rosbash, and Michael W. Young were awarded the Nobel Prize in 2017[84] for their discovery of genes and their mechanisms that create an internal biological clock, regulating each of our cells and the entire body.

These concepts were previously understood through common sense, but it is astonishing how precise the Quran was 1,400 years ago. As science delves deeper into understanding our bodies at the cellular and genetic levels, the Quran's insights become even more pertinent. How? When Allah mentioned that the Sun is a way to count seasons and time, it was apparently true without needing to delve into detail. Allah also mentioned that He has given us the Night for rest and the Day for work, in general. If we combine these revelations with the discovery of the circadian rhythm and the biological clock—driven by the appearance of the Sun and Moon—it gives us a profound, deeper meaning. We were able to conceive ideas of calculating season, day, and night outwardly, but now we know it extends even to the cellular level, where 'time' is counted by the Sun and Moon. I am sure it has more multifaceted meanings as we discover more through scientific exploration; however, this apparently simple revelation alone shows how comprehensive yet precise the Quran is in describing nature and human biology.

"[He is] the cleaver of daybreak and has made the night for rest and the sun and moon for calculation. That is the determination of the Exalted in Might, the Knowing" – Surah Al-An'am (6:96)

"Say, "Have you considered: if Allah should make for you the day continuous until the Day of Resurrection, what deity other than Allah could bring you a night in which you may rest? Then will you not see?" – Surah Al-Qasas (28:72)

"It is He Who made the sun to be a shining glory and the moon to be a light (of beauty), and measured out stages for her; that ye might know the number of years and the count (of time). Nowise did Allah create this but in truth and righteousness. (Thus) doth He explain His Signs in detail, for those who understand." – Surah Yunus/Jonah (10:5)

I can go on and on, but that would make this book more voluminous and defeat its purpose. So, I will present some more statements from the Quran that demonstrate why the Quran is so distinct from any other scripture and why it remains relevant for our modern times and beyond:

Surah Al-Ambiya wherein a single ayah Allah has revealed the fundamentals of Astrophysics and Biology.

"Allah has created every moving (living) creature from water. Of them there are some that creep on their bellies, some that walk on two legs, and some that walk on four. Allah creates what He wills. Verily! Allah is Able to do all things." - Surah Al-Noor (24:45)

In another ayah, Allah has mentioned the fact of the evolution of life on Earth: the origin of this universe, the origin of life, and the inner structure of all creation.

"Have not those who disbelieve known that the heavens and the earth were joined together as one united piece, then We parted them? And We have made from water every living thing. Will they not then believe?" - Surah Al-Ambiya (21:30)

Another apparently simple but fascinating scientific fact is the concept of pairs. We know that animals and plants exist in pairs, which is easy to observe. The Quran goes one step further, claiming that everything exists in pairs, 'what you know not.' What are these? Even with the current level of science, we have come to amazing discoveries. All matter is created in pairs. Every particle of matter has its corresponding antimatter. We now know at the atomic level that they all exist in pairs. But today, we understand that this pairing even occurs at the particle level with quarks. They all exist in pairs: Up and Down Quarks; Charm and Strange; Top and Bottom. The shocking revelation is that if you separate a pair of quarks with enormous force, the two quarks instantly create their own pairs—out of nothing, apparently. Scientists don't know how, but they've observed it. I think I won't be able to do justice to how this 'pairing' concept extends. Let's hear from Neil DeGrasse Tyson, in his lecture 'The Unknown Universe Explained by Neil DeGrasse Tyson' (from 37:31 to 41:26 minutes):

"The total number of quarks in this universe are six. Six quarks. Murrey Gell-Mann got it wrong. He thought there were only three but there are six. They still call quarks. Here's what spooky about quarks. You can never isolate one in free space. You can't! You know why? because here's a pair of quarks that are bound together and you're gonna go try to separate them. So, I challenge you to do that. So, you grab one side and the other and you start pulling and pulling and pulling. Well, quarks have a particular property that the force that brings them together gets stronger the more you pull them apart, not weaker. That's spooky unto itself but here's what happens. You pull them together so far; you're pumping energy to it at such a level that the moment you successfully separate them the energy you put in them spontaneously becomes another pair of quarks. So, the one you pulled out here another quarks manufactured out of the energy you pumped in. $E = mc^2$. The equivalence of mass and energy. The other quark. The energy you pumped into that it makes a second quark. So, you started with one pair, you separate them now you have two pairs and at no time did you ever isolate a single quark. That's how quarks behave. They don't ever want to be lonely. That's spooky to me. Quarks. Always in pairs."

See, what the Quran has said about pairs-

"Glory is to Him, Who has created all the pairs of that which the earth produces, as well as of their own (human) kind (male and female), and of ***that which they know not***." - Surah Ya-seen (36:36)

Most recently, in the Quantum physics, the entanglement of particles showed that the pairing has a "spooky" behavior that they communicate, instantly, even when they are billion/trillion miles apart – doesn't matter how far they are. How that happens is something scientists haven't figured out yet, but they have started using it in quantum computers and other technologies. As the Quran is not only for in our time but for the time the Human would live in this world (side interesting note that Quran has hinted that Allah brings new creation and restarts the creation – what does that mean, that's another whole conversation), this verse of "paired" must have more explanation to it. The Superdeterminism (based on the Quantum Entanglement observation) is pointing out that this world that we live in could be just a projection of the "reality". I would leave it to you if you would like to research more on this. I have given the reference of the Superdeterminism paper and read for yourself.

"Indeed, all things We created with predestination" – Surah Al-Qamar (54:49)

"He directeth the ordinance from the heaven unto the earth; then it ascendeth unto Him in a Day, whereof the measure is a thousand years of that ye reckon. (5) Such is the Knower of the Invisible and the Visible, the Mighty, the Merciful, "- Surah As-Sajda (32:5-6)

Similarly, Isaac Newton defined time as a constant, which contradicted the Quran. Just a few hundred years later, Albert Einstein brought science closer to the Quran again with his Theory of Relativity, asserting that time is relative.

"He arranges [each] matter from the heaven to the earth; then it will ascend to Him in ***a Day,*** the extent of which is ***a thousand years of those which you count.***" - Surah As-Sajdah (32:5)

In the aforementioned Quranic verses, so many fundamental scientific facts are declared that sometimes it feels too good to be true: the universe was once all joined together and then astonishingly separated and is being expanded; all living things are created from water and then formed into all the creatures that we see surrounding us; time is not constant but is relative. The surprises continue for those who have never read or contemplated the Quran with a knowledge of science.

Origin of Homo Sapiens and Creation of Human and prophet Adam (a.s.):

In *Surah Al-Noor,* Allah has clearly mentioned the origin of life as well as the evolution of species:

"Allah has created every [living] creature from water. And of them are those that move on their bellies, and of them are those that walk on two legs, and of them are those that walk on four. Allah creates what He wills. Indeed, Allah is over all things competent." - Surat An-Noor (24:45)

Allah also mentioned that He created Adam, the first man, like a potter forms clay. In *Surah Al-Rahman,* Allah tells us that He has created humans from clay, just like pottery.

"He created man from clay like [that of] pottery" - Surah Al-Rahman (55:14)

What does it mean? Why use the analogy of pottery? What difference would it have made if Allah had given the analogy of a mold for creating humans? We know that in pottery, the potter starts with a lump of clay and slowly and gradually, through the guidance and influence of the potter, shapes it into the desired object. At the beginning of the potter's work, you would not get any idea of the final object due to its sheer dissimilarity in look and feel. Even at the midpoint of creation, it would hardly resemble the final product. Now, if you introduce the dimension of time into this process, it may take a short period or a while to create an object, depending on the complexity of the design. So, in theory, it could take a minute, an hour, a year, or even a million years. Allah also mentioned in the above verse from *Surah An-Noor* that He has created all living things from water, and some walk on two legs, some on four, and some slither.

I am so intrigued by these verses:

"Have they not considered how Allah begins creation and then repeats it? Indeed that, for Allah, is easy. Say, [O Muhammad], "Travel through the land and observe how He began creation. Then Allah will produce the final creation. Indeed Allah, over all things, is competent."- Surah Al-Ankabut 29:19-20)

I have been pondering this for quite some time, but the more I think about it, the deeper I delve into a state of intellectual intoxication, awe, and humbleness.

Is this pointing to human evolution? Could there be further evolution of humans or animals in general? What could be the 'final creation'? Let's explore more in light of the Quran and science.

The creation story in Quran:

"How can you disbelieve in Allah when you were lifeless and He brought you to life; then He will cause you to die, then He will bring you [back] to life, and then to Him you will be returned."- Surah Al-Baqarah (2:28)

"And [mention, O Muhammad], when your Lord said to the angels, "Indeed, I will make upon the earth a successive authority." They said, "Will You place upon it one who causes corruption therein and sheds blood, while we declare Your praise and sanctify You?" Allah said, "Indeed, I know that which you do not know." - Surah Al-Baqarah (2:30)

"Do not the Unbelievers see that the heavens and the earth were joined together (as one unit of Creation), before We clove them asunder? We made from water every living thing. Will they not then believe?" - Surah Al-Ambiya (21:30)

"Allah has created every [living] creature from water. And of them are those that move on their bellies, and of them are those that walk on two legs, and of them are those that walk on four. Allah creates what He wills. Indeed, Allah is over all things competent." - Surat An-Nūr (24:45)

"He created man from clay like [that of] pottery"- Surat Al-Raĥmān (55:14)

"Who created you, proportioned you, and balanced you? In whatever form He willed has He assembled you." - Sura Al-Infitr (82:7-8)

Adam (a.s.) was pre-planned to be sent to Earth. Allah declared this to the Angels long before creating Adam. According to Dr. Jeffrey Lang[85], the fruit from the tree was part of training to be able to make independent decisions—i.e., free will. Through this training, Adam (a.s.) made a choice, which happened to be wrong, and was deemed prepared for Earth.

The Angels already knew that humans would cause corruption and bloodshed on Earth. How did they know this? It could be that beings similar to humans were already on Earth creating corruption and bloodshed, or Allah had informed them about humans' characteristics of doing both evil and good. However, Allah also stated that Angels are limited in knowledge. I didn't find any passages in the Quran where Allah foretells the Angels about the evil-doing characteristics of humans before their creation. If that's the case, then the alternative hypothesis is that humans (or beings like humans) were already on Earth.

Every living thing is created from water. Humans are living things, so they are also created from water. Science is so aligned to the description of life on earth.

Adam (a.s.) was also created from clay. Allah uses the metaphor of a potter. A potter creates an object in stages, through evolution, with utmost care, proportions it, and perfects it so that the object is fit for its purpose and yet beautiful. Humans in the hominoid chain are best proportioned for superior intelligence—the body's upright position and the proportion of brain volume compared to any other animal in the history of Earth's biology illustrate this. Humans became ready to accept the responsibility of being the caretakers of the Earth because of this superiority. Allah did not specify whether it took one second, one minute, or one million years, so the time lapsed for the proportioned body, brain, and intelligence was left unspecified.

Allah breathed into Adam (a.s.) His spirit and taught Adam (a.s.) names, and taught mankind to write with a pen. These are two unique attributes that Allah mentioned about Adam and no other creation. What differentiates us, humans, from all other animals? We are the only species on this Earth that quests for the purpose of its creation and is able to speak a language.

"Have they not considered how Allah begins creation and then repeats it? Indeed that, for Allah, is easy. Say, [O Muhammad], "Travel through the land and observe how He began creation. Then Allah will produce the final creation. Indeed Allah, over all things, is competent."- Surah Al-Ankabut (29:19-20)

"Here you are - those invited to spend in the cause of Allah - but among you are those who withhold [out of greed]. And whoever withholds only withholds [benefit] from himself; and Allah is the Free of need, while you are the needy. And if you turn away, He will replace you with another people; then they will not be the likes of you." - Surah Muḥammad (47:38)

Read the above verses carefully. What led us to think that we are the final creation? The explanation of these verses is primarily for different nations like the Mongols, Aryans, Arabs, etc. By the phrase '...will not be likes of you,' is Allah referring to superficial ethnic or racial constructs? However, Allah has mentioned in *Surah Al-Hujurat* that He divided humans into nations and tribes solely for us to recognize and know each other. Thus, it may not be as simple as explaining nations, races, and ethnicities with the example '...will not be likes of you.' This points to much deeper concept.

Traveling through the earth and understanding how we were created, here are a few scientific observations and theories of human evolution from hominids to Homo sapiens:

- Homo sapiens, modern humans like us, have evolved over 12 million years.
- Hominins (such as Homo erectus and Homo sapiens, for example) have engaged in warfare for hundreds of thousands of years.[86]
- The brain of Homo sapiens provided the capabilities that we refer to as superiority over other animals, primarily because of the proportionately large size of the head, which can accommodate a large brain. 'Humans (Homo sapiens) are the most abundant and widespread species of primate, characterized by bipedalism and large, complex brains. This has enabled the development of advanced tools, culture, and language.'[87]

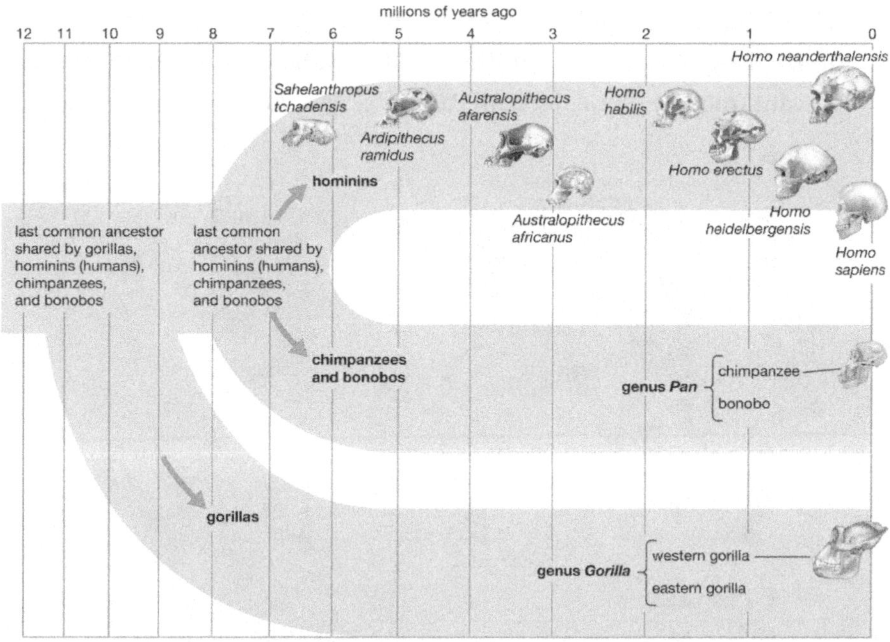

Figure 16: Depiction of human evolution – current theory[88]

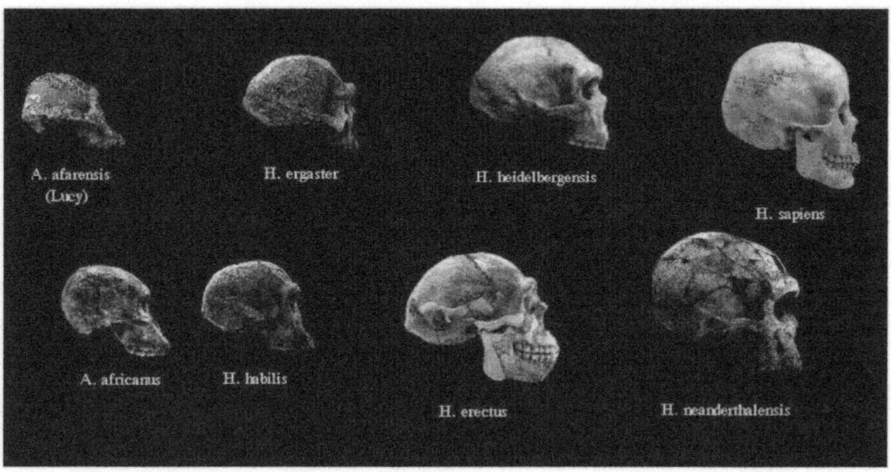

Figure 17: homo sapiens' skull that fits a largest brain ever[89]

- Homo sapiens spread across the earth from Africa and, around 50,000 to 70,000 years ago, passed through the cradle of civilization, i.e., the Levant (modern Syria, Jordan, Palestine, and the Arabian Peninsula).

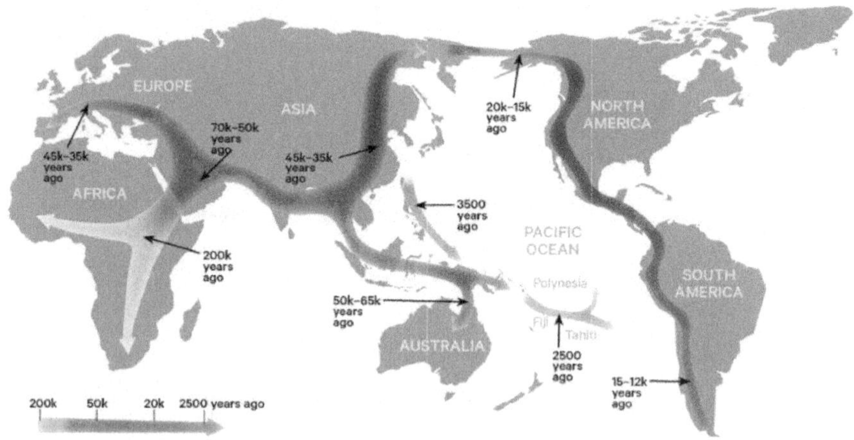

Figure 18: Human Migration: Out of Africa Theory[90]

After examining the Quranic story of the origin of life and human evolution and juxtaposing it with the current scientific understanding of human evolution, it is intriguing to see how these two perspectives are converging more closely every day.

Lifestyle choices, such as material life, charity, and food and drinks that are forbidden or allowed:

Islam is a way of life designed to avoid harm and achieve the best outcomes. The Quran forbids alcohol, drugs, excessive consumption of food and materials, and mandates fasting for 8% of the year while recommending additional fasting days throughout the year. Now we understand the power of autophagy and how it benefits the human body (refer to *Chapter VI: Navigate Out of the Destruction: Public Health Crisis*). Islam mandates waking up before sunrise and recommends going to sleep early and waking up early. We are aware of the harms of not sleeping at night and sleeping through the sunrise. Islam requires the performance of five daily prayers, which combine elements of meditation as well as physical exercises similar to yoga. Charity is mandatory in Islam – this obligatory charity is directed towards specific groups such as the poor, sick, and needy (seven categories of people are eligible for this mandatory charity). That charity is a tool to bring justice and equality in the society.

Civilization test

The religion, if to be taken as a way of life, must not conflict with civilization; rather, it should foster the creation of civilization. It is unthinkable that the creator of humans, who created such intelligent beings capable of understanding the universe and creation, comprehending math, science, and technology, would stand in the way of building human civilization. Thus, if the way of life comes from God, it must not only stand by, but it should also be the triggering force of a civilization when human society lacks one, and a fostering force when it has an existing civilization.

In fact, Islam continued one of the early Western civilizations, the Roman Empire. According to Professor Paul Freedman of Yale, '*There are four heirs to the Roman Empire. One is the Byzantine Empire, the Eastern Roman Empire, which calls itself the Roman Empire. It doesn't call itself the Eastern, doesn't call itself the Byzantine; it calls itself the Roman Empire, even though it does so in Greek. The second heir are the barbarian kings... They are attempting to prop up the remnants of Roman culture, civilization, and material society. The third heir, in some ways, is Islam...*'. We will soon see how Islam built upon the civilization passed from the Greco-Latin civilization.

Let's consider what Western intellectuals say about Islam's ability to create and maintain a civilization. It's a relatively long excerpt from the lecture of Professor Paul Freedman at Yale[91], because I couldn't explain it better than him:

"So, what is it about Aristotle, what is it about Diascordes, what is it about Ptolemy, of all of these scientists and philosophers that is of such fascination to the Islamic world? All of this emphasis that we've made on Islamic culture and its openness to other influences may seem strange to you in light of the reputation Islam has in modern America, or at least in many circles of modern America and Europe, as being obscurantist, or anti-modern, or religiously inflexible. I teach a group of retired people where I live, just outside New York, and we're studying Islamic Spain. And they are astounded at what I've just described, at the openness, at its tolerance, at its curiosity about classical and Persian sciences. And I was surprised because this is not new information. This is not something that historians have just come up with and just discovered. If you read medieval history textbooks of a hundred years ago, it's in there. Everybody knows that Aristotle was translated from Arabic into Latin. "Everybody knows", everybody who studied the Middle Ages knows. And I said to them, because you can't say to older people, "Oh, well you know your education is actually not very good, "the way we say to you all the time. Or, "Your attention span is not very good, because all you're doing is you're plugged in to your social world". No, these people went to college in the tough old days, allegedly, and they're like, "God, I thought Islam was just this sort of frozen religion that had never changed." So, you don't have that disadvantage. You don't have that idea, and so I'm not going to browbeat you with it on the basis of the experience of teaching seventy-year-olds. But there it is...I don't want to go into a long discussion about, "Islam, right or wrong?" Or, "Islam, progressive or regressive?" I will say this: there are those who believe, wrongly in my opinion, that there's always been this "clash of civilization", as it's sometimes called, between the progressive Christian West and the obscurantist Islamic East. I don't accept that, in part for reasons you've just heard. There is no consistent Islamic tradition of the maintenance of dogma, or the conversion of the world by force. Insofar as that exists now, it is, in my opinion, a modern phenomenon. It is a phenomenon that results from an encounter with the West beginning around the time of Napolean's conquests of Egypt, perhaps. It's about two centuries old. There's another kind of belief that at some point things changed. There's a book by Bernard Lewis, the most eminent

Western scholar of Islamic culture, called "What Went Wrong". And so, Lewis' assumption is that the world that I'm describing, the Abbasid caliphate, is an open society and at some point, and for some reason, the Islamic world closed itself. It became less susceptible to outside influence, more suspicious of it, more dogmatic, more anti-modern, more fixated on literalism, what in the Western Christian tradition would be called fundamentalism, and on tradition. I don't really like this either, because it sees all progress as the property of Western civilization. And it's not that I am not interested in Western civilization. I've taught it. I've taught it because I liked it. I'm not somebody who believes that it's all a tale of oppression, but I don't think that anybody who diverts from the path of Western civilization at some point is going off the cliff, or off the trail, and into the woods. There are a lot of different civilizations out there. There's a third related idea that the Arabs are just intermediaries. Yeah, it's great, they translate Aristotle so that the real guys who can really use Aristotle, Thomas Aquinas et al, can get started. I don't accept that, either, because they do more than that. ***They do an awful lot of original research in medicine, in mathematics, in philosophy.*** *But, within all of this, to my mind, fruitless speculation, there is kernel of what is an interesting problem.* ***And the interesting problem is, why were the Arabs so much more successful in assimilating conquered cultures than other invaders were? Say, for example, the Germans.*** *You don't get this kind of efflorescence of culture under the barbarian occupants of the former Roman Empire. We're talking, not just about cultural survival, keep in mind, but about and expansion of science and allied arts. I'd say there are maybe four factors that encouraged the Arabs conquest to absorb these new influences. They're not in themselves explanations, but they are certainly background factors. The fact that the conquest was quick and relatively painless, and that it was not really a religious war. Two, and I think here very important, the elimination of frontiers. I mentioned this briefly before. You get Persian as well as Greek astronomy. From India you get things like chess, so called Arabic numerals, which actually, as we all know, come from India. These things come into Arab and Persian worlds from India and eventually to Europe as well, in a world in which there are no frontiers between India and North Africa. They could go these thousands of miles* *peacefully. The elimination of linguistic boundaries. Arabic becomes the language of learning, as much as Latin would be in the European Middle Ages, much as English has tended to become in our era. So, Maimonides, the great Jewish philosopher, wrote largely in Arabic. The Christians of Spain, so called Mozarabic Christians, studied Arabic, taught in Arabic, wrote in Arabic.*

And finally, number four, the attitude of the conquerors and the conquered. The attitude of the conquerors was what Peter Brown...will call, ***"a garden protected by our spears". This is a quote from one of the conquerors. The Arab conquerors considered these to be wonderful civilizations that they were not going to pillage or destroy, but rather protect. "A garden protected by our spears."*** *But they were planning on enjoying the garden, not merely standing on the outside defending it for other people to enjoy. The conquerors were confident in their religion, so confident that they didn't need for others to recognize it or convert. It also gave them the confidence to accept new ideas from Greek civilization, from Persian civilization, from India. But there's also the attitude of the conquered. Brown says that, "as the storm of the Arab armies rolled over the horizon, the population of the Near East sat back to enjoy the sunshine." The Islamic conquest was of benefit, and perceived as of benefit, by most of the people who were conquered. A kind of counter example in a way, explain this. In Cordoba, the capital of Umayyad caliphate, or soon-to-be caliphate of Spain, a group of Christians around 850, were so upset at the contend attitude of the Christians of Islamic Spain – who were, if not a majority, probably about fifty percent, close to fifty percent at this time – these more fanatical, or at least more serious Christians, were so angry that all of their compatriots seemed to be just fine with Islamic rule that they got up in the marketplace of Cordoba and denounced Muhammad as a charlatan, as a false god, and as not a prophet. And while Islam is tolerant, that is something that you couldn't do. So, they did the thing that was most defiant of the regime, really the moral equivalent of burning yourself in the marketplace, and indeed they were imprisoned, told to recant, and when they didn't recant, they were executed. There are about fifty of these "Martyrs of Cordoba", as they're called. But they have to seek martyrdom because* *they have to look for it, they have to create it, because almost all of the rest of their compatriots are perfectly happy to be Mozarabic christens, practicing the freedom of their religion under a beneficent regime. Beneficent in the eyes of these Martyr Christians, but nevertheless the regime of the devil. This shows you something about the nature of the Arab conquest and occupation."*

"Let me just speak briefly about a couple of aspects of what the Islamic world was interested in studying...Let's start with mathematics. The great accomplishment of this time is the introduction of Arabic numbers, which if you've ever tried to multiply or divide with Roman numerals, are superior. ***Arabic numbers come from India, and along with this system of numerals, they imported zero – both the number, or the non-number, and the concept. The concept of zero allows for things like decimal places, which are also developed at this time. From India the Arabs get the kind of very basic ideas of trigonometry, the sine function. But it is their own researches, their own progress, that leads to the discovery, or development, of the five other functions...the cosine, the tangent, the cotangent, the secant, and the cosecant, right? All of these are discovered by the Arabs.*** *They built on an edifice whose foundation is Indian mathematics. In the early ninth century, a scholar attached to that House of Wisdom of Baghdad, named* ***Al-Khwarizmi, writes a book with the title that can be translated as something like, The Book of Addition and Subtraction According to the Hindu Calculation.*** *And this is what incorporates zero and decimal places, and interesting enough this book is known only from its translation into Latin. The Latin version survives, whereas the original Arabic does not.* ***Whitin a century of the publication of this book, decimal fractions have been developed, square roots, the value of Pi to sixteen decimal places had been calculated. Al-Khwarizmi is also the author of a treatise on Algebra. The word "algebra" comes from al-Jabr, which is sort of restoring, restoring something that has been imbalanced and that you're going about to balance, which of course is, in a way, the visual nature of algebra. Al-Khwarizmi was also astronomer. He developed star tables that allowed one to locate the***

planets and stars at different times of year and at different latitudes. This is what allows the making of things like astrolabes or, later, sextants. *These are things that describe they sky at a particular place – that allow you then to keep time; and also, to navigate; to calculate time for things like prayers, or fasts, celebrations; also, to cast horoscopes."*

Then he continued how Islam brought other foundational knowledgebase to the civilization:[92] *"But this question of how much water is there versus how much land is there – a sense of the entire world – is a problem investigated by these geographers. Many of these guys are indefatigable travelers. So there's this book by Al-Muqaddasi, usually known in English as the Best Division for Knowledge of the Regions. Completed in 985 after twenty years of traveling. But the greatest traveler of the Islamic premodern world was ibn-Khaldun, who is much later but worth at least mentioning here, 1332 to 1406. And he started from his native Tunis and traveled as far as China and Indonesia. And then, finally, a scholar named al-Idrisi, another one of these travelers, geographers, was hired by the Christian king of Sicily, Roger the Second, in 1138 to put together a map of the world with accompanying descriptive texts. And it is an aspect of the respect accorded to the Arab geographers in the Christian world, and the fact that despite our tendency to see these two worlds as opposed – after all 1138 is the era of the Crusades – there's quite a fair amount of collaboration, interchange of knowledge between the Christian kingdoms of Europe, and the Islamic world – the Islamic kingdoms – of the Southern Mediterranean and the Middle East.*

Finally, medicine. We're not exhausting the subject studied by the Arabs, but I wanted to give you math, geography, and medicine as three examples. The main authority for the Arabs, the person that they translated with the most assiduity and interest was Galen, a physician who wrote in Greek at the time of the Roman Empire. And Galen is the person who is responsible for the transmission, if not invention, of the notion of the four bodily humors…There are lots and lots of medical writings and doctors in the Islamic world. The most famous is known in the West as Avicenna, Ibn-Sina, 980 to 1037. He is a Persian, active in Persia.

And he, like many of these doctors, was not just a physician, but a musicologist and a philosopher. He wrote medical writings on physiology, diagnosis, treatment, and medication. His work was translated into Latin and known in the West as the Cannon. The Cannon of Avicenna was the standard work taught in medical schools until the seventeenth, eighteenth century."

In short, Islam not only built a civilization, but it also extended the civilization that it had inherited from the Persians, Indians, and ultimately the Romans. You might also ask this question: 'Civilizations have been built by humans for thousands of years, who held various levels of religious beliefs, including monotheism, polytheism, idolatry, or even atheism. So, why should I take your word that Islam has anything to do with civilization?'

If you didn't ask this question, I would say you weren't using your intellect. Let's examine how the civilization was built by people who took Islam as their religion. For Islam, like most major religions, you need to get to the core of it, i.e., to the Book, the Quran. The Quran has a unique approach unlike most 'holy scriptures' you may have encountered, where faith and belief are sought from the believer. Instead, the Quran asks you to think—think hard, really hard. It is shocking for a religion to take such a stance, which many orientalists have criticized in the past: Islam asks you to be rational and not a blind believer.

Allah repeatedly encourages us to use our intellect and reason. He compares those who don't employ their reasoning to the blind, deaf, and dumb (*Surah Al-Anfal* 8:22). Elsewhere in the Quran, those who follow blindly, without questioning or seeking understanding, are likened to cattle, or even regarded as lower than cattle (*Surah Al-Furqan* 25:44, *Surah Al-A'raf* 7:179), because they obey without comprehension or inquiry. Imagine a scene where cattle are driven towards a lush field to graze or towards a slaughterhouse, and you'll notice they don't use reason to differentiate between the two. This isn't an insult to cattle, as they are created with that level of intellect, whereas humans are endowed with a far more advanced brain than any other creature on earth. Anthropologists have provided evidence that Homo sapiens, with their superior brain development, surpassed Neanderthals, enabling humans to dominate the earth. Our advanced cognitive abilities allow us to use language, writing, and to build civilizations. Therefore, when we are endowed with unmatched capabilities and yet choose to ignore them, acting like cattle, the Creator, in His justice, rightfully describes such individuals as blind, deaf, and dumb.

Reflecting on those verses, I often ponder how we can ascertain whether we are truly people of intellect, using our capabilities effectively. Is incessant questioning a mark of utilizing our intellect properly? Now, I believe this below verse, along with similar verses, serve as litmus tests.

"Indeed, in the creation of the heavens and the earth and the alternation of the night and the day are signs for those of understanding Who remember Allah while standing or sitting or [lying] on their sides and give thought to the creation of the heavens and the earth, [saying], "Our Lord, You did not create this aimlessly; exalted are You [above such a thing]; then protect us from the punishment of the Fire" – Quran (3:190-191)

They suggest that people of intellect engage in a multitude of scientific disciplines: Astrophysics/Astronomy, Engineering, Oceanography and Oceanology, Naval Shipbuilding, Commerce, Trade, Economics, Meteorology, Geology, Agriculture, Botany, Zoology, Life Science, and the study of Weather and Climate. This single verse encourages the exploration of these sciences. There are numerous other verses I can now connect with, where Allah guides us towards the sciences of Anthropology, History, Linguistics, Mathematics, Chemistry, Physics, the Evolution of Life, Embryology, Metallurgy, Geography, and more. Hence, if we are truly people of the Book, the Quran, we are called to be people of civilization and progress, not just in a materialistic sense, but in a genuine advancement for humanity. This reveals, once again, why Islamic civilization encompassed all the faculties of knowledge mentioned above. It's no wonder that if we read and contemplate the Quran, we would be people of all knowledge. There's no escape from it.

Here are just a few of the many verses related to the above, which I have picked for you to appreciate: Quran (21:30), (21:33), (21:104), (23:12-14), (21:32), (57:25), (55:19-20), (78:6-7), (51:47), (24:40), (96:15-16).

So, if you would like to give it a try, Islam definitely passes the first test of sustaining the civilization of the Western world.

Pass its own claims

The Quran is full of claims that, if covered here, would require a book or a series of books by themselves. As the purpose of this book is to direct you to those claims for your own further research, I will cover just a few highlights that we understand clearly. As we gain more knowledge of the natural sciences, we will be able to understand even more in the future.

In the Quran, Allah speaks with an authority like no other. He says that if you don't want to believe in Allah, then leave His creation. And then He says, but you won't be able to. It's so simple to understand, yet we often go to great lengths and complicate it unnecessarily. I offer a simple analogy to help appreciate this concept. Think about a character in your computer video games. No matter how impressive the capabilities of the game character are, it has no way to leave the world of computer memory and processors. This is because the entire game is built off the 'ingredients,' so to speak, of the computer. Similarly, the ecosystem it is created for and created within has no way for it to leave. Humans and all creation in this universe are made from the same ingredients of this universe; astrophysicists call it 'we are all made from stardust.' Thus, it's self-evident that the creations in this universe won't be able to break free from the boundaries of the universe.

Create a single *surah* (chapter) similar to one from the Quran—that's the challenge from God. Some people have tried but ended up committing plagiarism. When challenged to produce something similar to an existing work, you don't simply copy it; instead, you take the attributes and emulate them. What are the attributes of a Quranic *surah*? (a) It's unique—not seen like it in that language, (b) it combines rhythmic, poetic, and rhyming elements, (c) it conveys messages that touch on science, arts, literature, history, archaeology, anthropology, astronomy, and other intellectual disciplines, (d) it was revealed over the course of 23 years, with events unfolding throughout that period, (e) it stands the test of time as science and human civilization continue to evolve, among other attributes I have not yet covered.

And no one has been able to do it yet.

If the Quran were from a man or anything other than the creator, there would be contradictions. After 1,400 years, this unchanged book still reveals no contradictions from one verse to another, even though it was revealed over 23 years and not initially in written form. Prophet Muhammad (pbuh) verbally transmitted it, and his companions were writing and memorizing it.

You would lead a depressed life if you do not follow the messages that come to you through the prophets.

"And whoever turns away from My remembrance - indeed, he will have a depressed life, and We will gather him on the Day of Resurrection blind." – Surah Ta-Ha (20:124)

This is a very strong claim: if a human being turns away from the remembrance of the creator, then their life will be filled with depression. It's important to ensure that you don't confuse this with the root cause of clinical depression, which is a medical condition that can be caused by many biological factors, including the side effects of medication. However, this discussion concerns those who have everything normal in their lives except that they do not ponder the creator of this universe. For such individuals, life may feel depressing. Essentially, it is saying that the creator has endowed us with an inherent quest for purpose in life. That's why every human being eventually asks the same questions: Who created me? Why was I created? Where will I go after my death? Those who do not contemplate these questions may lead a life without purpose, which can result in depression. Look around you and decide if this is true or false.

Next is the claim that the land and sea have been corrupted by our own actions. *"Mischief has appeared on land and sea because of (the meed) that the hands of men have earned that (Allah) may give them a taste of some of their deeds: in order that they may turn back (from Evil)."* - Surah Al-Rum (30:41)

Look at the environmental disaster, pollution, and climate change that we are exacerbating through our own actions. We have extracted all the fossil fuels from the ground and are burning them as if it's a never-ending party. We are consuming and wasting more natural resources than we ever need. We are indiscriminately destroying forests and natural habitats, devastating the natural balance. We are creating and consuming chemicals of all sorts, polluting the earth, water, and environment, which is also causing many diseases such as cancers, impeding brain development, and metabolic syndromes like heart disease, high blood pressure, diabetes, dementia, etc. The public health crisis section has covered this in detail.

Fit for the entire humanity

Let's consider what Western intellectuals say about Islam's universality:

Professor Paul Freedman explained the universality of Islam in very simple terms. He said that Islam is a universally accessible religion that emphasizes practical conduct and legal principles, making it approachable for people from all walks of life. It advocates for ethical living, including abstaining from alcohol and gambling, and observing dietary guidelines, without demanding extreme asceticism. Rather than calling for the renunciation of worldly goods, it encourages the act of giving alms, highlighting a practical approach to supporting those in need. Its teachings are designed to be applicable and manageable for anyone seeking a righteous path. Overall, Islam presents a moderate and balanced way of life, emphasizing inclusivity and the feasibility of its practices for adherents globally.

Here's the direct quote in Paul Freedman's own words:[93]

"**Islam is a religious of conduct and law, not of mortification and purgation**. It emphasizes **upright behavior**: no drinking, no gambling, certain dietary restrictions. Not the renunciation of the world – it doesn't say, "Sell everything you have and give it to the poor." It says, "Give alms." **It is a moderate religion, actually**.

It is a "do-able" religion. These obligations may be somewhat inconvenient at times, Ramadan for example, but there is nothing in here to the degree that the New Testament, for example, prescribes behavior that most people are not going to follow. Or that traditional Judaism, possible but certainly onerous. Lots of obligations.

The other differences, more important, with Judaism is that **Islam would be very quickly, universal**. In other words, it would encourage conversion, although not, as we will see, with great enthusiasm. It is completely erroneous to think that these armies that burst forth from Arabia after the death of Mohammed were intent of getting everybody to follow Mohammed. They were intent on conquest, all right. But we'll see that their goals were a little more complicated than that of orienting everybody towards this new faith, whatever we're going to call it."

Islam is a universal religion, unlike most other ethnic religions (e.g., Judaism). There is no central principle in Islam that relies on ethnicity; rather, anyone who accepts the religion immediately becomes an equal part of it—there is no waiting period, nor any superiority or inferiority based on ethnicity or the time of joining. This universality is also supported by the concept of one nation. Understanding how God has structured the system to unite everyone under one God is not only very practical but also unique compared to other religions (this will be covered later in more detail).

Christianity can also claim to be a universal religion. Observing Christians around the world, one might assert this claim, which isn't incorrect, apparently. Even if we set aside Jesus's (a.s.) own claim in the Bible (reference: only for Jews - no Gentiles) in exchange for accepting the reality of 2.4 billion Christians, we must ensure that our 'sought after' religion passes all the 'tests' to be 'the Truth'. Otherwise, we risk falling into a 'Pick-and-build-your-own-religion' ideology, which would essentially be atheism—denying the divine God. If someone starts down that path, then refer to the Atheism chapter to understand why Atheism cannot be the solution to save this civilization.

One Nation: Islam is the only religion that claims the last prophethood. This significant claim distinguishes Islam from other religions, making it universal by uniting everyone under one nationhood. Islam accepts all prior prophets—Jesus, Moses, David, Jacob, Ibrahim, Noah, and Adam (peace be upon them all). Additionally, denying or disrespecting any prophet precludes one from being Muslim. The finality of prophethood precludes the emergence of new prophets. If prophethood were not sealed, as honest individuals, we would have to consider anyone's claim to verify its truth. Without this seal, we might be divided into many nations, each following a different prophet. Thus, the seal ensures global unity.[94] We are instructed to follow the chain of prophets from Adam to Prophet Muhammad (pbuh), who leads us to the monotheistic God—Allah. Therefore, we should be united as one nation under one God through the last prophet (pbuh).

Sometimes, following Prophet Muhammad (pbuh) might seem like abandoning the teachings of Moses or Jesus (a.s.). However, Prophet Muhammad (pbuh) did not introduce new teachings but continued those of all previous prophets. By accepting the last prophet, you accept the entire prophetic tradition. Importantly, accepting the last prophet (pbuh) does not mean submitting to someone else's authority. Islam lacks a centralized authority—there is no papacy or central figure to whom allegiance is due, except to God and all His prophets. Every Muslim is an equal member of this one nation, possessing the same authority as any other Muslim worldwide.

Islam, a religion followed by close to 2 billion people around the world, prescribes practices that are not only spiritual in nature but also have profound implications on physical health and societal well-being. These practices, deeply embedded in the daily lives of Muslims, reflect an innate understanding of human biology and the natural world. Let's explore how Islamic rituals such as waking up before sunrise for prayer, performing prayer, maintaining cleanliness, fasting, and giving charity harmonize with the natural disposition of human biology, promoting health, well-being, and social equity.

The Islamic practice of waking before sunrise for the Fajr prayer and sleeping shortly after the Isha prayer aligns with the human body's circadian rhythm. The circadian rhythm is an internal clock running in the background of the brain that cycles between sleepiness and alertness at regular intervals. It is influenced by light exposure, and aligning our sleep patterns with the natural light-dark cycle can improve sleep quality, mood, and cognitive function. The National Institute of General Medical Sciences highlights the importance of this rhythm for health, suggesting that the Islamic ritual of rising early and retiring early may support optimal biological and psychological functioning. Additionally, the practice of praying five times daily in Islam surprisingly parallels the circadian rhythm. I am looking forward to more research outcomes in this area soon.

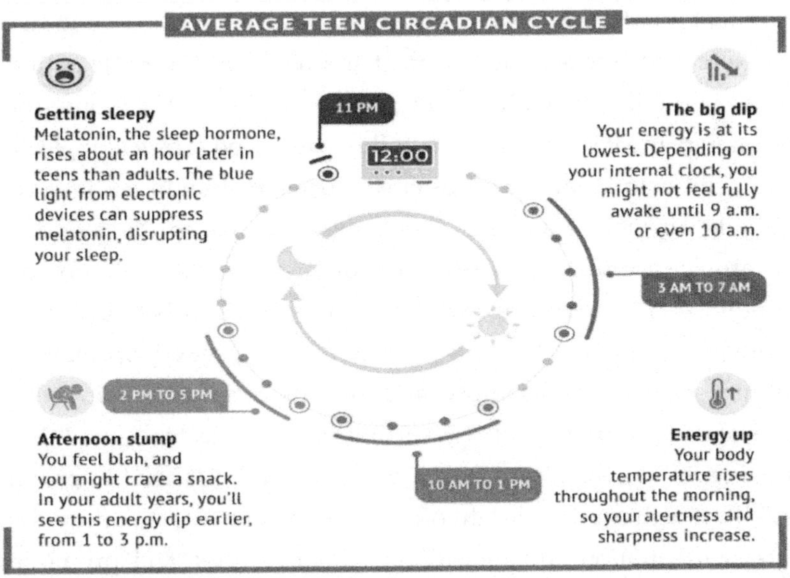

Figure 19: Circadian rhythm cycle of a typical teenager.[95]

Fasting during Ramadan, as well as on additional days recommended by Prophet Muhammad (every Monday and Thursday each week and an additional three days in the middle of the lunar month), is a combination of spiritual exercise that triggers 'miraculous' biological processes impacting our health and mental state. Autophagy, a process where cells degrade and recycle components, is a natural response to fasting. It aids in the removal of damaged cells, contributing to cellular repair and regeneration. This process, which perplexes researchers due to its seemingly self-destructive yet immensely beneficial roles, aligns with Islamic fasting practices, suggesting divine insight into human biology that promotes health and longevity.[96]

The daily prayers (*Salah*) in Islam incorporate physical movements that include standing, bowing, prostrating, and sitting. Performed five times a day, this ritual serves not only as a spiritual practice but also as a form of physical exercise. These activities disrupt an imbalanced lifestyle pattern, such as sitting on the couch all day and binge-watching TV, because they require taking breaks to connect fully with God—psychologically, physically, and emotionally. You can't stay up late at night because you have to wake up before sunrise. When these actions in the five daily prayers are performed as ordained—uninterrupted, with focused concentration, long enough prostrations, and pauses in between, apart from receiving reminders from the words of God—they help maintain physical fitness, improve flexibility, and increase blood circulation. Here are the stats: a minimum of 17 sit-ups, 17 leg stretches and back straightening in the bending (*ruku*) position, and 34 head-to-ground prostrations. Furthermore, Salah offers mental benefits by providing moments of meditation and reflection, reducing stress, and promoting mental clarity. The physical prostration, where the head is placed below the heart, enhances blood flow to the brain and is a unique posture associated with humility and serenity.[97]

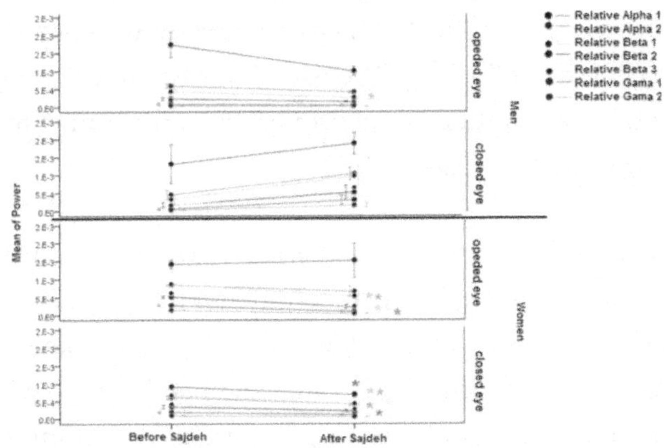

Figure 20:The Effect of Prostration on the Prefrontal Brain Activity

The forehead is mandatorily placed on the ground without any barrier in the middle. For centuries, Muslims performed this on the ground or on a material directly connected to the ground (a conducting material). However, there is a question about whether using non-conducting artificial carpets hinders this purpose. A formal study needs to be conducted before speculating on that. Scientific research is still ongoing regarding how the body and head directly touching the ground benefits us physically—our brain runs on approximately 12 watts of bio-electricity, and the ground is an electrically neutral body.[98] The spiritual benefits are evident, but the Quran also clearly suggests seeking solutions to problems through patience and physical worship (salah). If physical prayer, as mentioned above, aids blood flow and stimulates other biological positives, it can help control anxiety or stress and promote clear thinking. While the Quran does not mention these biological reactions, it is a matter of intellectual reasoning, which is a central theme repeatedly emphasized throughout the Quran.

Islam places significant emphasis on cleanliness through practices such as ablution (*wudu*) and the use of *Miswak* for teeth cleaning. These rituals directly impact physical health by reducing the risk of infections and promoting oral hygiene. Ablution involves washing and messaging of the hands, face, eyes, arms, and feet, which can prevent the spread of diseases and promote general well-being. The use of *Miswak*, a natural toothbrush, has been found to have antibacterial properties, contributing to oral health and preventing dental diseases.

The practice of mandatory charity (*Zakah*) and voluntary charity (*Sadaqah*) in Islam is not only a spiritual obligation but also a sophisticated economic system designed to reduce wealth inequality and promote social justice. This redistribution of wealth ensures that the needs of the poor are met, reducing societal tensions and fostering a sense of community. The act of giving also has psychological benefits, improving the giver's mental health and sense of satisfaction. The practice reflects an understanding of the interdependence between individual well-being and societal health, advocating for a balance between personal wealth and social responsibility. It's an economic master plan to alleviate social injustice and inequality. For example, the top 20% in America owns $107 trillion, and *Zakah* could amount to almost $2.5 trillion, which would not only alleviate poverty and income inequality in the USA but also address the dire situation of global inequality.[99] It purifies the money spiritually. Sharing your blessings with the poor in society allows you to sleep better and feel good. At the end, you can hoard money but can't feel good about yourself. A study conducted in Britain found that donating to the poor can improve blood pressure.

The practices prescribed by Islam resonate deeply with the natural dispositions of human biology and societal organization. Through synchronization with the circadian rhythm, the promotion of autophagy via fasting, the physical benefits of Salah, the emphasis on cleanliness, and the sophisticated system of charity, Islam offers a holistic approach to health and well-being. These practices demonstrate an intricate understanding of the human body, mind, and society, providing insights into how spirituality and biology can be interwoven to enhance life on both individual and communal levels. The wisdom embedded in these rituals transcends religious boundaries, offering valuable lessons on living a balanced, healthy, and harmonious life.

Governance through Representation and Consultation

Islam inherently seeks to avoid both anarchy and tyranny. It teaches the importance of maintaining some form of government rather than falling into anarchy. Additionally, Islam regards tyranny as the worst kind of governance, insisting that rulers be subject to the same laws as their citizens. Although this principle may not be visible in many parts of the world where Muslims are the majority today, it is important to note that the Muslim world has been in decline for several centuries. Thus, comparing its current state to its flourishing periods is not a fair comparison. In fact, democracy bears a closer resemblance to Islamic practices than other forms of governance such as monarchy, anarchy, or autocracy. I also find many similarities between the U.S. Constitution and Islamic practices. The first Muslim ruler, known as a *Caliph* in Arabic, Abu Bakr, of Arabian Peninsula was elected by the community in Madinah (currently located in Saudi Arabia). In his inauguration speech, he stated:

"I have been given the authority over you, and I am not the best of you. If I do well, help me; and if I do wrong, set me right. Sincere regard for truth is loyalty and disregard for truth is treachery. The weak amongst you shall be strong with me until I have secured his rights, if God wills; and the strong amongst you shall be weak with me until I have wrested from him the rights of others, if God wills. Obey me so long as I obey God and His Messenger. But if I disobey God and His Messenger, you owe me no obedience. Arise for your prayer, God have mercy upon you."[100]

Isn't it similar to the tyranny clause of the US Constitution? Yes, the process differs from the one-person-one-vote system, but it is closer compared to any other systems available in the world today.

Islam places a high value on consultation and advisership in governance. The Quran encourages the use of consultation in all our affairs, including governance, by stating that those who practice consultation in their decision-making are the most successful. Here's one example from the Quran:

"...and consult them in the matter. And when you have decided, then rely upon Allah. Indeed, Allah loves those who rely [upon Him]" – Surah Al-Imran

However, the most important aspect is not what is explicitly mentioned, but what is not imposed in Islam. Islam does not dictate a specific structure of governance nor does it attribute any divinity to rulers. Instead, whatever structure the society develops through consultation, and whoever is best qualified to establish justice, fairness, and equity in the society, Islam is entirely supportive of that.

Chapter VI: Navigate Out of the Destruction

As we delve into the grave risks highlighted earlier and search for a way out, I would like to make a general statement. Surprisingly but predictably, Islam has direct references for solving these problems. I will cover these references, but I will inevitably fall short. The Quran adopts a comprehensive approach where each verse should be weighed against the entire Quran to fully appreciate its message. This means that if I were to cover each point comprehensively, each topic could easily be expanded into a chapter or even a book by itself. I will try to provide enough information so that you can begin to consider how Islam might be a solution to the problems highlighted earlier in the book. However, even though the Quranic references are well-suited to solve these problems, I strongly urge you to read the entire Quran yourself before implementing it in your life, your family, and in society. The last thing I would want is for people to take this small book and this chapter as a prescription without using their own intellect. As mentioned in the Quran, God wants us to use our intellect and reason before taking any action. When you read the Quran, you will find a strong emphasis from God on using our intellect and reason. By the way, you may find many similarities between the Quranic solutions and those in Christianity or Judaism, which is not surprising because God sent the same message to all the prophets from the beginning of humanity, from Adam to Muhammad (peace be upon them all). I would also like to note that the problems the West is facing aren't isolated but intertwined, thus the solutions cannot be implemented in isolation either. When you consider each issue, keep in mind the overall approach to the solutions outlined. In addition to the philosophical approach, the exact implementation details need to be worked out in the context of socio-economic-cultural aspects. Social institutions need to be developed to realize the benefits of the solutions. On a side note, while the problems aren't limited to the geographic West but also the ideological West, many of the approaches to resolving these issues are equally applicable to many parts of the world. However, as my primary focus is on the USA, I am omitting any connection to other parts of the world to keep this discussion focused and brief.

Structural racism

Islam was introduced to declare the end of racism, but ironically, hidden racism exists within the Muslim community, including unconscious negative biases even towards fellow Muslims based on their nationality and ethnicity. Surprisingly, this negative bias is often less severe towards non-Muslims than it is towards Muslims. Conversations often reveal that Muslims believe they are worse in many areas compared to others. This perception is influenced by the association of terrorism with Muslims over the last few decades, based on current affairs and incidents around the world. Muslims also see all the negative actions undertaken by Muslims and Muslim countries, fostering the perception that all 'bad and illicit' activities are perpetrated by Muslims. This is true on a smaller time scale (e.g., if the time scale is the last 50 years for instability and another 200 years of European colonization of Muslim countries), but if you broaden the time scale to, say, 1300 years, a very different picture emerges. However, not every ordinary person has the ability to zoom out to such a time scale and comprehend at that level. But let's get to the point. Allah clearly warned us against discrimination and bigotry towards other nations, tribes, and races.

“O you who believe! Stand out firmly for Allah as just witnesses and let not the enmity and hatred of others make you avoid justice. Be just: that is nearer to piety, and fear Allah. Verily, Allah is Well-Acquainted with what you do.” - Surah Al-Ma’idah (5:8)

Moreover, *Surah Al-Hujurat,* with just 18 verses, teaches us how to behave in a civilized society and treat other Muslims and fellow human beings fairly in the social landscape. The Quran delves into minute details on fundamental civic sense and behavior, but most of us are heedless of its teachings.

"O you who believe! Let not a group scoff at another group, it may be that the latter are better than the former; Nor let (some) women scoff at other women, it may be that the latter are better than the former, Nor defame one another, nor insult one another by nicknames. How bad is it, to insult one's brother after having Faith [i.e. to call your Muslim brother (a faithful believer) as: "O sinner", or "O wicked"]. And whosoever does not repent, then such are indeed wrong-doers. "- Surah Al-Hujurat (49:11)

The above ayah commands us not to mock or defame other men and women, as those targeted may be better than those who defame and mock them. The same verse also instructs us to stop name-calling. These microaggressions are prevalent in all modern civilized societies under the guise of tolerance and free speech, which creates a toxic divide within society. Do you think if someone mocks you, either privately or publicly, you could remain without animosity and keep a clean heart towards that person? It doesn't work like that. Humans aren't built for that. Once we stop these behaviors, we will be able to create a just society in peace and harmony.

Widening wealth gaps and income inequality

The widening wealth gaps presented in this book couldn't be clearer, unless someone chooses to ignore them, indicating that they are systemic. Such widespread disparities cannot occur unless they are supported by the very system in which they exist. This is the same story in all countries that follow the same system we have in the US. One of the driving causes is capitalism. You may be surprised or even offended when I suggest that capitalism can cause these issues, despite being the engine that has propelled great wealth generation in this country and much of the world. Allow me to explain.

Capitalism has brought enormous wealth and prosperity to society. However, the trickle-down economy, which is central to capitalism, is supposed to spread wealth throughout society. At its core, capitalism harbors the principle of profit maximization. This works to the extent that there is enough wealth dripping through the fists of the capital owners. And make no mistake, we have set a whole lot of 'exceptions' in our economic system to widen the flow of 'dripping wealth. So, why not keep making 'exceptions' to the system and let it run? Run it to the point of destruction? Or, being realistic, check out a model that is inherently designed with those guardrails in place and reflects the natural human disposition. Check out the Islamic economic model. Islam provides a unique economic system that resembles capitalism without the excessive materialism and includes measures to establish social justice in economics. The Islamic economic system comprises three primary components:

The principle of multifaceted ownership dictates that ownership falls to private, public, and state entities. Unlike capitalism, where private ownership is the de facto principle and all other forms of ownership are mere exceptions, or socialism, where public ownership is the default and private ownership is the exception, Islamic economics maintains all three forms of ownership side by side. In fact, capitalism and socialism have resorted to their 'exceptional' forms of ownership when their economic models began to prove unfit for society in an attempt to survive. The Principle of Economic Freedom involves personal limitations set by Islamic spirituality and intellectuality, but ultimately by the objective limitations set by God. Personal limitations have a profound impact on individuals as they acknowledge the human weaknesses God has created them with and continuously strive to overcome these limitations or remain aware of them to avoid societal harm and injustice. Objective limitations define the boundaries set in the sacred law, such as forbidding any economic activity based on usury, gambling, and alcohol. Most importantly, these limits influence the formation of governments and enforce the rule of law within the bounds of sacred law.

The final component of the Islamic economic system is the Principle of Social Justice, which sets this model apart from any other man-made economic models, including capitalism and socialism. Islam does not leave social justice to the relative definitions of humans; rather, it is explicitly and objectively defined in the sacred texts. This social justice consists of two general principles: general mutual responsibility and social balance. General mutual responsibility fosters interdependency among society members, ensuring that economic activity cares for society without causing harm, and ultimately creates a balanced society.

The Islamic economic model possesses two important qualities that distinguish it from capitalism and socialism, which represent two extreme views on individual aspirations. Capitalism suggests that individuals thrive when driven by personal desires, assuming that society will manage with complete freedom of economic choice for individuals, while ignoring any potential conflicts of interest with societal needs. In contrast, socialism prioritizes societal needs over individual desires. Both assertions have been proven incorrect by thousands of years of human history. Islam does not indulge in such euphoria about human behavior; instead, it sets limits and creates boundaries to address human limitations. The second quality is that the morality derived in Islamic economics is not based on material circumstances or natural conditions, unlike in socialism and capitalism. Instead, it stems from the means used to achieve goals, which must originate from the pure intention to fulfill duties defined by God and to please Him alone.

Islamic economics does not stand independently from the framework of religion; rather, the successful implementation of an Islamic economy is not only based on the Islamic framework but is also completely dependent on a solid framework of religion within society. This necessity for religion in societal life stems from the view that 'the social system must be laid out for humanity, and it is not feasible to leave humanity to devise the system for itself, as long as its understanding is limited and its intellectual circumstances are incapable of discovering the solution to the entire social problem.' This perspective contrasts with the personal natural benefits that humanity is capable of extracting from its surroundings through personal motivation, which guarantees its spontaneous drive toward natural benefits such as medication, pleasure, and comfort.

Islamic economics also differs from capitalism and socialism in terms of whether science can be used as a tool to derive economic policy. While science only gradually reveals the truth of an existing system or circumstance and does not create truth, Islamic economics is not established through experimentation. Instead, it uses a top-down approach based on the truth revealed by God.

Finally, due to humans' natural disposition toward personal motivation that often conflicts with social benefits, and the potential to solve social problems through a natural inclination toward religion, it has been proven without a doubt that Islamic economics is part of a comprehensive social organization. This makes religion the general framework for our Islamic economic model. The use of Islamic economic principles, such as Mudaraba (partnership of capital and labor) and forbidding usury, are examples of religious frameworks that dictate the Islamic economic model.

Islamic economics is more than a mere economic mode; it is a comprehensive socio-economic model. Pure economics examines the production of goods and services through the lens of the demand-supply paradigm. On the other hand, a socio-economic system investigates the rationale of whether a production should be undertaken from a higher moral aim. From a pure economics perspective, the Ricardian "Iron Law" of wages postulates that lower wages increase the mortality rate among workers, thus maintaining a low wage in the economic system. However, a socio-economic system would not settle on that discovery and fact; instead, it would seek a way to resolve this "iron law." The Islamic socio-economic system differs from a pure economic system not in the subject matters investigated—as the same production and demand-supply phenomena are examined—but because Islamic economics pursues this from an ideological angle. Fundamental to the Islamic socio-economic model is the establishment of social justice. However, the use of traditional scientific methods is insufficient to investigate justice and human rights, as these can only be derived from the principles of a comprehensive ideology. Thus, Islamic economics denounces usurious practices as an unjust system and prescribes "Mudarabah," a partnership where one party provides capital while the other provides labor, and both share the profits and losses. Islam as a religion provides a comprehensive solution for humanity, so it is natural that there would be moral doctrines that provide guardrails. However, the Islamic socio-economic model is not just a set of moral doctrines and advice; it is a system of life, like any other social and economic model, that not only gives moral doctrine but also provides a practical way of implementing these in society. The evidence of this includes commands to abstain from and oppose any kind of oppression, selfish exploitation, and injustice; establishing, collecting, and using Zakat for the equitable distribution of wealth to support the poor and needy; and putting responsibility on the Islamic government to ensure that inequality in society is addressed head-on. Despite its dissimilarity in the morally obligatory aspects of the Islamic socio-economic system in comparison to capitalism and socialism, Islamic economics is also geared towards improving the same conditions that those two systems aim to address.

Islamic economics sits evenly between the two extreme forms of economic systems, capitalism and socialism, while providing a more pragmatic economic system catered to society's holistic needs.

Apart from that, the economic system also impacts the levels of objectives: Necessity, Need, and Frills. In capitalism, there is no distinction between the production and distribution of goods and services. This is one of the reasons we do not see a purely capitalistic society in the world because it doesn't work in reality. For example, during the COVID-19 pandemic, the US government invoked the Defense Production Act to enforce the production of masks, ventilators, meat, etc. This is against the principles of capitalism's free market. So, either we have to have constant exceptions in whatever economic system we live in to support the levels of objectives, or we have to accept that the free market will somehow work it out. However, the Islamic economic system is designed to avoid such dilemma because the levels of needs are fundamental to Islam.

Public Health Crisis: Chronic Diseases

It's the lifestyle that triggered our healthcare disaster. Thus, to come out of this, the ultimate answer lies in living a natural life, stopping excessive consumption, and living for a purpose by avoiding materialism. If we don't, then the 'profiteering machine' of the food and pharmaceutical industries will find other ways to fool us again and again with their 'fancy' new research. I am sure you would agree that we can't afford another 50 years to survive at this rate of decline.

From where we are in the West, we can't resolve it all at once. This can be formulated into five stages of lifestyle transformation. The first two stages are absolutely critical and prerequisites for reaching the higher stages. However, even if we achieve the first two stages, the quality of life will fundamentally change, *insha'Allah* (if God wills). And it doesn't take much time to see the result. Depending on the current level of physiological and psychological states, preliminary benefits could be visible within 3-6 months, *insha'Allah*. By the way, Islam has introduced mandatory practices that promote a healthy lifestyle. I would also say that it's not only Islam; other religions like Christianity and Judaism also have similar lifestyle directives. If those were followed, they wouldn't be in this mess. After all, most religions originate from the same God, but we humans have twisted these due to our ignorance.

Stage 1: ***Change your food habit: Eat real food;*** Stage 2: ***Live a normal active life;*** Stage 3: ***Limit exposures to chemicals;*** Stage 4: ***Break the chain of excessive consumption and reject materialistic rat race;*** Stage 5: ***Limit artificial lifestyle;*** Final Stage: ***Live for a purpose***

Each of the stages needs an explanation on why to get there, what it entails, how it would benefit us, and how to achieve it in order to live a healthy life.

"Researchers examined data from 204 countries between 1990 and 2019. They found that there were more than 3.26 million early-onset cancer cases reported in those countries in 2019, up from 1.82 million in 1990, an increase of 79.1%." It has concluded that: "Encouraging a healthy lifestyle could reduce early-onset cancer disease burden."[101].

Stage 1: Change food habit: eat real food

You may ask, why do we need to choose real food? Is it rooted in our religion? Yes, it is. We have long ignored this because we didn't have to worry until the modern processed food industry invaded our lives. We always focused on "*halal*" (permitted) food because Allah has commanded this in the Quran and Hadith. However, we overlooked the adjective "*tayyiban*" (good) that Allah uses alongside "halal" when discussing food. What we took for granted as halal food was good food until we, humans, began contaminating it (in Dr. Robert Lustig's words, "what do you do to the food") through ultra-processing, turning it from good to potentially toxic. Want to see an example? We all know that olive oil is good for health. But we can turn this good oil into toxic oil. How? Just cook it at a high temperature. From the book *Metabolical*: "Trans-fats are very low in Real Food, but you can make them right on your stove from any unsaturated fat. In fact, you can turn one of the healthiest fats in your kitchen (olive oil) into the deadliest (trans-fat) with just extra heat. The reason? Unsaturated fats have cis-double bonds. If you heat an unsaturated fat past its smoking point, that cis-double bond can isomerize (flip) into a trans-double bond, and voila—a trans-fat... The lower the oil's smoking point, the easier it is to turn it into a trans-fat. Extra virgin olive oil has the lowest smoking point of all the fats, at 160 C (320 F)." A halal and good fat become halal and toxic trans-fat that will now cause all sorts of health problems rather than helping us. Interestingly, Dr. Robert Lustig suggests that we instead eat lard, as it's healthier for high-temperature cooking than any other oil: "*The exception to this smoking point rule: saturated fat—because there are no double bonds and therefore nothing to isomerize. Even though lard got a bad name as a saturated fat, it's way safer to fry in than any other oil.*"

Consider the Quran, which is so universal and eternal that 1400 years ago it advised not to indiscriminately eat what is halal but only to eat what is halal as well as good for your body. Additionally, what is good for one person may not be good for another. Thus, understanding what we eat is embedded in our religion.

"Eat from the good things with which We have provided you."- Al-Baqarah (2:57)

"O mankind, eat from whatever is on earth [that is] lawful and good..."- Al-Baqarah (2:168)

"Eat from the good things with which We have provided you."- Al-Baqarah (2:172)

"Say, 'Lawful for you are [all] good foods…"- Al-Maaida (5:4)

"And eat of what Allah has provided for you [which is] lawful and good."- Al-Maaida (5:88)

"Eat from the good things with which We have provided you."- Al-A'raaf (7:160)

"That eat of what Allah has provided for you [which is] lawful and good."- An-Nahl (16:114)

"Eat from the good things with which We have provided you."- Taa-Haa (20:81)

"[Allah said], 'O messengers, eat from the good foods…"- Al-Mu'minun (23:51)

The same applies to sugar. Honey is medicinal for the human body, and fruits, along with many other foods, contain sugar alongside essential nutrients. However, when we extract sugar from these foods, it becomes unhealthy. Why? Because we remove the most essential part needed for the digestion and a healthy metabolism: fiber. This creates a "volume" issue for our digestive system. An analogy would be that when we have a normal rate of rain, the earth can absorb it gradually. However, during heavy rain, the same amount of water poured onto the earth in a very short period results in flash floods that destroy properties and lives. Similarly, sugar (fructose, to be specific) floods the liver, damaging it and other organs. We should strictly moderate added sugar and avoid ultra-processed foods.

Disclaimer: Stages 1 and 2 are somewhat intertwined and should generally be implemented in parallel. However, certain actions in Stage 1 need to be completed to effectively transition into Stage 2 in a sustainable manner, which is why I have prioritized it. For example, consuming sugar and ultra-processed foods creates a vicious cycle that can prevent us from leading an active lifestyle, as these foods tend to make us lethargic and inactive.

You may ask, when we were young, we often used to eat sugary foods like candies, ice creams, desserts, etc., and we were perfectly fine. Even now, some people who eat sugary foods seem to be doing just fine. Yes, that's true. I lived the same way. I drank Coca-Cola and indulged in ice creams when I was a kid. But think about how often we used to eat them. Once a week? A few times a month? We always ate sugary food during Eid, and I had no health problems whatsoever for a long time until my mid-twenties. Eating in moderation certainly isn't a problem. In fact, a daily intake of 12 grams of sugar is generally regarded as safe. However, we can get much of that from fruit if we eat naturally. So, our bodies can handle the occasional sugar spike, but it should be truly "once in a while." Besides, our life is a complete system, so overall factors such as an active lifestyle, stress level, pollution, social life, faith, and worship, which are covered in the next stages, play significant roles in how my intake of sugary foods will impact me. At this stage, let's start with:

- Stop regular intake of all foods that have explicitly or implicitly added sugar. You will be surprised to find that almost every food is contaminated with added sugar. From fruit juice to coconut water, sugar is added. Soft drinks, beverages, juice, cereal, biscuits, chocolate, cake, baklava, bread, ketchup, etc.
- Foods that are ultra processed normally lack fibers to increase shelf life. Fiber is essential for a normal metabolic function (read the book

Metabolical by Dr. Robert Lustig for more detail) so avoid anything that is packaged for longer shelf life.

  - Eating fresh fruit is better than drinking juice for the same reason: to avoid consuming refined sugars. Additionally, sugar is often added to natural juice to make it sweeter.

- Processed foods usually have preservatives which preserve food so it doesn't need to be a genius to think what happens when that food gets into our digestive system. It's a tug of war between the digestive system and the preservatives.
- Take gaps between eating food (according to Dr. Robert Lustig: wait for 20 minutes for another serving). This will allow the food metabolism to trigger suppressing ghrelin and generating leptin to send signal to the brain that the body is metabolizing the last meal and don't need another meal soon.
- Eat in moderation. Fulfilling the stomach at all the time is like we're raving the car engine at all the time. For Muslims, we are advised in *Ahadith* to keep one-third of our stomach empty. "Nothing is worse than a person who fills his stomach. It should be enough for the son of Adam to have a few bites to satisfy his hunger. If he wishes more, it should be: One-third for his food, one-third for his liquids, and one-third for his breath." - *Al Tirmidhi*
- Fasting twice a week, on Mondays and Thursdays, was a practice keenly observed by the Prophet Muhammad (peace be upon him), as reported by *Al-Tirmidhi*. Interestingly, the benefits of this practice are now being recognized by medical science. Fasting triggers a process in our bodies known as autophagy, which was discovered by the Japanese scientist Yoshinori Ohsumi in 2016. Here are some scientific facts about autophagy: It can rapidly provide fuel for energy and building blocks for the renewal of cellular components, making it essential for the cellular response to starvation and other types of stress. After an infection, autophagy can eliminate invading intracellular bacteria and viruses. It also contributes to embryo

development and cell differentiation. Cells use autophagy to eliminate damaged proteins and organelles, a quality control mechanism critical for counteracting the negative consequences of aging. Disrupted autophagy has been linked to Parkinson's disease, type 2 diabetes, and other disorders prevalent in the elderly. Mutations in autophagy genes can cause genetic diseases. Moreover, disturbances in the autophagic machinery have been linked to cancer. Intense research is currently ongoing to develop drugs that can target autophagy in various diseases.[102]

Stage 2: Live a normal active life

This stage is a vital complement to the previous one, as it plays a crucial role in making sustainability achievable. Our bodies are designed for regular physical activity, and our metabolic system, brain function, and hormone secretion all work in harmony when we are active. For instance, engaging in activities such as walking can lower stress levels and enhance the overall performance of our metabolic system and body.

So, how can we accomplish this?

If your profession requires physical work, then you're in luck—you may not need this advice on physical activity. However, if your job doesn't involve much physical movement, consider incorporating physical tasks at home, walking to your workplace or to a transit station, engaging in gardening, or adding a physically demanding hobby. The bottom line is to try to be physically active.

If you're unable to incorporate physical activities into your routine, compensate by walking, cycling, jogging, or hiking regularly. It's always better to be outdoors; nature is beneficial. If going outside isn't feasible, consider the gym as a last resort. Aim to be active for at least an hour every day. One thing we often overlook is that exercises like using a treadmill can be seen as a recent construct with significant costs: time and money. Think about it—an hour spent walking, jogging, or running on a treadmill doesn't produce anything except burning calories that you've paid for. Other than staying active, you're not achieving anything productive. Here's an analogy: imagine you have a car that you seldom drive. To prevent damage to the battery, tires, and brakes, you need to drive it occasionally, maybe just around the neighborhood. Does this achieve the car's primary purpose of transportation? No, you're merely burning fuel and time to maintain its longevity. Instead, if you used the car for practical purposes, like dropping off your kids, commuting to work, or visiting a place, you'd fulfill both its function and ensure its upkeep. To make up for this perceived waste, try to fill the time with productive actions, such as listening to a podcast to gain knowledge, pondering your life, or intentionally relaxing to recharge for your next activity.

Muslims engage in several mandatory physical activities throughout the day. The five daily prayers (*salah*) involve a combination of mental, physical, and spiritual acts. Daily prayers are full of physical activity: individuals perform at least 17 (and up to 31) bends, 34 (to 62) partial push-ups, 5 (to 11) neck stretches, and stand straight for 20-40 minutes, depending on the duration of their prayers. Additionally, the ritual requires washing and cleansing the hands, face, mouth, and feet before each prayer. It is also recommended to brush teeth using a natural chewing stick known as *miswak*[103], derived from the Salvadora persica tree, before prayers. While I have only touched upon the physical aspects here, the greater benefits include meditation, devotion, and spirituality, which are also crucial for our psychological well-being.

Additionally, it's highly recommended to go to the mosque daily for the five daily prayers. By doing so, you achieve all the above-mentioned benefits, along with social interaction and connections with fellow human beings. During prayers at the mosque, you are required to stand shoulder-to-shoulder in a row, which is also scientifically proven to be beneficial. Human touch facilitates the flow of oxytocin, necessary for healthy living. According to NIH research, "Inter-individual touch can be a desirable reward that can both relieve negative affect and evoke strong feelings of pleasure."[104]

Stage 3: Limit exposures to chemicals and plastics

The above two stages should solve the majority of our problems. However, our modern world has been inundated with chemicals: plastic (and Styrofoam) containers, cups, bowls, utensils, insect sprays, sunscreens, dishwasher detergents, cleaning chemicals, paints, and the list goes on. Our modern life is surrounded by these chemicals. Read the warning signs on many plastic, rubber, and chemical products, and you will see that many are known to cause cancer, birth defects, or other reproductive harms. Here is a list of chemicals that are being proposed to have warnings added to their labels.[105]

I will add few specifics for your awareness:

Avoid using plastic items for warm and hot foods. Never put them in the microwave. Using plastic or Styrofoam cups for hot coffee or tea is harmful, but even the seemingly harmless paper cups often come with a thin plastic layer. This layer can create microplastic particles that enter our metabolic system.[106]

PFAS is a chemical that has been used indiscriminately in our products for decades. Here's what the NIH is now saying: "altered immune and thyroid function, liver disease, lipid and insulin dysregulation, kidney disease, adverse reproductive and developmental outcomes, and cancer."[107] What products contain PFAS chemicals? You would be horrified to see the list: cleaning products; water-resistant fabrics, such as rain jackets, umbrellas, and tents; grease-resistant paper; nonstick cookware; personal care products, like shampoo, dental floss, nail polish, and eye makeup; stain-resistant coatings used on carpets, upholstery, and other fabrics. Can you avoid them all? I doubt it. But I don't think it's worth surrendering to it and risking diseases like kidney disease, cancer, and liver diseases.

There are other chemicals that are hard for us to avoid because they are in the public sphere, such as water contamination, air pollution, pesticides, or other chemicals used on farms, etc. The more we can limit this exposure, the better support we will provide our bodies to recover, whatever they can.

Stage 4: Break the chain of excessive consumption and reject materialistic rat race

"Children of Adam! wear your beautiful apparel at every time and place of prayer: eat and drink: But waste not by excess, for Allah loveth not the wasters" (7:31)

The excessiveness of our consumption is causing anxiety in our lives and creating significant pollution on Earth. The development of countries is synonymous with excessive consumption, a concept ingrained in capitalism. For example, in the USA (and similarly in many other countries), excessive consumption is evident everywhere. The massive solar thermal power plant in the Mojave Desert of California, miles of solar panels destroying the desert ecosystem, leveling mountains in Utah for minerals, and massive farms in Oklahoma and Kansas are just a few examples of our excessive consumption. We eat more than necessary, discard 40% of our food (according to statistical data), build large houses for a few people that consume more land, require more building materials, and use more energy. Scientists and environmentalists discuss saving the earth by reducing the carbon footprint, but we should save ourselves from excessive consumption and waste to save the Earth. If we reduce our excessive consumption, our production would decrease, leading to less pollution, fewer toxic products (such as plastics and chemicals), and less of everything. Our actions, driven by greed and consumption, are wreaking havoc on this planet.

Then there is the rat race to create the ability for unlimited consumption. Most of us may not even realize that we are living a life where our success is defined by our profession, job title, income, the size of our house, the car we drive, or what our children accomplish following in our footsteps—essentially, the social status we hold in comparison to others.

Someone else defines what success means in our lives, and we race to reach that without even questioning their background or motives. Someone else dictates how to live our lives, and we immediately start to fit ourselves into that prescribed lifestyle. Someone defined that I have to work like a slave for the week and wait for the weekend to recharge, I have to go on vacation a few times a year to escape the nightmare we've created for ourselves, I have to enjoy summer—repeatedly, year after year, in a never-ending loop, and I have to earn tons of money until I'm 67 before I retire, when nothing is left of my youth to do anything meaningful for the purpose of my life.

We think these materials will bring us happiness until we find that they do not. It is like being thirsty for water but only being given salty water to quench your thirst, which only makes you thirstier until you collapse emotionally, psychologically, or physically.

Why don't those "make us happy" materials give us tranquility? Because we aren't created for that. As soon as we reach a height of success, we see the next height to reach, and then the next. But for what? As soon as that question starts to come to your mind, you get no answer. This materialistic system doesn't even want you to ask that question—it makes sure by keeping you busy all the time and not allowing you any free time alone to reflect—lest your eyes become wide open! Because once you know that you are going to leave all of the worldly success at any time or in just a matter of a few years—in 40, 60, or 80 years—in comparison to the life of eternity. You realize that you are collecting all "the stuff" that people in the past left in this world. Then what? That will make you anxious—what are you heading towards? Some of us can't take it anymore and declare that there's no life hereafter and just wish to let it end. Then it comes to their mind—why are they racing for materialistic success? Then they try to come up with new innovative thoughts. The rest of us who aren't foolish enough to declare that nonsense get scared because we aren't collecting anything for that journey and start hopelessly hoping for nothing.

Then we start taking drugs to continue living for materials: some of us take alcohol to forget reality; some of us take psychiatric drugs to keep us out of stress and depression; some take blood pressure or cholesterol drugs to keep the body running for the rat race; some take vacation pills every season, every month, or every weekend to forget the madness of the race; some take "materialistic success" drugs to show off to others that they are doing better than all those around them; every one of us is on some kind of drugs!

So, what can we do to break free from the relentless pursuit of materialism? Here are a few thoughts:

Define Concrete Material Goals: Start by setting clear and concrete goals for your materialistic pursuits. Ask yourself questions such as: How much money do you want to earn, and why is it important? How many degrees do you wish to attain, and what purpose will they serve? What size of a house do you need, and how does it align with your life objectives? Repeat this process for all other materialistic desires. This might seem straightforward, but failing to establish well-defined goals can lead you unknowingly into the materialistic rat race. Often, once you achieve a career, social, or financial milestone, you find yourself unsatisfied and immediately striving for the next one. How many times have you thought, if you just get that promotion, a certain salary increase, a particular position, or attain a specific social status, then "I'll be all set"? Yet, shortly after reaching these goals, you set new, even higher ones. The pursuit of material possessions never ends until our last breath. Imam Al-Ghazzali likened our thirst for worldly materials to drinking from a salty sea—the more you drink, the thirstier you become until you meet your demise due to the saltiness. Therefore, write down your materialistic goals and regularly evaluate your progress. Cultivate contentment with what you've achieved.

Avoid External Influences: Be cautious not to let external influences define your materialistic goals. It's easy to underestimate how much we are influenced by our surroundings. In psychology, this phenomenon is known as "social pressure," "social conformity," or "peer pressure." It can create an illusion of control over your goals when, in reality, you are merely reacting to societal influences. Remember that you must set these goals for yourself. To prevent others from shaping your aspirations, regularly assess whether your materialistic goals align with your personal values and desires.

Distinguish Material Desires from Spiritual Aspirations: It's crucial not to confuse your temporal materialistic desires with your pursuit of eternal success in the hereafter, which is guided by your life's purpose. The recommendations mentioned above primarily pertain to material possessions that you will inevitably leave behind when you pass away. However, for everything else that you will carry the outcome of those into the afterlife, do not limit yourself to modest goals. Instead, aim for objectives that are grand. Compete with others in acts of righteousness and in contributing positively to humanity. This is the ultimate path to success.

In summary, by setting clear materialistic goals, guarding against external influences, and distinguishing between material desires and spiritual aspirations, you can navigate the materialistic world while staying true to your higher purpose in life.

Stage 5: Limit artificial lifestyle

If you find yourself at this stage, you may already be doing well in your life. However, if you're seeking to truly elevate your life to the next level, consider embracing a more natural way of living by reducing your reliance on artificial products and services. To be clear: not everyone needs to reach this stage due to the availability and exposure to an artificial lifestyle. However, individuals who are exposed to excessive artificial life and living at the higher levels of Maslow's hierarchy of needs might find it necessary to reach this stage.

Artificial or synthetic products have undeniably improved our lives significantly, including innovations like electric lighting, televisions, computers, smartphones, and social media. These inventions are remarkable, and our civilization should continue to develop new products and technologies. However, unbridled and excessive use of these artificial amenities can disrupt the balance in our lives. It's crucial to remember that human evolution occurs at a gradual pace due to the inherent nature of our biology. Attempting to defy this natural pace is unwise.

For instance, for thousands of years, we satisfied our social needs by engaging with real people in person, allowing our brains to process social interactions at a manageable rate. In contrast, social media has completely altered this dynamic by providing a constant stream of social interaction without genuine physical contact. This change has led to our brains receiving dopamine from social media usage, potentially harming our neurons and undermining our natural sources of happiness. By limiting our time on social media, we can allocate more time to genuine, in-person human interactions.[108]

This is just one example. The closer we live to nature, the better our biological systems tend to function. Therefore, whenever feasible, consider reducing your reliance on artificial aspects of modern life and embrace the therapeutic benefits of immersing yourself in nature through every possible means at your disposal.

Final Stage: Live for a purpose

It's important to recognize that what follows isn't an isolated stage but rather an overarching principle that should permeate all stages of life. The preceding stages are aimed at promoting a healthy body and mind during our time in this world. However, what value is there in leading a profoundly healthy life here if we depart from this world unprepared for the eternal one? Throughout human history, billions of individuals, much like yourself, have come and gone. So, it behooves us to ask: Why are we brought into this world? What awaits us once we depart from it? If you've already discovered the answers to these questions, then kudos to you. The subsequent question is whether you are actively preparing for that journey.

But if you haven't yet arrived at those answers, it's crucial to pause whatever you're doing now and seek those answers. Our Earth has existed for approximately 4 billion years, humans have inhabited it for thousands of years, and our lifespan here is limited to around 100 years at most. That's an infinitesimal fraction of the Earth's history. You fall into one of two categories: either you're absolutely certain, with substantial evidence, that there is no God (as an atheist), or you need to explore the truth about the existence of God and adhere to His guidance for your own salvation.

If you remain uncertain and continue to drift through this fleeting life, you're ultimately deceiving no one but yourself. Imagine this situation as akin to someone on a cruise ship approaching the precipice of Niagara Falls. They know they will soon reach the edge but take no action because they haven't deciphered the physics of what happens when they go over the falls. Instead, they decide to enjoy their time on the cruise ship and neglect to contemplate the imminent plunge. Just remember, there's no return once you are at the edge.

Once you come to terms with this reality, dedicate your life to pursuing a career in the context of life's purpose. It doesn't matter which field or industry you are involved in, as long as it's not immoral or harming others, whether it's science, technology, engineering, construction, politics, business, food, entertainment, arts, or religion. Devote your efforts to contribute to the greater purpose of your eternal life.

Alcohol and Drug addiction crisis

It's rather a very simple solution to the very complex problem that the USA is grappling with. It's so simple that it may seem unrealistic but it worked for majority of the time. It's even mostly working for many parts of the world where people follow it. In Islam, all kinds of harmful drugs and alcohols are forbidden. This unequivocally mentioned in the Quran.

The prohibition of intoxicants, including drugs and alcohol, is a topic addressed within Islamic teachings, particularly in the Quran. Islam places a significant emphasis on the health, well-being, and moral state of its followers, advocating for a lifestyle that ensures the physical, mental, and spiritual welfare of the community. This section explores the Quranic perspective on the prohibition of drugs and alcohol, drawing insights from specific verses and their implications for Muslims.

One of the key verses in the Quran that addresses the consumption of alcohol and intoxicants is found in *Surah Al-Baqarah* (2:219): "They ask you about wine and gambling. Say, 'In them is great sin and [yet, some] benefit for people. But their sin is greater than their benefit.'" This verse acknowledges that while there may be some perceived benefits in alcohol and gambling, the harm they cause far outweighs these benefits, hinting at the eventual revelation of their prohibition.

The directive becomes more explicit in *Surah Al-Ma'idah* (5:90-91), which states: "O you who have believed, indeed, intoxicants, gambling, [sacrificing on] stone altars [to other than Allah], and divining arrows are but defilement from the work of Satan, so avoid it that you may be successful. Satan only wants to cause between you animosity and hatred through intoxicants and gambling and to avert you from the remembrance of Allah and from prayer. So will you not desist?"

As this problem influences many other problems, so solving this problem could be at the top of the list to start with.

Mental health epidemic

Following Islam may not cure mental health issues but it can help prevent them from arising. What are the causes of mental health issues?

First of all, I must acknowledge with full transparency that I do not have professional education in mental health, and I am in no way pretending to be an expert. I suggest consulting a medical professional if it's a medical mental health issue.

That said, the current state of the mental health epidemic is unprecedented, even compared to 50 years ago. The world was not much less stressful back then; we had World Wars, colonization, social disparity, racism, you name it. These issues haven't worsened, but what has deteriorated today includes the depletion of family structures leading to loneliness, an intense materialistic lifestyle and rat race, a lack of purpose in life, excessive consumption of food and materials, drastic changes in eating habits from natural to preservative-laden, highly processed foods, and a lack of social interaction. While I'm not stating that these factors are the definitive reasons for anyone's mental health issues, these are significant changes we've observed over the last 50 years. Let's explore these one at a time.

Depleted Family structure

Hold your imagination as I have covered it in the immediate next section on how Islam reinforce the preservation of family that's the building block of the society. So, we can recover the family structure through that.

Excessive consumption and food habit and Lack of purpose in life

If you have read the book sequentially, you should already have the answer. However, if not, please refer to the section "Public Health Crisis: Chronic Diseases," where I have discussed our excessive food consumption at length. The issue of excessive materialism and resource waste is covered later in this chapter, in the section "Excessive Materialism and Waste of Resources."

Social interaction and Loneliness

In terms of social interaction, all Muslims are commanded to interact socially. It is highly recommended for Muslims to go to the mosque, where they stand shoulder to shoulder and pray in congregation. They are required to visit the mosque once a week and meet with other community members. During the month of Ramadan, they go to pray for hours every night, totaling 30 times in the month. Islam defines neighbors as those living in 40 surrounding houses, and if someone does not have food or needs help, it is your responsibility to support them. These practices are also found in Christianity, but most of the West has moved away from Christianity, exacerbating social issues. However, Islam does not make these practices optional but mandatory. So, even if you do not like to interact socially that often, similar to how sometimes you don't want to eat vegetables even when you know they are good for your health, you are mandated to engage in social interaction. Metaphorically speaking, Muslims were eating "vegetables"—engaging in social interaction and receiving the benefits of mental health support—for free. This social interaction also addresses loneliness at a macro level. Finally, the family structure support in Islam (refer to the next section) provides the micro-level, day-to-day support to alleviate loneliness.

Depleted family values and loss of family bonds

One of the fundamental purposes of the Islamic lifestyle is the continuation of humanity through family. Islam has made marriage obligatory for everyone except those who face physical, mental, or economic challenges. The sanctity of the family is paramount in the Islamic social structure.

The Prophet Muhammad (pbuh) has explicitly advised young men, those of who can afford to maintain a family and support his wife should marry. (Sahih al-Bukhari, Book 67, Hadith 3 and Sahih Muslim, Book 16, Hadith).

The most significant aspect of upholding family values is creating a respectful environment where men are respectful and just toward women. Much injustice has been done to women in the name of religion by all religious communities. However, Islam aims to break that chain and establish justice between men and women. God has given clear instructions to men to be respectful and just:

"O you who have believed, it is not lawful for you to inherit women by compulsion. And do not make difficulties for them in order to take [back] part of what you gave them unless they commit a clear immorality. And live with them in kindness. For if you dislike them - perhaps you dislike a thing and Allah makes therein much good." - Surah An-Nisa (4:19)

Islam accords women the highest respect. Mothers are held in such high regard that an authentic hadith from the Prophet (pbuh) states if someone's mother is displeased with them, they cannot enter heaven. Family values emphasize the importance of caring for parents, which is given utmost importance in the religion.

"And your Lord has decreed that you not worship except Him, and to parents, good treatment. Whether one or both of them reach old age [while] with you, say not to them [so much as], 'uff,' (i.e. even being slightly annoyed) and do not repel them but speak to them a noble word. And lower to them the wing of humility out of mercy and say, 'My Lord, have mercy upon them as they brought me up [when I was] small.'"- Surah Al-Isra (17:23-24).

Here, the Quran further reinforces the duty towards parents:

"And We have enjoined upon man [care] for his parents. His mother carried him, [increasing her] in weakness upon weakness, and his weaning is in two years. Be grateful to Me and to your parents; to Me is the final destination." - Surah Luqman (31:14)

A man and a woman form the new family and Islam instructs both to love and be kind to one other.

"And among His signs is this, that He created for you mates from among yourselves, that you may dwell in tranquility with them, and He has put love and mercy between your [hearts]: verily in that are Signs for those who reflect." - Surah Al-Rum (30:21).

A quick comparison of Quran and Bible where the beginning of the story of Adam and Eve, all the blames were put on Eve and told that sufferings of women's life on earth is due to their treachery. Let's see first what the Bible says. The key verse that directly involves Eve in this event is Genesis 3:6, which states:

"When the woman saw that the fruit of the tree was good for food and pleasing to the eye, and also desirable for gaining wisdom, she took some and ate it. She also gave some to her husband, who was with her, and he ate it."

In the biblical account of the fall of Adam and Eve found in Genesis 3, after they ate the fruit from the tree of the knowledge of good and evil, God pronounced several curses as consequences for their actions. Specifically for Eve, and by extension to all women, the curses are detailed in Genesis 3:16. The verse states:

"To the woman he said, 'I will make your pains in childbearing very severe; with painful labor you will give birth to children. Your desire will be for your husband, and he will rule over you.'"

On the contrary, Quran never blames Eve for Adam to slip. Rather Quran says that, both are equally responsible for the slippage. There's no blame game and women are not in any cursed life whatsoever. Let's check what Quran says about Adam and Eve:

The Quranic narrative of Adam and Eve (*Hawwa* in Arabic) and their slip (note the word choice: it doesn't say "sin," but "slipped") from obedience to Allah presents a significantly different perspective from the Biblical account, especially concerning blame and curses. The Quran emphasizes the joint responsibility of both Adam and Eve for their mistake and does not single out Eve as the primary cause of the slip. Furthermore, no curse is placed on Eve or women in general as a result of this event.

The Quran mentions the story of Adam and Eve in several chapters (*Surah* in Arabic), highlighting their joint action in disobeying Allah but without attributing the blame to Eve. For example:

Surah Al-A'raf (7:19-22) narrates the temptation and the slip in a way that implicates both Adam and Eve without singling out Eve:

"O Adam, dwell, you and your wife, in Paradise and eat therefrom in [ease and] abundance from wherever you will. But do not approach this tree, lest you be among the wrongdoers. But Satan whispered to them to make apparent to them that which was concealed from them of their private parts. He said, 'Your Lord did not forbid you this tree except that you become angels or become of the immortal.' And he swore [by Allah] to them, 'Indeed, I am to you from among the sincere advisors.' So, he made them fall, through deception. And when they tasted of the tree, their private parts became apparent to them, and they began to fasten together over themselves from the leaves of Paradise. And their Lord called to them, 'Did I not forbid you from that tree and tell you that Satan is to you a clear enemy?'"

Surah Taha (20:121) also mentions the slip without placing the blame on Eve but went one step ahead to clarify that Adam disobeyed and made the mistake:

"And Adam disobeyed his Lord and erred."

"And We said, 'O Adam, dwell, you and your wife, in Paradise and eat [therefrom] in [ease and] abundance from wherever you will. But do not approach this tree, lest you be among the wrongdoers.' But Satan caused them to slip out of it and removed them from that [condition] in which they had been. And We said, 'Go down, [all of you], as enemies to one another, and you will have upon the earth a place of settlement and provision for a time. We said, "Go down from it, all of you. Then Adam received from his Lord [some] words, and He accepted his repentance. Indeed, it is He who is the Accepting of Repentance, the Merciful. And when guidance comes to you from Me, whoever follows My guidance – there will be no fear concerning them, nor will they grieve.'"- Surah Al-Baqarah (2:35-38)

Unlike the Biblical narrative, the Quran does not mention any curses being placed on Adam or Eve as a direct consequence of the disobedience. The consequences of their action were their expulsion from Paradise and the decree that humanity would live a mortal life on earth, facing challenges and toils. However, these consequences are not framed as curses but as part of the divine wisdom and plan for humanity. Dr. Jeffrey Lang had shown that these verses (*Surah Al-Baqarah* 2:30 – 33) are explaining that God created Adam and Even to send to the Earth as part of divine plan and through their "training" they were prepped up and were sent live a short life that's an opportunity. Importantly, the Quran also emphasizes the forgiveness granted to Adam and Eve after their repentance. For instance, *Surah Al-A'raf* (7:23) recounts their plea for forgiveness, which Allah accepts:

"They said, 'Our Lord, we have wronged ourselves, and if You do not forgive us and have mercy upon us, we will surely be among the losers.'" Allah immediately accepted their repentance and forgave them.

"Then Adam received from his Lord [some] words, and He accepted his repentance. Indeed, it is He who is the Accepting of repentance, the Merciful" – Surah Al-Baqarah (2:37)

This aspect of the story underscores the merciful nature of Allah and the concept of repentance and forgiveness in Islam, rather than focusing on blame or eternal punishment.

Women and Men are given the equal opportunities and equal rewards in the Quran. Male is not getting higher status because they are men or women are given higher status because they are women but their righteousness will earn higher status to God.

"O mankind, indeed We have created you from male and female and made you peoples and tribes that you may know one another. Indeed, the most noble of you in the sight of Allah is the most righteous of you. Indeed, Allah is Knowing and Acquainted" – Surah Al-Hujurat (49:13)

Islam also provides a unique view of responsibilities of men and women without dehumanizing anyone. Islam has put roles and responsibilities in the family where men and women, due to their biological uniqueness, are responsible to something over others. For example, men are responsible to provide the livelihood for the family where wife has the right on husband's assets. However, husband doesn't have any right on whatever the wife possesses and she's not at all be held responsible for providing livelihood in the family from her assets. Her assets and wealth are protected.

"Indeed, the Muslim men and Muslim women, the believing men and believing women, the obedient men and obedient women, the truthful men and truthful women, the patient men and patient women, the humble men and humble women, the charitable men and charitable women, the fasting men and fasting women, the men who guard their private parts and the women who do so, and the men who remember Allah often and the women who do so - for them Allah has prepared forgiveness and a great reward." Surah Al-Ahzab (33:35).

I know a major question and concern about Islam is the authority and disciplining of women. Prophet Muhammad (pbuh) is the role model who exemplified living by the Quran. No historian, whether Muslim or not, has ever claimed that he mistreated his wives. On the contrary, he managed family disputes in a disciplined manner. Do you know how? He chose to leave the house and live alone for a month. Once tensions had eased, he returned home, arbitrated, and resolved the disputes through conversation. He never resorted to physical force as a means of discipline. Thus, we must be cautious not to mistakenly label cultural behaviors as Islamic practices.

So, when a society is built upon a social contract, namely marriage, and both parties are respectful to each other with clear instructions to show utmost respect to men, women, and parents, the loosening bonds can be repaired to prevent society from becoming fragmented.

Long Injustice to the Black and Poor

Islam commands adherence to justice, even if it goes against oneself, relatives, or parents. There is no excuse for participating in or inflicting injustice on others in Islam. Furthermore, Islam celebrates the diversity of ethnicities and commands us to enrich one another through this diversity.

"O you who have believed, be persistently standing firm in justice, witnesses for Allah, even if it be against yourselves or parents and relatives. Whether one is rich or poor, Allah is more worthy of both. So, follow not [personal] inclination, lest you not be just. And if you distort [your testimony] or refuse [to give it], then indeed Allah is ever, with what you do, Acquainted. "– Surah Al-Nisa (4:135)

"O ye who believe! stand out firmly for Allah, as witnesses to fair dealing, and let not the hatred of others to you make you swerve to wrong and depart from justice. Be just: that is next to Piety: and fear Allah For Allah is well-acquainted with all that ye do." - Surah Al-Maidah (5:8)

There are numerous verses in the Quran that command Muslims to stand for justice. These are not merely statements from stories or conversational topics. If you read the verses from *Surah An-Nisa* and *Surah Al-Ma'idah,* you will see a clear command for every Muslim to stand for justice indiscriminately—even against oneself. It couldn't be clearer than that. Moreover, the verse from *Surah Al-Ma'idah* serves as a reminder and warning from Allah against any form of discrimination and bigotry against others, including nations, tribes, and races. Justice must be individualized—one person's wrongdoing cannot be attributed to an entire community, race, or nation.

Muslims should have been the torchbearers of human rights and humanity in general. However, many of Allah's commands have been forgotten, and some have engaged in bigotry, which is unequivocally forbidden in the Quran. Do you not think that mockery and jokes about them constitute a form of backbiting, if not outright bigotry? If you backbite an individual, you may be able to seek forgiveness from that person, but how do you seek forgiveness when you have slandered an entire nation? *Surah Al-Hujurat* warns us about the severity of backbiting.

"O you who believe! Avoid much suspicion, indeed some suspicions are sins. And spy not, neither backbite one another. Would one of you like to eat the flesh of his dead brother? You would hate it (so hate backbiting). And fear Allah. Verily, Allah is the One Who forgives and accepts repentance, Most Merciful." - Surah Al-Hujurat (49:12)

Allah may forgive if His commands are disobeyed—that is between you and Him—but when the rights of a fellow human being are violated, either physically or emotionally (through backbiting and slandering), repentance is not possible until they forgive you. In one hadith, the

Prophet (pbuh) said that the truly poor person is the one who arrives with all their good deeds but is forced to give them all away because of their wrongdoings to others. The Hadith is as follows:

The Prophet (pbuh) is reported to have said: "Do you know who is bankrupt?" The Companions replied, 'The bankrupt amongst us is the person who has no money or property." The Prophet (ﷺ) said, "The bankrupt from amongst my Ummah is the one who will come on the Day of Resurrection with a good record of *Salah* (prayer), *Sawm* (fasting) and *Zakah* (charity). But he also cursed someone, slandered against someone, unlawfully took the property of another, killed someone or beat someone. Then all of these abused persons will receive parts of his (abuser's) *Hasanaat* (good deed). When all of his (abuser's) *Hasanaat* have been removed from his record after he (abuser) pays back for what he owes, then the aggrieved persons' sins will be transferred to and thrown on him (abuser) and he (abuser) will be thrown into the Fire." (Related by *Muslim* and *Tirmidhi*)

Islam came to declare the end of racism. On top of that, *Surah Al-Hujurat*, has just 18 verses but each of the verse teaches us how to behave in a civilized society and treat other Muslims and fellow human beings fairly in the social landscape. The Quran goes into minute-level detail on fundamental civic sense and behavior but most of us are heedless to its teaching.

"O you who believe! Let not a group scoff at another group, it may be that the latter are better than the former; Nor let (some) women scoff at other women, it may be that the latter are better than the former, Nor defame one another, nor insult one another by nicknames. How bad is it, to insult one's brother after having Faith. And whosoever does not repent, then such are indeed wrong-doers."- Surah Al-Hujurat (49:11)

The verse commands not to mock or defame others, lest those targeted may be more virtuous than their detractors. It also instructs us to stop name-calling. Such microaggressions, prevalent in modern societies under the guise of tolerance and free speech, create a toxic divide. Do you think you could remain without animosity and maintain a clean heart towards someone who mocks you, whether privately or publicly? It's not in human nature to do so. Stopping these behaviors is essential for fostering a just society.

Climate change and pollution

Humans are sent as caretakers of the Earth, but we have engaged in rampant environmental destruction due to ever-increasing consumption. This excessiveness also leads to significant pollution, which many believe is accelerating climate chaos. The development of countries has become synonymous with excessive consumption. In the USA, for instance, the massive solar thermal power plant in the Mojave Desert, endless solar panels destroying the desert ecosystem, mountain leveling in Utah for minerals, and vast farms in Oklahoma and Kansas exemplify our overconsumption. We consume more food than necessary, discarding 40% of it (according to statistical data), build oversized houses for few occupants, using more land, materials, and energy.

Scientists and environmentalists advocate for reducing our carbon footprint to save the Earth, but we must also curb our own excessive consumption and waste. By doing so, our production will decrease, leading to less pollution, fewer toxic products (like plastics and chemicals), and overall, less waste. Our actions, driven by greed and consumption, are wreaking havoc on the Earth—both land and sea. Land is devastated by deforestation, extraction of fossil fuels and minerals at alarming rates, and subsequent burning that renders it uninhabitable. The seas suffer as well, with plastic pollution forming floating islands and dying coral reefs, while glaciers melt rapidly.

So, what does Islam say about this? Remarkably, it not only offers solutions but also pinpoints the root cause. The insights it provides are so profound that one might think the Quran is referring to what we have been doing to the earth in recent years.

"Mischief has appeared on land and sea because of (the meed) that the hands of men have earned that (Allah) may give them a taste of some of their deeds: in order that they may turn back (from Evil)." - Surah Al-Rum (30:41)

A Muslim cannot deny our contribution to the climate impact on the land and sea, as the Quran clearly states that many mischiefs result from our own actions. If we cease these actions, we can alleviate their impacts. We know we are engaging in the mass destruction of forests, overconsumption of fossil fuels, plastics, and other chemicals, among other activities. Therefore, we must reverse our actions to mitigate the detrimental effects of these practices.

Excessive materialism and waste of resources

If you weren't aware, Islam was once criticized for being overly materialistic compared to Christianity, where monasticism and celibacy were seen as ways to be religious. However, this perception has shifted for Christianity over the last several hundred years, particularly after the Christian reformations and the rise of the prosperity gospel. This shift has made Islam appear almost "monastic," although it is far from it. Islam has remained consistent, continually advocating for balance in all aspects of life. This principle is reiterated throughout the Quran, a point so profound that I feel compelled to mention it again for emphasis:

"O children of Adam! Wear your beautiful apparel at every time and place of prayer; eat and drink, but waste not by excess. For Allah loves not the wasters." Surah Al-A'raf (7:31)

This couldn't be clearer: Do not waste and do not commit excess.

"Fair in the eyes of men is the love of things they covet: women and sons; heaped-up hoards of gold and silver; horses branded (for blood and excellence); and (wealth of) cattle and well-tilled land. Such are the possessions of this world's life; but in nearness to Allah is the best of the goals (to return to). (14) Say: shall I give you glad tidings of things far better than those? For the righteous are Gardens in nearness to their Lord with rivers flowing beneath; therein is their eternal home; with companions pure (and holy) and the good pleasure of Allah. For in Allah's sight are (all) His servants. — (15) "- Surah Al-Imran (3:14-15)

More on worldly life in this Surah to keep the worldly life in perspective with the hereafter:

"Everyone shall taste death. And only on the Day of Resurrection shall you be paid your wages in full. And whoever is removed away from the Fire and admitted to Paradise, he indeed is successful. *The life of this world is only the enjoyment of deception (a deceiving thing)*" - Surah Al-Imran (3:185)

He continued the warning in many places in the Quran:

"Know that the life of this world is but amusement and diversion and adornment and boasting to one another and competition in increase of wealth and children - like the example of a rain whose [resulting] plant growth pleases the tillers; then it dries and you see it turned yellow; then it becomes [scattered] debris. And in the Hereafter is severe punishment and forgiveness from Allah and approval. *And what is the worldly life except the enjoyment of delusion.*" - Surah Al-Hadeed (57:20)

"And adornments of gold. *Yet all this (i.e. the roofs, doors, stairs, elevators, thrones of their houses) would have been nothing but an enjoyment of this world.* And the Hereafter with your Lord is (only) for the Muttaqûn." - Surah Al-Zukhruf (43:35)

If this is an overarching directive, there are specific instructions for reduced consumption: 30 days of mandatory fasting, Prophet Muhammad's (pbuh) recommendation to fast twice a week, and an extra three days a month, while keeping the stomach one-third empty. This isn't to say that eating less is the sole solution, but imagine if we had adhered to this practice—what could we have achieved? The disaster in our climate due to excessive food production, where we consume three times more than necessary (speaking about America), and many other problems mentioned earlier in the book could have been mitigated. Then, by addressing all other forms of overconsumption and living a balanced life in every aspect, we could create a more normal world. Combining this with all other resolutions would transform the USA.

Pornography

Pornography is a modern problem facilitated by technology. Although the Quran does not explicitly mention pornography, its teachings provide profound guidance on modesty, chastity, and the sanctity of human relationships that effectively counteract this issue. A practicing Muslim is guided in such a way that even consuming pornographic content, let alone participating in the industry, is contrary to the teachings of the Quran. It is evident how women are objectified in the pornography industry. As previously mentioned in this book, the human trafficking of women and girls, subjecting them to horrific lives, is part of this industry. Islam holds women and modesty in the highest regard.

These principles can be applied to address the problem of pornography, guiding individuals towards a path of spiritual and moral purity.

Guarding Personal Modesty

One of the foundational principles in the Quran regarding personal conduct is the importance of guarding one's modesty. Surah An-Noor (24:30-31) instructs both men and women to lower their gaze and guard their private parts, highlighting the significance of personal modesty:

"Tell the believing men to reduce [some] of their vision and guard their private parts. That is purer for them. Indeed, Allah is Acquainted with what they do. And tell the believing women to reduce [some] of their vision and guard their private parts..."

This directive serves as a preventive measure against the consumption of pornography, which exploits and distorts the natural human inclination towards sexual curiosity and attraction.

Fostering Strong Marital Bonds

The Quran places great emphasis on the sanctity of marriage as a bond that fulfills emotional and physical intimacy between spouses. Surah Ar-Rum (30:21) mentions:

"And among His signs is that He created for you from yourselves mates that you may find tranquility in them; and He placed between you affection and mercy. Indeed, in that are signs for a people who give thought."

By encouraging strong, loving, and respectful marital relationships, the Quran indirectly addresses the void that often leads individuals to seek fulfillment in harmful ways, including pornography.

Avoiding Lewdness and Indecency

The Quran explicitly prohibits lewdness and indecency, which are intrinsic to pornography. Surah Al-A'raf (7:33) states:

"Say, 'My Lord has only forbidden immoralities - what is apparent of them and what is concealed - and sin, and oppression without right, and that you associate with Allah that for which He has not sent down authority, and that you say about Allah that which you do not know.'"

Pornography is a manifestation of such immoralities, promoting a culture of lewdness that the Quran warns against.

Encouraging Reflection and Self-Purification

The Quran also emphasizes the importance of self-reflection and purification of the soul (Surah Ash-Shams 91:9-10), encouraging individuals to recognize the harmful effects of sins on their spiritual and moral well-being. By fostering a mindset of self-improvement and consciousness of Allah's commands, individuals are more likely to resist temptations, including the allure of pornography.

Quran's comprehensive guidance on modesty, chastity, the sanctity of marriage, and the prohibition of indecency provides a strong foundation for addressing this issue. By adhering to these principles, individuals can cultivate a healthy perspective on sexuality and relationships, steering clear of the destructive path of pornography. The Quran, thus, offers a timeless solution to modern challenges, guiding believers towards a life of purity, dignity, and spiritual fulfillment.

We've covered the problems impacting the country and outlined how Islam inherently approaches these challenges that threaten the very core of civilization. As I started this chapter, this book aims to trigger a journey by unveiling the Quranic teachings and directives to the rational minds in the West, encouraging them to benefit from the Quran. I could cite many other verses from the Quran to show how it provides solutions to these problems. In that case, the book would have to cover almost the entire Quran because it offers guidance for these and all other human challenges. So, my humble request is for you to read the Quran for yourself. I can at least promise that you will not be disappointed.

Chapter VII: Let the Journey Begin

Even though the title may suggest a grandiose change, for America, the adjustment is simpler than in other parts of the world. It's more about slightly turning the wheel toward the destination rather than making a U-turn, as many might have assumed from reading thus far. This is because most Americans are followers of an Abrahamic faith, which is the foundation of Islam. Nearly 74% of the U.S. population adheres to one of the Abrahamic faiths, and approximately 71% of them are Christians. Thus, it's a relatively straightforward shift for those 70% who already have roots in the Judeo-Christian faith. The other 22% of the U.S. population are "nones," i.e., religiously unaffiliated, who have primarily lost trust in religions not because they have explored the truth, but because they have been put off by the actions and behaviors of the so-called followers of these faiths. For them, the change might even be easier since they aren't replacing one faith with another but filling a gap. However, every change can seem daunting if you don't see its value or benefit. As humans, we always ask, "What's In It For Me?" or WIIFM before embracing any changes. Assuming you have read up to this chapter, you might already be convinced that Islam could be the solution for both this material life as well as the hereafter and, to the extent necessary for continuing this Western civilization. If not, I would suggest revisiting the earlier chapters before proceeding. It would be a waste of your time to read this chapter if you don't think Islam offers a solution. The rest of the chapter will not make sense otherwise. For the sake of the book's length, I will cover the two Abrahamic faiths: Christianity and Judaism, and the non-religious affiliated folks. I will address other religious groups in another publication, as they require a completely different approach due to their belief structures.

"And do not insult those they invoke other than Allah, lest they insult Allah in enmity without knowledge. Thus, We have made pleasing to every community their deeds. Then to their Lord is their return, and He will inform them about what they used to do." - Surah Al-An'am (6:108)

"You will surely find the most intense of the people in animosity toward the believers [to be] the Jews and those who associate others with Allah; and *you will find the nearest of them in affection to the believers those who say, "We are Christians." That is because among them are priests and monks and because they are not arrogant."* - Surah Al-Ma'idah (5:82)

"And do not argue with the People of the Scripture except in a way that is best, except for those who commit injustice among them, and say, 'We believe in that which has been revealed to us and revealed to you. And our God and your God is one; and we are Muslims [in submission] to Him.'" - Surah Al-Ankabut (29:46)

The first step you need to take is to ask yourself this question: Who created me, what is the purpose of my life on this earth, and what will happen after my death?

Once you ask that question, you can't rest until you get to the bottom of it because you will realize that this entire universe wasn't created for mere play. Your existence on Earth isn't a simple "incident" where you stumbled upon this planet and then everything ends with your death.

Every religion offers an answer, but I challenge you: most of us accept answers from others rather than discovering them through personal exploration. You may disagree and claim that your convictions to your religion came from your own exploration. If you are a religious person, have you read your religious text thoroughly and then the Quran? This is true not only for followers of other religions but also for many Muslims who haven't read the Quran from beginning to end with understanding on their own. So, don't feel bad if you haven't.

Once you have read your religious scripture and the Quran, take stock of your daily life: How are you living day-to-day—is it in alignment or complete contradiction to your faith? Consider whether current scientific knowledge contradicts or supports your beliefs. I'm not suggesting that you must choose between science and faith (as discussed in the section "Believing in Science" under Chapter IV: "What Are Our Choices?"), but I am encouraging you to reconcile your daily actions with your religious teachings. Are you consistently disregarding your scripture? If so, why? And why do you continue to hold onto these contradictions? Reflect on these questions.

If you're an atheist, this problem is more prominent. Many people who believe that God doesn't exist are convinced by their "heroes" whom they follow, as well as by observing the "unintellectual" behavior of fellow humans who believe in some sort of religion.

You may counter that you are too busy with life and don't have time to pause and reflect. Then the final part of the original question—"What will happen after your death?"—returns to haunt you. Like many before you—your parents, grandparents, and ancestors—you are living your life on this earth, which will soon end. In the grand scheme of humanity's history, our lifetimes are but a blink of an eye. Metaphorically speaking, we are all on a bus ride, passing time until our journey reaches its stop, the final destination, and we are dropped off. Will that place be cold? Hot? Rainy? Are we collecting the appropriate clothing and convertible currency for that destination? What currency will be accepted there? If we are deluding ourselves with thoughts that "things will be just fine" or "we'll see when we get there," remember, it's a one-way ticket. No one has returned from there, and neither will you. Now is the time to prepare and collect the wherewithal.

Next, I have outlined a simple journey from prominent faiths, or the absence thereof, to Islam. This is by no means an exhaustive account but a starting point where you can begin your journey and make necessary adjustments to fit your circumstances. Let's begin the journey towards incredible truth!

From Christianity

Jesus, peace be upon him, is one of the honored and highly revered prophets sent by Almighty God. He is the Messiah who was promised to the Jews by God. He was born miraculously of the virgin Mary, without a father, and his mother is one of the most revered women in humanity. With permission from God, he performed many miracles, such as healing the sick, resurrecting a dead person to life, and more. However, he cannot be God. If you believe in Almighty God and in all the prophets before Jesus, then take a moment and think rationally:

- If being born without a father from a virgin mother is considered miraculous enough to confer divinity, then why shouldn't another individual, born without a father and without a mother, also be considered divine? I am referring to Prophet Adam (peace be upon him), who was created without a father or a mother. By the same logic, shouldn't he be considered more divine than Prophet Jesus?
- If, for the sake of argument, some claim that existing from the beginning confers divinity upon Prophet Jesus, then shouldn't someone without a beginning deserve even more divinity? I am referring to Melchizedek, the high priest mentioned in the Bible, who is described as having no beginning. Moreover, Jesus had a beginning (he was born), lived to a certain age, and then died (though it is claimed he was resurrected. As a side note, Muslims believe, based on a Quranic verse, that Jesus (peace be upon him) did not die on the cross but was taken up by Allah). Then why would it be rationally appropriate to attribute divinity to Prophet Jesus over Melchizedek, who does not even have an end? We should be consistent, shouldn't we?

- As mentioned earlier, the Trinity was added to some versions of the Bible and later removed as a fabrication (or copy error). Why would you continue to believe in it even after the removal of that phrase? But some scholars in Christianity, such as Nabeel Qureshi, have continued to push that and sometime using science to reason the Trinity: the three forms of water (H_2O) i.e. liquid, solid, and vapor. Then ask yourself: if you have a molecule of H_2O in a liquid state and you destroy it, what would the "solid or vapor" state of H_2O be? You would say, "Hey, I just destroyed the molecule, so it's all destroyed." Yes, you are making a reasonable scientific claim. Then ask yourself: if there are three persons (like the three states of water molecules) in one God, and when Jesus, according to their claim of the Trinity as God the Son, died on the cross, then the God (essence, just like the molecule) would be dead. Unless you claim that the spirit from the body is returned to the essence of God. In that case, you're claiming that the God's spirit was split (or given out) and then returned, which is not befitting for the Almighty God. However, if you are like many Christians in the world and your belief in the Trinity is more about personal faith rather than a scientific and rational claim, then I would suggest not presenting any such reasoning as it does not advance the argument to prove the Trinity.

If you are like those Christians who have experienced God and the Spirit personally in your life and your faith is built upon those inner feelings and private experiences with God, then I would ask you to consider these:

- First of all, no one can argue with your inner feelings and private experiences with God, so we can stop here. There's no point in continuing the conversation because the fundamental purpose of having a conversation between two human beings is to listen to each other's points of view and come to terms through rationality as human beings. What you are claiming as your experience with the

Christian God, many Muslims claim similar inner feelings and personal spiritual experiences with their God, Hindus claim the same spiritual experiences, and atheists claim a "similar" lack of spiritual experience. Why would you dismiss their inner feelings and spiritual experiences over yours?

- Look at your surroundings, the environment, the Earth, the solar system, the galaxy, and the universe. If you've studied these as part of your education, then what do you see? You've studied mathematics, physics, chemistry, biology, sociology, anthropology, and other academic disciplines. Do you observe any rationality, laws, and systemic approaches in all these areas?
    - The earth and moon rotate in a precise calculation.
    - The speed of lights is determined.
    - The Hydrogen and Oxygen reacts and bonded together with a precise rational formula and created H_2O. All the chemical reactions are same.
    - The microbes use a disease vector logically, we've seen such example in Covid in 2019, Spanish flue in the Europe and Americas, Black Death in medieval Europe, etc. and we can see the predictability of rise and fall of such pandemics.
    - Weather and climate changes follow certain patterns and repeat it in a cycle that can be predicted to a large extent.

- As a Christian or of any faith, you must believe that the omnipotent and the almighty God has created all these phenomena, including you, in so precise manner and with logic and rationality and reasoning. Did you give a thought on why that same God would come to you without any reasonable explanation that you can't express logically? How would you reconcile those two phenomena?
- However, if you put your blind faith because there's no alternative, I would urge you to please continue reading further – Islam came to complete the religion of God that was revealed to humanity through

all the prophets beginning from Adam through Moses and Jesus (peace be upon them all) and perfected and completed through the last prophet Muhammad (peace be upon him).

Now, let's examine whether Jesus (peace be upon him) ever claimed divinity or identified himself as God.

- Most prophets in the Bible are referred to as the "son of God," a term commonly used among the prophets in the Greek tradition. Thus, Jesus is not distinct from other prophets in this regard. Moreover, David was called the "begotten" son in the Bible, indicating no significant difference between him and other prophets according to Christian scripture. However, as Muslims, we do not accept the term "begotten."
- Jesus never claimed divinity but, like other prophets of his time, stated that salvation comes through him—a belief consistent with the roles of prophets like Noah, Abraham, and Moses (peace be upon them all).
- Jesus did not advocate for his worship but instead directed his disciples to worship the one God.
- Jesus expressed his dependence on the Father (God), stating that he could do nothing without Him.
- Jesus displayed all the characteristics of a human being: he was born through normal childbirth, circumcised, acquired knowledge, made mistakes like human, was baptized as a Jew, and required food, among other human traits. He never explicitly declared his divinity.
- Finally, according to the Bible, he died like any mortal, which contradicts any claim of his divinity that may arise from interpretative additions to the scripture.

I would like to conclude the points that Jesus is a prophet of God and not divine God himself by taking these passages from the book "How Jesus Became God: by Bart D. Ehrman.

"They don't pass any of our criteria. They are not multiply attested in our sources; they appear only in John, our latest and most theologically oriented Gospel. They certainly do not pass the criterion of dissimilarity since they express the very view of Jesus that the author of the Gospel of John happens to hold. And they are not at all contextually credible. "Find the details in the reference section.

Now take a look at Islam, which regards Jesus as one of the most prominent prophets of God:

- Muslims pray in the manner that Jesus prayed: by placing their faces on the earth.
- Muslims pray to God in the way Jesus (peace be upon him) did: seeking help from God alone (referencing the Bible: only the Father has the power).
- Muslims are required to afford due rights to all Christians as People of the Book and followers of the prophet Jesus (peace be upon him).

Islam perfects the religion of Jesus. Prophet Muhammad (pbuh) received the final testament, the Quran, from the same God. So, what can you do to understand the religion of Islam?

- Get a copy of the Quran in English or your preferred language. It's not a vast book, but it is very different from any book you are accustomed to reading. The Quran does not follow chronological order like an ordinary book but is a thought-provoking text with repeated reminders that challenge humans to use their intellect across almost all facets of scholarship: history and stories, archaeology, philosophy, anthropology, biology, astronomy, environmental science, and more. You should read it once to create a sitemap of the contents, and then read it again to establish connections across the contents.
- Watch for the similarities and contrasts between the Quran and the Bible. The Quran contains only the words of God, unchanged, unlike the Bible, which includes words from God, the disciples, and other

known or unknown authors some of whom never met Jesus (peace be upon him). In Islam, the words of the disciples (called companions) and of the Prophet Muhammad (pbuh) are recorded in separate books, known as *Ahadith* (Sayings of the Prophet), and other scholarly texts that are distinct from the Quran. The Quran is unchanged and undisputed because it comes directly from God and is preserved through word-for-word memorization and in written form. The *Ahadith* undergo scrutiny; some are considered highly authentic while others are deemed acceptable or weak. I encourage you to read the Quran, which is undisputed and preserved down to "the dots," metaphorically speaking.

- Look out for the story of Prophet Adam and Eve, the scientific facts on the creation of the universe, the earth, life, and all other creations. You should see substantial differences, and you can clearly distinguish the truth and how the Quran fits with humanity and Western civilization.
- Watch for the stories of all other prophets, and you should find that prophets are mentioned as sinless, unlike in the Bible.
- Listen to the Quran in Arabic. The Quran has an audible aspect that is declared in the Quran itself, which would help you appreciate the content of the Quran with its unique approach. There are many recitations and listen to any reciter that you like. My favorite is *Mishary Rashid Alafasy's* recitation on YouTube or Spotify.

Once you have read the Quran and are convinced that it is the word of God, do not keep this knowledge to yourself. Create a community in your neighborhood and town so that you can support each other. We are highly social creatures. Often, we ignore the truth and facts, even when we know they are true and correct, simply because our friends and relatives disagree with those facts. We need a support system. Therefore, do not isolate yourself with your discovery of Islam unless you have an exceptionally strong personality. Create a support system and discuss together to navigate toward the truth. Islam is a religion aligned with the innate nature of humanity; thus, being in a community is a foundational aspect of it. To fully appreciate the religion and enjoy the benefits of the beauty of Islam, spread the word to your friends, family, and acquaintances, and build a supportive community.

From Atheism and Agnostics

I would first like to start by saying that one of the many reasons behind your denouncing religion, possibly the leading one, is the arrogant behavior or lack of intellect demonstrated by many believers in God. I often watch discussions and debates between atheists and Christians, Jews, Muslims, etc., and feel empathetic toward the atheists or agnostics because I can clearly see why most of them become atheists. Surprisingly for atheists or agnostics, those dogmatic, cruel, or intellectually devoid assertions are not rooted in the religion of God. I can assert this safely based on the Quran—as the unaltered and unchanged words of God. We, the religious people, often repeat what we are accustomed to from the religious community we grew up in. I feel bad, but not ashamed, to say that when I see Carl Sagan, Christopher Hitchens, Richard Dawkins, Neil DeGrasse Tyson, or even Sam Harris (though some atheists are also arrogant and indecent in their opposition) paired with Bill O'Reilly, Sean Hannity, or some other religious zealot who has never thought beyond their religion and yet goes gung-ho to fight atheists. They don't just fail miserably but also do more disservice by potentially pushing the next religious person on the fence toward agnosticism. Let's consider an example.

Richard Dawkins – Christmas Lecture at The Royal Institution's titled: "Waking up in the Universe" in 1991. At 47:26 minute he made a profound call to show how absurd it sounds when we don't use our intellect or reasoning:

"Imagine the scene to scientists arguing and one of them says, 'I believe that the dinosaurs went extinct because a comet hit the earth. ***Why do I believe that because that's what my father and grandfather believed and that's what people in my country have always believed.'*** 'But I believe that it was a virus that drove the dinosaurs extinct. ***Why do I believe that because my father and grandfather believed it and that's what people in my country have always believed.'*** Or suppose the conversation went like this 'Never mind the evidence I just know that a comet struck the earth because it's been privately revealed to me that a comet struck the earth but I just know that it was a virus. Because I just know it. Because I just know it. Because I have faith that it was a virus.'

If you overheard conversations like that, you'd think they were pretty odd scientists, wouldn't you? You'd see no reason to believe any of them growing up in the universe. Partly means, evolving from simple to complicated, inefficient to efficient, brainless to brainy but it also means growing out of parochial and superstitious views of the universe. Growing up to a proper scientific understanding of the universe based upon evidence public argument rather than Authority or tradition or private revelation. Growing up means trying to understand how the universe works not copping out with supernatural ideas that only seem to explain things that actually explain nothing well."[109]

I mentioned earlier how I see the atheists' point of view, where they really want to understand the universe using their intellect and reasoning. So, what does religion say about that? I am not advocating for a return to the Bible, as that's the primary reason many were pushed toward atheism. Instead, I am referring to a book that has remained unchanged for 1,400 years. Check this out! You might find yourself in awe, as if Richard Dawkins were reading from the Quran, expressing outrage in the same way Allah does about people who do not use their reason and intellect. To some extent, Richard Dawkins' words and the Quran's messages match word for word. Islam demands that humanity not follow blindly after their forefathers or others but instead use reason. Islam has given the highest status to those who are intellectual and use reason, while it labels those who do not use reason as the worst of God's creatures. This reasoning is based on the origin of the universe, life on Earth, and the history of humanity—that is, using the entire creation of this universe to be observed and learned from. I have highlighted both Richard Dawkins' words and the statements from the Quran:

"And when it is said to them, "Follow what Allah has revealed," they say, "***Rather, we will follow that which we found our fathers doing." Even though their fathers understood nothing, nor were they guided?***" -Surah Al-Baqarah (2:170)

"Indeed, the worst of living creatures in the sight of Allah are the deaf and dumb who do not use reason." - Surah Al-Anfal (8:22)

The Quran doesn't just ask us to use reason; it insists that we shouldn't even pursue something without first acquiring knowledge about it. So, you should be clear that you are not asked to jump into Islam without conducting your own inquiry.

"And pursue not that of which you have no knowledge; for every act of hearing, or of seeing or of (feeling in) will be enquired into (on the Day of Reckoning)." Surah Isra (17:36)

I have mentioned 26 verses in *chapter III: "Searching for Solution"* that you can go back and read again to appreciate Islam's insistence on using intellect. I could go on with many other examples, but you've got my point if you want to. Having said that, let's make our case.

If you come from a background where you found your religion to be incompatible with your rationality or the current state of science, I can empathize with your dilemma. This book is for you, as I agree that most religions force us to stop thinking. However, if you have the same argument against Islam, I would challenge you because you probably haven't read the Quran from beginning to end with an open mind. Most importantly, you may have formed your objections based on arguments with other Muslims. I wouldn't blame you for this because often, we Muslims confuse Islam with local cultures and try to impose these as "Islam." Therefore, my request to you is to read the Quran with an open mind and through the lens of intellect. You might be surprised to find that the Quran actively encourages humans to use their intellect and reason. The Quran asks at least 26 times, "Wouldn't you use reason/intellect?" and equates people who don't use reason and blindly follow a religion to cattle. I am looking for those who use reason and their intellect.

However, if you have outsourced your reasoning to other smart intellectuals and simply accept their verdict, know that you are doing yourself a disservice. Richard Dawkins, Sam Harris, and Neil DeGrasse Tyson are undoubtedly smart and intellectual, but their expertise is specific to their own fields. Their opinions on Islam are conjectural in nature. I have watched their lectures and speeches and read their writings. They have almost never read the Quran from end to end but have picked out a few verses here and there, and they often use analogies from the Bible to judge the Quran. There are many statements and quotes they have mentioned in their lectures or writings that sound as if they were reading from the Quran, without knowing it as they never bothered to read the book. I mentioned above one such example from Richard Dawkins's Christmas Day lectures he critiqued religions by saying that people follow religion just because of their forefathers and the culture and society they were born into, without using reason. What an irony! By the way, Richard Dawkins and others are slowly changing their positions on religion as well. In his own words, on a Piers Morgan show, he stated that he is not a militant atheist[110] at all (even though he had declared himself a "militant atheism" in a Ted Talk presentation[111] right after the 9/11 terrorist attacks in America). Anyway, my request to you is please do your own research and don't rely on others for the most important pursuit of your life.

Following are some scientific reasonings to consider if you're a scientifically minded person.

Creation of the Universe: The Universe was created from nothing. The Earth and all celestial bodies were once joined together and then separated astonishingly. The universe is expanding. Yes, I am reading this from the Quran. I have mentioned the references in other sections but read the Quran to learn more about the creation of the universe. By the way, the Quran may seem similar to the Bible if you haven't read the Quran yourself. The Quran also states that the universe was created in six *'yaum,'* which translates to 'day.' However, *'yaum'* also mean epochs or stages. How do you know if the Quran is referring to 'epochs' instead of literal days, and we're not making this up? First, consult an Arabic language expert if you are not one yourself. Then, read the Quran where Allah mentions that the *'yaum'* used to describe the creation of the universe is relative (thousands of years in our count). It cannot be more profound than that because the Bible claims the universe was created in six days (even specifying morning and evening), and some allege that the Quran was 'taken' from the Bible. This not only debunks that claim but also suggests that the message must have been lost or distorted when it was written in the Bible by another man hundreds of years later.

Origin of Life: Islam does not specify the age of the Earth or the universe, nor does it claim any specific date for the Earth's formation or the emergence of Homo sapiens. In the Quran, the origin of life is described as originating from water, from which all forms of life have evolved.

"Allah has created every [living] creature from water. And of them are those that move on their bellies, and of them are those that walk on two legs, and of them are those that walk on four. Allah creates what He wills. Indeed, Allah is over all things competent." - Surat An-Noor (24:45)

When reading these Quranic verses, you might often think that you are reading modern scientific claims. I leave it to you to explore this further through your reading.

Evolution: I have discussed this in the Appendix, so please refer to that for more details. Briefly, the Quran mentions the creation of Adam, the proportioning of human beings, and suggests that creation will be repeated. These are all profound claims that you are unlikely to encounter until you read the Quran for yourself.

Bottom line: continue reading this book's appendices on Atheism and read the Quran for yourself before making any decisions about your life. After that, if you are still unsure, my request to you would be this: if you are uncertain about accepting Islam as your religion, at the very least, believe in one God, believe in the messengers, do right, forbid evil, and God will guide you. Why? Because if you have a rational mind, you will find that the probability of there not being a creator is extremely small, if not nonexistent, compared to the probability of there being a creator. Therefore, as a rational individual, you should logically side with the higher.

From "None" Affiliation

If you're not an atheist or agnostic but identify as 'unaffiliated,' it means you have renounced any specific religion due to personal or intellectual reasoning. You likely still believe in a higher being but aren't convinced that any religion fits your criteria. Here is my request for you:

Like atheists and agnostics, the majority of your arguments against religion are likely due to the lifestyle and behavior of religious people and societies. Additionally, you may have read religious texts and were not convinced by those scriptures. Assuming you've read the previous sections on Christianity or Atheism (if not, please go back and read them, as you may find many of your questions answered), I will not repeat myself but will reinforce the request to read the Quran with an open mind. Try to set aside preconceived notions about the geopolitical landscape and so-called 'Muslim' countries. You will discover for yourself how far Muslims are from their Book, a topic I touched upon at the beginning of the book. You may even find yourself advising the Muslims around you afterward. In fact, that's the beauty of Islam—it's universal and transcends tribalism or any ethnic affiliation. In Islam, every Muslim is equal to another Muslim worldwide. There is no central papal or church system in Islam. It's between you and God—that's the beautiful and liberating experience that awaits you.

From All Others

Regardless of your current beliefs, approach the Quran with an open mind. Read it once without judgment. Then, read it again to form a holistic understanding of the entire book, and if needed, read it a third time. Also, listen to the original Quran in Arabic. There are many recitations available; listen to a reciter whose style resonates with you. My favorite is Mishary Rashid Alafasy's recitation, available on YouTube[112] or Spotify[113].

Finally, I am only human, with many limitations. Therefore, I might not have fully explained why Islam is the most natural choice, or you might agree with the choice but not my approach, or you might simply remain unconvinced for any reason. Nevertheless, I urge you minimally to believe in a single creator who fashioned this universe and to reject any partnership with anything else from His creation on Earth. Always strive to do good and avoid all that is evil: lying, backbiting, stealing, ingratitude, harm, and other crimes against fellow human being and the creations of God. Once you practice this and use your intellect to reflect on the creation of the Earth and the universe, you will surely, God willing, be guided to the truth. The Creator who made you and me will not leave you unguided! Our Creator is just and cannot be unjust to anyone. God bless you!

Conclusion

The great achievement of American exceptionalism has reached a point where the foundation of this civilization is being eroded. Depleting family structures, a widening gap of wealth and inequality, physical and mental health pandemics, structural racism, excessive consumption, and out-of-control materialism, along with catastrophic pollution and climate impacts, are undermining the very foundation of America. However, the answer cannot be to deny the science and scientific knowledge that have enabled modern civilization. We have witnessed the benefits of the sciences in our everyday lives. Also, due to our shortsightedness, we've seen the growing phenomenon of intellectuals renouncing God, having experienced the shortcomings of the people of faith. Those with a scientific mindset are caught in the middle, seeing that the scientific method works, yet finding that the holy scriptures often oppose not only the scientific facts but also common-sense facts. They have been left with no option but to renounce religion as a logical consequence of their deep understanding of the natural world and the universe, which operates entirely within the realm of rationality. America needs to navigate out of this destruction, not by shutting down rationality and science, as that would only expedite the spiral down to the end of civilization. This was precisely the case in the fourth century when Greek knowledge was discarded after the Roman Empire embraced Christianity as the religion of the empire. Why? Because it was deemed pagan knowledge. The result? A thousand-year-long "dark age" in Europe. Meanwhile, a vibrant civilization emerged from a place that no one had anticipated or expected. There was a spark that brought the light of civilization, inheriting Greek, Persian, Roman, and ancient Indian knowledge into the Arabic language. Essentially, Islamic civilization carried the torch of Greek knowledge, which the current Western civilization is now carrying forward. Take it from Professor Roy Casagranda: "what we are told that the Dark Ages the Middle Ages the medieval period starts with the fall of Rome in 476 and doesn't end until sometime around 1492 that it lasts a thousand years there's a thousand years without knowledge but I just showed you that there were actually extraordinary developments that were taking place including calculus 600 years before Newton. Ibn Al-Haitham stated Newton's first law of motion 600 years before Newton. He actually described Kepler's first law of planetary motion 500 years before Kepler."

The West, particularly the most powerful country in the world, the United States of America, is now faced with an imminent threat. In response, a knee-jerk solution could be to lead a "bi-polar" life—for lack of a better term—*Living in Science without embracing it and Dreaming in Faith without practicing it*. In other words, many of the "faithful" maintain their religion by creating two worlds: they use science in everyday life while living a "perceived religious" life that is not reflected in their actual religion. This is because they either read scripture merely as stories or literature, thus living a life of duality. This approach may prolong the survival of religion but at the cost of losing the next generation dramatically. There is no turning back; we cannot deny the science that has driven our civilization, but we cannot ignore faith either, as science does not answer the deeply ingrained human question: what's the purpose of our life?

Meanwhile, the civilization we know is in turmoil, spiraling down towards self-destruction. There is a way out by firmly grasping the steering wheel to regain control, where science and religion do not contradict but complement each other. Christianity could undergo another reformation to return to the "original" message of Jesus (peace be upon him) and thus become rational, or we could accept the truth from the same God who created the earth, sent all the prophets, and delivered the final message. This message not only advanced the knowledge that reinvented the science from the Greeks and Romans but also aligns with all rationality, reasoning, and intellect that drive our current civilization. Alternatively, we could pursue both paths. We can delay further, or we can steer the ship, if you will, towards the truth. The sooner we act, the better for the West.

قُلْ يَا أَيُّهَا النَّاسُ قَدْ جَاءَكُمُ ال ٥حَقُّ مِنْ رَبِّكُمْ فَمَنِ اهْتَدَى فَإِنَّمَا يَهْتَدِي لِنَفْسِهِ وَمَنْ
ضَلَّ فَإِنَّمَا يَضِلُّ عَلَيْهَا وَمَا أَنَا عَلَيْكُمْ بِوَكِيلٍ ﴿١٠٨﴾

“Say, "O mankind, the truth has come to you from your Lord, so whoever is guided is only guided for [the benefit of] his soul, and whoever goes astray only goes astray [in violation] against it. And I am not over you a manager." – Surah Yunus (10:108)

The Quran is the final message in the chain of monotheistic religions from God. Many people think that if they have read the Bible, the Quran must be the same. Surprisingly, even many Muslims share this misunderstanding. The Quran, preserved and unchanged, is uniquely different from other holy books. At one point, Islam was even criticized for being overly materialistic and rational. The Quran states that all messages to past prophets contained the same essence, but most were either lost or altered. The Quran presents these messages so cohesively that it is regarded as the ultimate guidance for humanity, urging the use of reason, science, and the establishment of social justice. Theoretically, one could create a synthetic faith by cherry-picking from all religions, and arguably, what we see today in the West resembles this approach. Thus, if we do not want to deceive ourselves, we should not repeat the same actions and expect different results. Islam is a universal religion; it does not belong to any ethnicity or race. It is for all humanity Wherever you are, whoever you are—Islam is for you. There is no central papal authority, religious leader, or central religious relic that you must blindly follow—everyone is equal under Islam, and we all have equal access to God, regardless of language, color, ethnicity, or geographic location. Read the Quran for yourself. Share it with friends and family. Discuss it as a community. Do not keep it to yourself. We all stand to benefit from it.

يَا أَيُّهَا الرُّسُلُ كُلُوا مِنَ الطَّيِّبَاتِ وَاعْمَلُوا صَالِحًا إِنِّي بِمَا تَعْمَلُونَ عَلِيمٌ ۝٥١ وَإِنَّ هَٰذِهِ أُمَّتُكُمْ أُمَّةً وَاحِدَةً وَأَنَا رَبُّكُمْ فَاتَّقُونِ ۝٥٢

“[Allah said], "O messengers, eat from the good foods and work righteousness. Indeed, I, of what you do, am Knowing. And indeed this, your religion, is one religion, and I am your Lord, so fear Me." – Surah Al-Mu’minun (23:51-52)

As we conclude this book and embark on our journey, I invite you to consider the enduring righteousness advocated by all prophets throughout human history. If my efforts, constrained by my human capacity, fail to fully convey the profound beauty and benefits of the last message from God, the Holy Quran, I continue to cherish a dream. At the very least, I dream of a future where, in the West, we embrace a twenty-first-century civilization in which Christians, Muslims, Jews, and all other people of faith coexist harmoniously. United under the guidance of the same one God worshiped by prophets Abraham, Moses, Jesus, and Muhammad (peace be upon them all), we aim to establish justice, fairness, and equity in society. This vision is not merely a hope for religious unity but a call to recognize and live by the shared principles and values that span our faiths, fostering a more inclusive and compassionate world. America will remain a beacon of hope to the world by steadfastly upholding justice both at home and abroad, standing firm against any form of injustice. Ameen!

Appendix A: Golden Age of Islamic Civilization

"The duty of the man who investigates the writings of scientists, if learning the truth is his goal, is to make himself an enemy of all that he reads, and ... attack it from every side. He should also suspect himself as he performs his critical examination of it, so that he may avoid falling into either prejudice or leniency." You may have noted, correctly, that this is the proper approach to analysis of scientific findings, to either support or contradict those findings based, as much as possible, on logical and objective critique. Who is the source of the quote — was he a Greek, British, or an American scientist? Actually, his name is Hasan Ibn *al-Haytham*[114], a polymath. Also known as the father of modern optics. He was born in Basra, Iraq in 965 CE during the Islamic Golden Age.

Take one aspect of science that you see every day - the stars in the sky. Did you know that if you list all the "named" stars you will find that two-thirds of those stars are named in Arabic? Why is that so? The reason lies behind the concept of "naming rights". Any invention, new idea, or discovery gets its name from its inventors. That is the norm. That's why you see the early scientific names were predominantly in Greek. Neil deGrasse Tyson has explained this in one of his talks at "The Science Network". The early planets are named after Greek gods because they are either discovered by Greeks or standardized by them. Similarly, when Arab Muslims discovered many stars or standardized many astronomical inventions, those were named in Arabic. Muslims also invented modern Chemistry (the word Chemistry came from the Arabic word Alchemy), Algebra, Algorithms, early Robots or machine automation, etc. The University of Karueein, the oldest existing and continually operating educational institute, founded in 859 AD was established by a Muslim woman in Fez, Morocco. The list goes on and on.

When my daughter got into high school, she bought a book on world religion and civilization and I was thundered to see that the Islamic civilization (forget about the Golden Age) was completely omitted. It covered Christianity, Judaism, Hindu, Buddhism, Zoroastrianism, etc. but not a single word for Islam. I wish I had the copy of that book but I didn't know that one day I am going to write this book on the Islamic Golden Age. Anyway, in recent book that my son is using has mentioned of Islam and some references of Islamic civilization which is better than nothing. I copied the above few paragraphs in verbatim from James M. Powell's book to show that even after the attempt, unconscious or may be conscious, to ignore the fact of golden age of Islamic civilization from much of high school in this country, those facts are sipping through the scholarly works. Now let's see some of the accounts of the tremendous contribution of the Islamic Civilization to the humanity. There are many books written to it by Muslims, Christians and non-religious scholars so I will not do justice to the goal of this book if I redo all those here again. I would rather point out few interesting accomplishments and contribution to the human civilization that have lingering impact that you and I are benefiting even today. I will show with excerpt from the research works of the renowned scholars and then list out books and lectures that you can read and watch for yourself.

Let's start with an overarching statement from a Western scholar written just few years ago about the accomplishments and contribution of Islamic Golden Age of Islamic Civilization to the Western civilization. Let's read this excerpt from the book *Medieval Studies* by James M. Powell that unequivocally shows medieval Europe's state on scientific knowledge and how Islamic Golden Age contributed to the revival of true science in Europe that sparked the renaissance.

"If we conceive the Middle Ages as extending from approximately A.D. 500 and 1500, science on a large and meaningful scale did not intrude into the Latin West until the second half of the twelfth century, when the effort to appropriate Greco-Arabic science by translation into Latin was well underway.

Before that, only a miniscule part of Greek science had been available in Latin. During the early Middle Ages, western Europe subsides on a meager scientific fare that had been absorbed into handbooks and encyclopedic treatises associated with the names of Chalcidians, Macrobius, Martianus Capella, Boethius, Isidore of Seville, Cassiodorus, and the Venerable Bede. The science embedded in these treatises was usually superficial, and frequently inaccurate or contradictory. Nothing illustrates the sorry state of affairs better than the virtual absence of Euclid's *Elements,* without which astronomy, optics, and much of mechanics were impossible.

The influx of Greco-Arabic science into western Europe had already begun and would soon overwhelm the incipient rational science that had been gradually evolving within the context of the old learning.

The new positive attitude toward learning undoubtedly encouraged Europeans to seek out Arabic and Greek scientific and philosophical texts. They now behaved much as the Arabas before them. Just as many Arabic speaking scholars actively sought, rather than passively received, Greek science and philosophy following the rapid spread of Islam, so also did Latin scholars of the twelfth century travel to the sources of the new knowledge and actively and vigorously appropriate it.

The achievements of the international brigade of translators that labored in Spain, Sicily, and northern Italy were truly monumental. Within a period of approximately 130 years, they made available in Latin much, if not most, of the cumulative scientific knowledge that had been produced by the civilizations of Greece and Islam. Among these treasures were the works of Aristotle and the commentaries of Averroes (Arabic name: **Abu'l**

Walid Muhammad ibn Rushd), which together would dominate scientific thought for the next 400 years; Euclid's *Elements*; Ptolemy's *Almagest*, the greatest astronomical treatise until the *De revolutionibus of Copernicus; Alhazen's (*Arabic name*:* **Ibn Al-Haytham***)* Optics, the Algebra of al-Khwarizmi (Arabic name: **Muhammad ibn Musa Al-Khwarizmi**); and the medical works of Galen, Hippocrates, and Avicenna (Arabic name: **Ali Ibn-Sina**)"[115]

Let's now go into significant areas of civilization and scientific contribution of Islamic Civilization to the world, humanity in general and Western renaissance in particular.

Knowledge based society

House of Wisdom, at the time Caliph Al-Ma'mun and later in the 9th century, sparked the knowledge-based society, especially, through the Translation Movement that accumulated the knowledge from Greek, Persian, Indian knowledges. Being ignorant and irrational were considered unacceptable by the society. Here's from S. P. Scott, "During the most splendid period of Islamic Spain, ignorance was regarded as so disgraceful that those without education concealed the fact as far as possible, just as they would have hidden the commission of a crime."[116]

"Andalusian rulers now had the luxury of peace and prosperity, with scholars enjoying their generous patronage. Al-Hakam, mirroring al-Ma'mūn's obsession with books, would use the vast sums of money at his disposal to satisfy his own obsession. He would send men to the East to obtain copies of all the books they could lay their hands on, enabling him to build a great library within the royal palace next to the Great Mosque of Córdoba, which would soon hold almost half a million books - the largest library in Christian Europe at the time had no more than a few hundred manuscripts."[117]

How about great library of Alexandria? If you read the popular history in the West, you may be taught that Amr ibn al-Aas had burned the library in 642 AD with a supporting quote from him, "If those books are in agreement with the Quran, we have no need of them; and if these are opposed to the Quran, destroy them". First of all, that doesn't make sense according to the Quran as the Quran has almost forced human to use the intellect. Not only that, the Quran has started with the revelation that reminds human "Read…". Also, scholars have questioned the motive and truthfulness of that story. " Later scholars—beginning with Father Eusèbe Renaudot's remark in 1713 in his translation of the History of the Patriarchs of Alexandria that the tale "had something untrustworthy about it"—are skeptical of these stories, given the range of time that had passed before they were written down and the political motivations of the various writers."[118] As a matter of fact, the library was destroyed multiple times and one of the most realistic final destruction could be in 391 AD. Regardless, we should be careful about the history as we tend to be biased towards what fit to our narrative so I would warn myself and the readers to be careful about it. Rather, we should take account of the implication and outcome of that period and see what transpired from that time. Did we have knowledge-based society from that 391 AD event? Certainly not. The medieval time of the Western civilization was called as "medieval" because it was the dark age. What about the era after 642 AD? Did the society plunged into darkness of ignorance. Completely contrary to that! Just as Quran relentlessly forced to use reason, intellect and observations to the natural phenomenon, it ushered a golden age of knowledge and science by the Islamic civilization for next at least five to seven centuries that you will see in the subsequent sections. Had the knowledge and libraries were so hated, how could the Islamic civilization bring all the knowledge-based inventions. The math would add up with such fabricated history. I will cover all those but here's a quote from Dr. Roy Casagranda that summarize it well, "...birth of a new civilization and that civilization was the Arab civilization. The Arabs were in fact in the process of putting together their empire that they had carved out of the Roman Empire and attached it to the Persian Empire. Two empires that they had conquered and they were in the process now of translating all the texts that they had in those libraries into Arabic and they really only start to get some serious successes in the eighth century and beginning of the ninth century and that's where the literature is coming from. It's coming from the Arab world and by the time we get to the 11th century, the Arabs have actually done some remarkable stuff. They invented modern agriculture, they invented modern agriculture, they're the first guys to put ice on a ship and pack fresh food on top of the ice and then use it to distributes fresh food across the Indian ocean. They're the guys who figured out the coffee industry they're the guys who set up a mass distribution network for sugar. They built the first large-scale dam so that they could irrigate higher ground. They're the guys who set up the first waterwheel so that you could power stuff like you could power a mill for example using a waterwheel. They figured out lenses, they created the first camera. They were doing cataract surgery. They are the guys who realized that prevention was better than medicine. They're the guys who figured out all objects in the universe exert gravity on all other objects in the universe. They're the guys who realized that light had a finite speed that it traveled in waves that could be broken up into its constituent colors. They invented the world's first-ever scientific method 600 years before Bacon does it again. They stated Newton's first law of motion 600 years before Newton. Kepler's first of planetary motion 500 years before Kepler. Remarkable stuff you've never heard of it before because that too got written out of history."[119]

University

"The University of Al Karaouine, founded in 859 AD, is listed in The Guinness Book Of Records as the world's oldest degree-granting university.[54] The Al-Azhar University was another early madrasa now recognized as a university. The madrasa is one of the relics of the Fatimid caliphate. The Fatimids traced their descent to Muhammad's daughter Fatimah and named the institution using a variant of her honorific title Al-Zahra (the brilliant).[120] Organized instruction in the Al-Azhar Mosque began in 978."[121]

Mathematics

Islamic civilization made significant contributions to mathematics during the medieval period, particularly between the 8th and 14th centuries. Scholars in the Islamic world built on and greatly expanded the knowledge they inherited from the Greeks, Indians, and Persians. Key contributions include:

Algebra: The term itself comes from the title of a book by the Persian mathematician Al-Khwarizmi, "*Al-Kitab al-Mukhtasar fi Hisab al-Jabr wal-Muqabala*" (The Compendious Book on Calculation by Completion and Balancing), written around 820 CE. This work laid the foundations for algebra and introduced systematic methods for solving linear and quadratic equations. In his book The Compendious Book on Calculation by Completion and Balancing, Al-Khwarizmi deals with ways to solve for the positive roots of first and second-degree (linear and quadratic) polynomial equations."[122]

Development of Arabic Numerals: Although originally developed in India, the system of writing numbers that we use today was transmitted to Europe through Arabic texts. This numeral system included the concept of zero, a crucial development in the history of mathematics.

Trigonometry: Islamic mathematicians like Al-Battani and Ibn Muadh made significant advancements in trigonometry, developing new trigonometric ratios and refining the sine and cosine functions. These works were crucial for navigation, astronomy, and surveying.

Geometry: Scholars such as Omar Khayyam worked on generalizations of the Euclidean geometry and contributed to the theory of proportions. Alhazen (Ibn al-Haytham) made significant contributions to the understanding of optics through geometric studies.

Calculus Precursors: Ideas that led to integral calculus were developed by scholars like Alhazen and Thabit ibn Qurra, who worked on sums of integral powers and area calculations.

Mathematical Tables: The creation of mathematical tables for functions like sine, cosine, and tangent was advanced during the Islamic Golden Age, facilitating calculations for astronomers and other scientists.

Number Theory: Islamic mathematicians like Al-Karaji and Al-Khazini explored the theory of numbers, including work on perfect numbers, combinatorics, and number sequences.

The work of Islamic scholars was transmitted to Europe through translations into Latin in the later medieval period, profoundly influencing the Renaissance and the development of modern mathematics.

Physics

"Ibn al-Haitham (known in Western Europe as Alhacen or Alhazen) (965-1040), often regarded as the "father of optics" and a pioneer of the scientific method, formulated "the first comprehensive and systematic alternative to Greek optical theories." He postulated in his "Book of Optics" that light was reflected upon different surfaces in different directions, thus causing different light signatures for a certain object that we see. It was a different approach than that which was previously thought by Greek scientists, such as Euclid or Ptolemy, who believed rays were emitted from the eye to an object and back again. Al-Haytham, with this new theory of optics, was able to study the geometric aspects of the visual cone theories without explaining the physiology of perception. Also, in his Book of Optics, Ibn al-Haytham used mechanics to try and understand optics. Using projectiles, he observed that objects that hit a target perpendicularly exert much more force than projectiles that hit at an angle. Al-Haytham applied this discovery to optics and tried to explain why direct light hurts the eye, because direct light approaches perpendicularly and not at an oblique angle. He developed a camera obscura to demonstrate that light and color from different candles can be passed through a single aperture in straight lines, without intermingling at the aperture."[123]

Medicine

"The Canon of Medicine (Arabic: al-Qānūn fī al-Ṭibb; Latin: Canon Medicinae) is an encyclopedia of medicine in five books compiled by Muslim Persian physician-philosopher Avicenna (Ibn Sina) and completed in 1025. Perhaps one of the most famous and influential early books, that continued to influence later creations. It presents an overview of the contemporary medical knowledge of the Islamic world, which had been influenced by earlier traditions including Greco-Roman medicine (particularly Galen), Chinese medicine, Persian medicine, and Indian medicine. Its translation from Arabic to Latin in 12th century Toledo greatly influenced the development of medieval medicine. It became the standard textbook for teaching in European universities into the early modern period.

...William Osler, Sir William Osler, 1st Baronet (July 12, 1849 – December 29, 1919) was a Canadian physician and one of the "Big Four" founding professors of Johns Hopkins Hospital, described the Canon as "the most famous medical textbook ever written," noting that it remained "a medical bible for a longer time than any other work.

...George Sarton, George Alfred Leon Sarton (31 August 1884 – 22 March 1956) was a Belgian-American chemist and historian. He is considered the founder of the discipline of the history of science as an independent field of study. His most influential works were the Introduction to the History of Science, wrote in the Introduction to the History of Science.

...The Qanun is an immense encyclopedia of medicine. It contains some of the most illuminating thoughts pertaining to distinction of mediastinitis from pleurisy; contagious nature of phthisis; distribution of diseases by water and soil; careful description of skin troubles; of sexual diseases and perversions; of nervous ailments."[124]

Astronomy

Islamic civilization made significant contributions to astronomy during the Medieval period, particularly during the Islamic Golden Age from the 8th to the 14th century. Scholars in the Islamic world advanced astronomical knowledge through comprehensive studies, observations, and translations of ancient texts from Greek, Persian, and Indian sources. Here are some key contributions:

- Astronomical Instruments: Muslim astronomers refined and invented numerous astronomical instruments like the astrolabe, which helped observers calculate the time of day or night and determine the altitude and position of celestial bodies.
- Observatories: They established sophisticated observatories, such as the ones at Maragheh[125] and Samarkand, which were crucial for the empirical study of astronomy.

- Star Catalogs and Maps: Islamic astronomers compiled extensive star catalogs and maps. Al-Sufi's "Book of Fixed Stars" is a notable example, improving on the earlier work of Ptolemy and providing detailed descriptions of stars and their positions.
- Mathematical Astronomy: They developed and applied trigonometry to better understand celestial movements and distances. Al-Battani and others made significant improvements to Ptolemaic models, offering more accurate calculations of the solar year and the length of seasons.
- Theoretical Developments: Astronomers like Al-Biruni and Alhazen contributed theories on phenomena such as eclipses, the Earth's circumference, and the nature of light. Their work laid the groundwork for modern astronomical science.
- Influence on Later Science: Islamic astronomical works were translated into Latin in the late Middle Ages, influencing European astronomy during the Renaissance, including scientists such as Johannes Kepler and Nicolaus Copernicus.[126]

"Sufi's Cluster" likely refers to the "Beehive Cluster," also known as Brocchi's Cluster. This open cluster in the constellation Cancer is visible to the naked eye under good conditions and resembles a nebulous mass, like a swarm of bees. The connection to "Sufi" comes from the Persian astronomer Al-Sufi, who described it in his famous book "Book of Fixed Stars" in the 10th century. In his work, Al-Sufi provided detailed information on many stars and clusters visible in the night sky, contributing significantly to the field of astronomy.[127]

Civic society

The law of divorce in Islamic Spain was the foundation of Europe and America's managing the divorce in the society. This may sound simpler but you may be surprised that the Bible, except extreme cases like fornication or leaving Christianity, doesn't allow divorce at all. The most extreme measure was to enforce the divorcee to remain single even after those rare cases. That had created a huge issue in Islamic Spain especially of its Christian citizens. The law today we see in America, i.e., women entitled to the family wealth and alimony after divorce is a legacy from that law in Islamic Spain. Dr. Roy Casagranda jokingly said in his lecture that "In Texas for example, we do community property divorce, we got that from Mexico. Mexico is Catholic. It didn't have divorce. When the Arabs ruled Spain they got sick of all the deadbeat husbands who were divorcing their wives for younger models and then leaving the children to be raised by those divorced wives who no longer had a source of income so there are all these kids living in the streets so what they did in Spain was they created a system where all the property generated from the moment of the marriage is start to the moment that the marriages and got split in half, period. End story, that's community property law so you know you'll hear this thing that conservatives will say I'm worried about Sharia law, well, then don't get divorced because that's Muslim law."

Richard Bulliet, a world-renowned professor of history at Columbia University has mentioned in his lecture, titled "Religion and the State in Islam: From Medieval Caliphate to the Muslim Brotherhood" that Islamic law was more in large served the justice in equitable fashion to the citizens in the majority of the history of Islamic civilization. In his own words: "...and the fact of the matter is more and more scholarly studies are showing that Islamic law was perceived as and functioned as the law of the land for Muslims and non-Muslims alike and administered a comparatively equitable fashion and we have studies about what happens when Muslims sued Christians and vice versa it appears to be quite equitable according to the documents we have so that the Islamic law at the level of social order actually did it seems support the idea of an orderly society and no-anarchic society regardless of the misbehavior of the ruler."

Architecture and Urban Development

The Islamic Golden Age created cities around the world, and their remnants are still visible in modern-day India, Pakistan, Spain, Azerbaijan, Turkmenistan, Iran, Morocco, Egypt, Syria, Turkey, and of course, the Middle East. Today, you can visit Spain to see the Alhambra and Medina Azahara to appreciate their architecture and construction. Here are key points summarizing these contributions:

Architectural Innovation: Islamic architecture is known for its intricate tile work, large domes, and arches, often featuring geometric and arabesque designs. Notable structures include the Alhambra in Spain, the Dome of the Rock in Jerusalem, and the Great Mosque of Córdoba.

Urban Planning: Islamic cities were well planned with defined street layouts, public baths, souks (markets), and residential areas organized to promote community cohesion and efficient commerce. Baghdad, Damascus, and Cairo are examples of cities developed with complex urban planning principles that included advanced infrastructure and public services. "The most famous legacy was a palace-city complex built a few miles outside Córdoba, known as Medinat al-Zahra' (the word medina meaning 'city')."[128]

Gardens and Palaces: The concept of paradise gardens, which are enclosed and lush with vegetation, water features, and symmetric layouts, was an essential element of Islamic palatial architecture. Examples include the Generalife gardens of the Alhambra[129] and the gardens of the Taj Mahal in India.

Mosques and Madrasas: The development of mosque architecture was pivotal, serving both religious and educational purposes. Mosques were centers of community and learning, often attached to madrasas (educational institutions). The architectural design of mosques evolved to include large minarets, expansive prayer halls, and detailed calligraphy.

Water Management Systems: Islamic architects excelled in developing water management systems within their architectural designs, as seen in the use of aqueducts, fountains, and pools that not only served practical purposes but also enhanced the aesthetic appeal of the environments.

Cultural Synthesis: Islamic architecture often incorporated elements from earlier civilizations like the Byzantine, Persian, and Indian, creating a unique blend that spread across different regions. This synthesis is evident in the Indo-Islamic architecture of the Indian subcontinent and the Moorish influences in Andalusia, Spain.

These contributions reflect a rich legacy of not only architectural innovation but also sophisticated urban planning that has influenced modern architecture and city planning principles globally.

Appendix B: The revival of Muslim countries

Today, a renowned scientist writes: "...how many [Nobel prize winners] were Muslims? And it's like one, maybe two...now, how many Nobel Prizes are won by Jews? It's like the fourth of the Nobel Prizes...how many Muslims are there in the world. It's like a billion Muslims. How many Jews? Fifteen million, tops. So, you do the ratio of these numbers; had Islam not collapsed in its intellectual standing in the year 1100 and you just do the ratios, they would have every single Nobel Prize today. So, the fact that it's not only just a few but it's near zero is deeply worrying. I am concerned about what's lost. What brilliance may have expressed itself and did not in that community over the past thousand years." That was not the thinking of a Muslim but of Neil deGrasse Tyson, the American astrophysicist.

Let me ask you now — did you ever pause and ask why the situation of Muslims today is in such darkness? Yet, during the Middle Ages Islamic civilization brought much light to Europe, in mathematics, medicine, astronomy, and more. Though Tyson correctly points to the consequence of the loss of the Islamic Golden Age, he was in haste to blame Imam Al-Ghazali for demonizing mathematics and triggering the decline. In fact, al-Ghazali had said the complete opposite: "Mathematics comprises the knowledge of calculation, geometry, and cosmology; it has no connection with the religious knowledge and proves nothing for or against religion; it rests on a foundation of proofs which, once known and understood, cannot be refuted." Al-Ghazali also wrote: "Great indeed is the crime against religion committed by anyone who supposes that Islam is to be championed by the denial of these mathematical sciences. For the revealed Law nowhere undertakes to deny or affirm these sciences, and the latter nowhere address themselves to religious matters."

Nonetheless, al-Ghazali warned the seekers of knowledge to be careful about, metaphorically, jumping into the ocean of knowledge unless they are well trained in swimming. But the Muslims of his time took the easy route to "cut the head to cure the headache" and instead of focusing on both Islamic foundational knowledge as well as natural sciences, they discouraged seeking knowledge about the natural sciences. What high costs human civilization is paying by having kept the multitudes of Muslims away from that light of knowledge. Now, how do we bring back that enlightened civilization that would bring good not only to the Muslims but also to humanity?

Other Western intellectuals have also wished for a strong Islamic civilization. Karen Armstrong, a well-known author of books on world religions, in her book Muhammad, A Biography of The Prophet, wrote: "Islam Isn't going to disappear or wither away; it'd have been better if it had remained healthy and strong. We can only hope that it is not too late." In fact, we ought to demonstrate far better than we do in every aspect of life. It's a promise from Allah. "And thus We have made you a just community that you will be witnesses over the people… "(Qur'an 2:143). So, if we follow what Allah has commanded of us, we should be the exemplar nation on this earth. But we are far from that.

Now the question we should ask is why our situation is like this. Contrary to the Islamic Golden Age that endured for close to a millennium, Muslims are now amongst the most backward and ignorant people in the world. Also, Muslims have become synonymous with being oppressed, and many times it is a Muslim regime oppressing their own people. The poorest of the countries in the world is Muslim, the most corrupted country is a Muslim country, the most backward country is a Muslim country, and the most persecuted people in the world are Muslims. Some of the causes of the collapse of Islamic civilization are that the society became more focused on materialism instead of spirituality and knowledge; there were, and continue to be, damaging political, social, and economic effects of long colonial rule; and among the masses of Muslims there has been complacency, loss of unity, religious extremism, etc.

Finding Our Way Out of Dysfunction and Malaise

It's not enough to just analyze what we had and how we lost it. We need to find a way out of the current dysfunction and malaise. Make no mistake, all the wonders of the Islamic Golden Age didn't just happen by themselves but were initiated and achieved by the Arabs from the Arabian Peninsula who were uncivilized and also discounted and largely ignored by the two great civilizations of that time: the Persians with 1,200 years of imperial history and the Romans with 900 years. A great civilization in Arabia, however, came into existence and in a short span of time became a dominant civilization that paved the way for the Islamic Golden Age. What was the instrument that sparked the light, bright enough to bring people out from the darkness of ignorance? Arabs were given only two things by Prophet Muhammad (s) — the Qur'an (revealed to him by Allah) and the Prophet's sunnah.

That, by itself, guidance from a Divine source, enlightened the Arabs and taught them the fullest love of Allah and fear of Him alone; and so, they were launched to the heights of civilization for the next several hundred years. We are in great need of that Divine spark to release the dynamic of revival in our time. The revival could bring a great deal of material success in every aspect of life. But is that enough? What good would it be if we focus only on worldly success? The value and consequences of our efforts must be transferable to life in the hereafter. Our efforts must be relevant to the ultimate purpose of our life. After all, isn't this worldly life negligible compared to the infinite life of the hereafter? The ultimate success of a Muslim ought to be success in the hereafter. And that's the purpose of our life on this earth.

Purpose of Life

We believe that Allah has created us and, therefore we should look to Him for answers. Who would be better to answer why we were created than our own Creator? If we want to know the purpose of a machine, we are unfamiliar with, we would ask the manufacturer of the machine. If we want to know how to use a new smartphone, we would look to the manufacturer of the phone. The manufacturer provides us with the user manual and specifications detailing the purpose of the machine or device and how to use it. We look into the user manual and find everything we need to know. Similarly, we need to look into the user manual of Islam, the Qur'an, to find answers to all our questions. Did Allah tell us why we were created and what the purpose of our life is? Yes, He did. Allah has created us to serve Him, and nothing else, i.e., *ubudiyah* (عبودية) — servitude to Allah. "And I did not create the jinn and humankind except to serve Me" (Qur'an 51:56).

There are countless ways we can implement *ubudiyah*. It has two parts: 1) the prayers and other rituals of worship and, 2) all other actions in this worldly life that are done for the sake of Allah. Part one is clear to most of us. So, let's re-imagine a framework within which to implement the second part of the *ubudiyah*: start with an oath that we will uphold the *ubudiyah* in our every action. After that we will trace the purpose of our daily activity back to the Qur'an and sunnah. That means that all of our intentions, words, and deeds are within the framework and criteria of what Allah has commanded and what He has forbidden. If we're firm on that commitment, then we can start the journey of the revival in our time.

There are many things that we need to do to bring about an Islamic revival, and there are many ways to go about that. The ultimate goal is to be in the state of *ubudiyah* (servitude to Allah SWT) and follow, to the best of our ability, every command that Allah and His messenger (s) have given to us in the Qur'an and *ahadith*. However, in a practical sense, our immediate focus should be on the deficits that are evident in the contemporary Muslim ummah. Only then can we utilize our limited resources most efficiently.

There are many things that we need to do to bring about an Islamic revival, and there are many ways to go about that. The ultimate goal is to be in the state of *ubudiyah* (servitude to Allah SWT) and follow, to the best of our ability, every command that Allah and His messenger (s) have given to us in the Qur'an and *ahadith*. However, in a practical sense, our immediate focus should be on the deficits that are evident in the contemporary Muslim ummah. Those deficits of our time can be shortlisted can be short listed and targeted to recover. Only then the revival of the Muslim countries out of the can be realized.

- Understand the Quran in Arabic
- Learn fundamental natural science
- Stand for justice
- Relearn the civic responsibilities
- Stop excessive consumption
- Fight the unconscious bias and racism
- Participation in the democratic process
- We can't afford division among Muslims
- Work hard while believing in Qadr (the Destiny)
- Early "retirement" from job and save your youth
- Living a healthy life for purpose
- Learn how to handle information wisely
- Pray *Tahajjut* (night prayer) and perform non-obligatory fasting
- Stop backbiting and slandering
- Knowledge-based society and economy
- Collaboration among Muslim countries

Appendix C: Literary, Scientific & Mathematical analysis of verses in the Bible

I am copying those statements from Dr. Zakir Naik and Dr. William Campbell's famous dialogue:

- The Bible speaks about the creation of the universe. In the beginning, Book of Genesis (1), it says that almighty God created the Heavens and the Earth in six days and talks about an evening and a morning, referring to a 24-hour day. Today scientists tell us that the universe cannot be created in a 24-hour period of six days. The Qur'an too speaks about six *"ayyams"*. The Arabic word singular is *"yaum"*, plural is *"ayyam"*. It can either mean a day of 24 hours, or it is a very long period, an *"yaum"*, an epoch. Scientists say we have no objection in agreeing that the universe - it could have been created in 6 very long periods.
- Genesis (1:3 - 5) says that light was created on the first day." Genesis (1:14 - 19) says that "The cause of light - stars and the sun, etc. was created on the fourth day". How can the cause of light be created on the 4th day - later than the light which came into existence on the first day?
- Genesis (1:9 - 13) says that earth was created on the 3rd day. How can you have a night and day without the earth? The day depends upon the rotation of the Earth.
- Genesis (1:9 - 13) says that earth was created on the third day. Genesis (1:14 - 19) says that the Sun and the Moon were created on the fourth day. Today science tells us that earth is part of the parent body, the Sun. It cannot come into existence before the Sun.
- Genesis (1:11 - 19) says that the vegetation, the herbs, the shrubs, the trees - they were created on the 3rd day and the Sun was created on Day 4. How can vegetation come into existence without sunlight, and how can they survive without sunlight?
- Genesis (1:16) says that God created two lights, the greater light, the Sun to rule the day, and the lesser light the Moon, to rule the night. The actual translation, if you go to the Hebrew text, is 'lamps. Lamps

having lights of their own. And that you will come to know better, if you read both the Verses – Genesis (1-16 & 17). Verse no.17 says that "And Almighty God placed them in the firmament, to give light to the earth." Indicating that the Sun and the Moon has its own light - which is in contradiction with established scientific knowledge that we have. There are certain people who try to reconcile, and say that the six days mentioned in the Bible, actually refers to epochs - like the Qur'an long periods - not six, 24-hour days. It is illogical - you read in the Bible, evening, morning - It clearly states 24 hours, it indicates. But even if we agree with the illogical argument - yet they will only be able to solve the 1st scientific error of 6 days creation, and second, of first day "light" and 3rd day "earth." The remaining four, yet they cannot solve. Some further say that if it is a 24-hour period, why cannot the vegetables survive for one 24-hour day without sunlight? But you cannot say the days mentioned are 24 hours as well as epochs. If you say it is a long period, you solve Point-1 and 3, the remaining 4 points are yet there. If you say the days are 24 hours a day, you solve only Point-5 and the remaining 5 are still there - It becomes unscientific.

- Regarding the concept of Earth, there are various Scientists who have described how the world will end? Hypothesis - Some may be right; some may be wrong. But either the world will perish or the world will live forever. Both cannot take place simultaneously – It is unscientific. But this is exactly what the Bible says. It is mentioned in the Bible, in the book of Hebrews (1:10 & 11), and the book of Psalms (102:25 & 26), that" Almighty God created the Heavens and the Earth, and they will perish." Exactly the opposite is mentioned in the book of Ecclesiastics (1:4), and the book of Psalms (78:69), that "The earth will abide forever." One has to be unscientific - Both cannot take place. The world cannot abide forever as well as perish – it is unscientific.
- Regarding "the Heavens", the Bible says in Job (26:11), that "The pillars of the Heaven will tremble." The Qur'an says in Surah Luqman

(31:10), that "The Heavens are without any pillars - Don`t you see?" The Bible says heaven has got pillars.

- Not only do the Heavens have pillars - the Bible says in the first book of Samuel (2:8), as well as the book of Job (9:6), and the book of Psalms (75:3), that "Even the earth has got pillars."
- In the field of "Diet and Nutrition" The Bible says in the book of Genesis (1:29), that "God has given you all the herbs bearing seeds, the trees bearing fruits - those that bear seed, as meat for you." The New International Version says" The seed-bearing plants, and the trees bearing fruits bearing seeds are good for you, all of them." Today, even a layman knows that there are several poisonous plants like wild berries, datura, plants containing alkaloid, polyander - that if you ingest, if you eat there are high possibilities you may die.
- The Bible has a scientific test on how to identify a true believer. The Gospel of Mark (16:17 & 18): "There will be signs for true believers and among the signs - In my name they shall cast out devils, they shall speak foreign tongues, new tongues, they shall take up serpents - And if they drink deadly poison, they shall not be harmed - And when they place their hand over the sick, they shall be cured."
- In the field of medicine, the Bible says in the book of Leviticus (14:49 - 53) - it gives a novel way for disinfecting a house from plague of leprosy… disinfecting a house from the plague of leprosy. It says that "Take two birds, kill one bird, take wood, scale it - and the other living bird, dip it in water…and under running water - later on sprinkle the house 7 times with it." Sprinkle the house with blood to disinfect against plague of leprosy?
- The book of Leviticus (12:1 - 5) says that "After a woman gives birth to a male child, she will be unclean for 7 days, and the period of uncleanliness will continue for 33 days more. If she gives birth to a female child, she will be unclean for two weeks, and the period of uncleanliness will continue for 66 days." In short, if a woman gives birth to a male child, she is unclean for 40 days. How come a woman

remains unclean for double the period, if she gives birth to a female child, as compared to a male child.

- The Bible test for adultery - How to come to know a woman has committed adultery. In the book of Numbers (5:11 - 31) says, in summary: "The priest should take holy water in a vessel, take dust from the floor, and put it into the vessel - And that is the bitter water 'And after cursing it, give it to the woman and if the woman has committed adultery, after she drinks it, the curse will enter her body, the stomach will swell, the thigh will rot, and she shall be cursed by the people. If the woman has not committed adultery, she will remain clean and she will bear the seed."
- The Bible says regarding 'Hydrology' in Genesis (9-13 - 17): "After God, at the time of Noah, submerged the world by flood, and after the flood" subsided, He said... 'I put up a rainbow in the sky as a promise to humankind never to submerge the world again, by water. Rainbow is due to the refraction of sunlight, with rain or mist. Surely there must have been thousands of rainbows before the time of Noah, peace be upon him. To say it was not there before Noah's time you have to assume that the law of refraction did not exist - which is unscientific.

The Bible has also full of contradiction even with basic numbers:

- It is mentioned in Ezra (2: 1), and Nehemiah (7:6): "When the people returned from exile, from Babylon, when king Nebucheldeser of Babylon, when he released the men from Israel, they came back from captivity" - and the list of the people are given. The list is given in Ezra (2:2 - 63), and Nehemiah (7:7 - 65); the list is given with the names as well as number of people released. In these 60 Verses there are no less than 18 times - the name is exactly the same but the number is different. There are no less than 18 contradictions in less than 60 Verses, of these two chapters.

- In Ezra (2:64) it says that the total congregation numbered 42,360. And if you read in Nehemiah (7:66), also the total is 42,360. But if you add up Ezra (2), it does not come to 42,360 but to 29,818. And if you add up Nehemiah (7), even then it does not come to 42,360 but to 31,089.
- In Ezra (2:65), it says that there were 200 singing men and women - Nehemiah (7:67) says that there were 245 singing men and women. Were they 200 - or were they 245 singing men and women?
- It is mentioned in the 2nd Kings (24:8), that Jehoiachin was 18 years old, when he began to reign Jerusalem, and he reigned for 3 months and 10 days. 2nd Chronicles (36:9), says that Jehoiachin was 8 years old when he began to reign and he reigned for 3 months, 10 days. Was Jehoiachin 18 years when he began to reign, or was he 8 years old?
- It is mentioned in the 1st Kings (7:26), that in Solomon's temple, in his molten sea, he had 2,000 baths. In the 2nd Chronicles (4:5), he had 3,000 baths. Did he have 2000 baths or did he have 3,000 baths?
- It is mentioned in the First Kings (15:33), that Basha died in the 26th year of the reign of Asa. And 2nd Chronicles (16:1), says that Basha invaded Judah in the 36th years of the reign of Asa. How can Basha invade 10 years after his death?

Appendix D: What should a Muslim look like?

As a matter of fact, there are not just one but many attributes that Muslims should have that identify them and make them stand out from the crowd. Those who only exhibit one or two may be overlooked, but when it's a set of identifiers, it is more difficult to dismiss someone. Rather, I would argue that it would be very distinctly noticed, similar to how neon signs are unignorable. Just like when you see a U.S. Marine or a military man, you can easily recognize him by his approach, physical posture, and speech, even if he is not wearing his uniform. See for yourself what the Quran and Sunnah say about a Muslim.

- Muslims hate to harm and never kill a fellow human being because it's explicitly mentioned in the Quran that if one person kills another person unjustly then as if he or she is killing the entire humanity. [Quran, Hadith]
- Muslim would strive to learn the highest possible scientific knowledge in the field of their interest because God has asked to investigate and deeply ponder the creation of the earth, heaven, flying of birds, the origin of life, creation of the universe, embryology, … so that they get an understanding of their creator.
- Muslim won't put themselves in undue burden because God explicitly promised them that they are created weak and there's no burden in the religion. So, if someone is putting them in undue burden then they are doing something wrong.
- Muslims will have clean intention behind anything they do as God will judge their intention for any action.
- Muslim will not be unjust to others and in return, not let others to be unjust on them.
- Muslim men and women wear loose clothes that cover their body to below their knees to maintain modesty, as taught to us by our Prophet (pbuh) and told in the Quran.
- Muslims meet and greet people with a smile. That's sunnah of the Prophet (pbuh).

- Muslims maintain good hygiene as ordered by Allah and modeled by the Prophet (pbuh).
- Muslim men usually keep their beard - "keep the beards and cut the mustaches short" is recommended by the Prophet (pbuh).
- Muslims keep the body clean and healthy: they wash their face, arms, legs and wipe their head 5 times a day and brush and massage (miswak) their teeth - those are order from Allah and practice of the Prophet's Sunnah.
- Muslims aren't anxious or stressed out in the face of adversity but maintain their patience because Allah has mentioned that He loves who are patients and He is with those who seek solution to a problem through patients. [Surah An-Nisa]
- Muslims control their anger when they become aggravated because it's in the Quran and the Prophet (pbuh) warned to not be controlled by the devil and also mentioned that whoever controls their anger is the true strong person. [Surah Al-Imran, Hadith]
- Muslims are confident and fear none but Allah because none has any power to do harm or bring any benefits except Allah. [Surah At-Tawba]
- Muslims walk with humility and do not boast or show off. Allah taught us that through the advice of wise Luqman (a.s.) [Surah Luqman]
- Muslims don't yell when debating because the loudest voices are those who have the voice of a donkey. [Surah Luqman]
- Muslims don't waste time in vain talks and vein activities as time is the most precious commodity given to them. [Surah Al-Asr, Sura Al-Mu'minun]
- Muslims don't gossip or backbite because this is considered as an abhorrent act in the eyes of Allah. [Surah Al-Hujurat]
- Muslims stand for justice and are impartial regardless of their kinship with the perpetrators. [Surah An-Nisa]

- Muslims aren't racist and cannot be a bigot. Be it towards a fellow muslim or non-muslim or to an entire nation or ethnicity - Allah has explicitly ordered against such action. [Surah Al-Hujurat and Al-Ma'idah]
- Muslims don't mock or make fun of others because they know that those same people could be better than themselves. [Surah Al-Hujurat]
- Muslims live in community, centered on masajeed and take care of their community while they have their individual rights and responsibilities. Those are ordained by Allah and exemplified by the Prophet (pbuh) through his entire life. [Quran; Sunnah]
- Muslims shouldn't be overweight or obese as the Prophet (pbuh) instructed us to keep one third of the stomach empty when eating and drinking. They also fast for 30 mandatory days in Ramadan. Moreover, our prophet (pbuh) highly recommended Muslims to fast on Mondays and Thursdays as well as 3 middle days (Ayaam Al-Bid) of every lunar month. [Sunnah; Surah Al-A'raf]
- Muslims are not wasteful rather they take care of the earth as Allah sent human as Khalifa (representative) on the earth [Surah Al-A'raf; Surah Al-Baqara; Quran]
- Muslims don't drink alcohol, don't gamble, and don't watch inappropriate or indecent contents. [Surah Al-Ma'idah]
- Muslims eat only halal food that is good and avoid eating drinking or inhaling anything toxic or harmful for their body because Allah has ordered them to do so. [Surah Al-Maidah]
- Muslims maintain modesty between boys and girls, and avoid unnecessary interaction between the two genders. [Surah An-Noor]
- Muslims don't identify or associate themselves with the LGBTQ+ movement as it is explicitly forbidden in the Quran. [Surah Hud; Quran]

- Muslims are just in transactions and don't give less than the true value of the exchange. They are not also engaged in bribery. [Surah Al-Baqara; Surah Al-Mu'minun]
- Muslims are upfront and explicit in business transactions because they have to keep the contract in writing along with witnesses. [Surah Al-Baqarah]
- Muslims don't take interest when they lend money and avoid interest bearing transactions and businesses. [Quran]
- Muslims always give good advice and never deceive or lie to others. [Quran; Hadith]
- Muslims always side with the oppressed and against the oppressors - regardless of their religious identity. [Surah An-Nisa]
- Muslim men protect the dignity of women, take care of their family and are respectful in their dealings with any women and their wives [Surah An-Nisa, Sunnah]
- Muslims children are respectful to their parents and take care of them. [Surah Al-Isra; Hadith]
- Muslims have low divorce rates because divorce is the least liked action in the eyes of Allah. Even when they are dealing with a separation, they are respectful and civil. [Surah An-Nisa; Surah An-Noor]
- Muslims consult with others before making decisions and once a decision is made, they go with that without any hesitation. Also don't regret on the outcome, whatever it may be. Nothing befalls good or bad without the permission of Allah [Surah As-Shura; Quran]
- Muslims don't insult others' deities even when they disagree with them because Allah ordered them not to use foul languages. [Quran]
- Muslims do not use harsh words when conversing or debating with regular Christians and Jews because they are ordered to use good words. [Quran]

- Muslims are literate, because the Quran started with the order to read and reminded us the blessing Allah bestowed us with the ability to write. [Quran]
- Muslims will give you commitments about future event with "InshaAllah" i.e., he will do everything possible to meet the commitments - and there's no lapse from his side and rely on Allah to allow him to succeed [Surah Al-Kahaf]
- A neighbor of a well-off Muslim, would be assured to not only get full protection but also food, shelters, and all kind of supports whenever they need it - forty houses are the neighbor who have rights on a Muslim. [Quran; Hadith]
- Muslims take care of their relatives as their relatives have rights on them. Also, they never sever ties with their relatives - because whoever does it they are never to enter in the Jannah. [Quran; Hadith]
- Muslims are content in their life with whatever materialistic wealth he earns, be it big or small, because Prophet (pbuh) had explicit instruction: whoever wakes up in a morning with healthy body, roof over your head and a day worth of provision - as if he has everything in this world. [Hadith]
- Muslims don't pollute the earth because Allah has warned against the corruption on the earth and sea that will wreak-havoc to the climate. [Quran]
- Muslims are generally physically and psychologically strong because Prophet Muhammad (pbuh) has encouraged and instructed explicitly to be so. A strong Muslim is better than a weaker Muslim even though both are good. [Hadith; Quran]
- Muslims leave the plate of their food clean without any leftover because waste of food is strongly disliked by Allah and prophet Muhammad (pbuh). The prophet (pbuh) recommended through his own example to eat food to the last bit and leave the plate clean. [Quran; Hadith]

- Muslims go to bed early and wake up before sunrise for Fajr prayer and go out to find Allah's bounty. Because the Quran instructs us to wake up for night prayer (tahajjut) and strongly reprehend who stays at bed up until the sun rise. [Quran; Hadith]
- When inflicted with fear of overwhelming crisis and opposing forces, Muslims show their passion through their actions and words: "Allah is my protector and He is sufficient for me in overcoming all crisis." [Quran]
- Muslims are naturally scientific minded because the Quran repeatedly asks the mankind to observe, ponder, and make reasoning out of that observation- and always keep the mind open for evidence. [Quran]
- Muslims are very logical in their dispositions because Allah said in the Quran that the worst of creature in His creation are those who do not use their reason and intellects. [Surah Al-Anfal]
- Muslims are active listeners because they learned from the prophet of Islam (pbuh) as he showed the best example of how to listen: facing towards the speaker with full physical and mental attention. [Sunnah]
- Muslims feed the poor as Allah commands them to feed the hungry, take care of poor, and do charity. [Surah Al-Mu'minun]
- Muslims are very keen and careful to protect orphans because Allah and His prophet (pbuh) repeated it so many times to take care of the orphans. [Quran; Hadith]
- Muslims take action to the best of their abilities while relying on Allah for the outcome when injustice, indecency, wrongdoing, etc., become prevalent in society. This is because Allah explicitly mentioned that He will not change the status of a nation until they make efforts to change themselves. However, it's important to note that Allah never burdens anyone with more than they can bear. [Surah Al-Baqarah; Surah Ar-R'ad]

- Finally, when a Muslim is asked about their faith, they are proud of their Muslim identity and say: indeed, we are among the Muslims. [Quran]

Appendix E: Reference Texts

Professor Paul Freedman

In his lecture "14. Mohammed and the Arab Conquests" under the course "The Early Middle Ages, 284—1000" at Yale (2012) said:

"**Islam is a religious of conduct and law, not of mortification and purgation**. It emphasizes upright behavior: no drinking, no gambling, certain dietary restrictions. Not the renunciation of the world – it doesn't say, "Sell everything you have and give it to the poor." It says, "Give alms." It is a moderate religion, actually.

It is a "do-able" religion. These obligations may be somewhat inconvenient at times, Ramadan for example, but there is nothing in here to the degree that the New Testament, for example, prescribes behavior that most people are not going to follow. Or that traditional Judaism, possible but certainly onerous. Lots of obligations.

The other differences, more important, with Judaism is that **Islam would be very quickly, universal**. In other words, it would encourage conversion, although not, as we will see, with great enthusiasm. It is completely erroneous to think that these armies that burst forth from Arabia after the death of Mohammed were intent of getting everybody to follow Mohammed. They were intent on conquest, all right. But we'll see that their goals were a little more complicated than that of orienting everybody towards this new faith, whatever we're going to call it."

"How Jesus Became God" by Bart D. Ehrman

"They don't pass any of our criteria. They are not multiply attested in our sources; they appear only in John, our latest and most theologically oriented Gospel. They certainly do not pass the criterion of dissimilarity since they express the very view of Jesus that the author of the Gospel of John happens to hold. And they are not at all contextually credible. We have no record of any Palestinian Jew ever saying any such things about himself. These divine self-claims in John are part of John's

distinctive theology; they are not part of the historical record of what Jesus actually said.

Look at the matter in a different light. As I pointed out, we have numerous earlier sources for the historical Jesus: a few comments in Paul (including several quotations from Jesus's teachings), Mark, Q, M, and L, not to mention the finished Gospels of Matthew and Luke. In none of them do we find exalted claims of this sort. If Jesus went around Galilee proclaiming himself to be a divine being sent from God—one who existed before the creation of the world, who was in fact equal with God—could anything else that he might say be so breathtaking and thunderously important? And yet none of these earlier sources says any such thing about him. Did they (all of them!) just decide not to mention the one thing that was most significant about Jesus?

These narratives are found in Matthew 28, Mark 16, Luke 24, and John 20–21. Read through the accounts and ask yourself some basic questions: Who was the first person to go to the tomb? Was it Mary Magdalene by herself (John)? or Mary along with another Mary (Matthew)? or Mary along with another Mary and Salome (Mark)? or Mary, Mary, Joanna, and a number of other women (Luke)? Was the stone already rolled away when they arrived at the tomb (Mark, Luke, and John), or explicitly not (Matthew)? Whom did they see there? An angel (Matthew), a man (Mark), or two men (Luke)? Did they immediately go and tell some of the disciples what they had seen (John), or not (Matthew, Mark, and Luke)? What did the person or people at the tomb tell the women to do? To tell the disciples that Jesus would meet them in Galilee (Matthew and Mark)? Or to remember what Jesus had told them earlier when he had been in Galilee (Luke)? Did the women then go tell the disciples what they were told to tell them (Matthew and Luke), or not (Mark)? Did the disciples see Jesus (Matthew, Luke, and John), or not (Mark)? Where did they see him? —only in Galilee (Matthew), or only in Jerusalem (Luke)? "

Understanding brain signals

Electroencephalography (EEG) brain signals, such as alpha, beta, theta, delta, and gamma waves, are crucial for understanding brain activity and health, as well as psychological states. Each type of wave has its own range of frequencies and is associated with different states of brain functioning and consciousness.

Alpha Waves (8-13 Hz)
Significance: Alpha waves are typically associated with a state of relaxed alertness and calmness. They are more prominent when one is calm, meditative, or in a resting state but still alert. High levels of alpha activity are linked to a reduction in stress, anxiety, and depression.

Healthy Brain: A healthy adult brain exhibits alpha waves predominantly in the posterior part of the brain when the eyes are closed but awake.

Beta Waves (13-30 Hz)
Significance: Beta waves are associated with active, analytical thought and alertness. These waves are present during focused mental activities, problem-solving, decision making, and when engaged in focused work or conversation.

Healthy Brain: A balanced amount of beta activity is necessary for effective functioning in daily tasks. However, excessively high levels of beta waves are associated with anxiety, stress, and restlessness.

Theta Waves (4-8 Hz)
Significance: Theta waves are linked to creativity, intuition, daydreaming, and fantasizing. They are also associated with deep relaxation, meditation, and REM (Rapid Eye Movement) sleep. Theta activity fosters memory consolidation and emotional processing.

Healthy Brain: Theta waves are commonly found in sleep and in deep meditative states. In waking hours, high theta activity in adults may indicate ADHD or other attention issues, but it can also signify high levels of creativity.

Delta Waves (0.5-4 Hz)
Significance: Delta waves are the slowest EEG waves, associated with deep, dreamless sleep and regenerative processes in the body. They play a crucial role in healing and renewal.

Healthy Brain: Predominant during deep sleep, delta waves are crucial for effective restorative sleep. In waking states, unusually high delta activity may indicate brain injuries or other neurological issues.

Gamma Waves (30-100 Hz)
Significance: Gamma waves are associated with higher mental activity, including perception, problem-solving, and consciousness. They are involved in cognitive functioning, learning, and information processing.

Healthy Brain: Gamma activity is important for cognitive functioning, memory, and learning. Healthy gamma wave activity is associated with a heightened state of awareness and insight.

Each type of wave serves as a window into the brain's functioning and health, offering insights into cognitive states, emotional states, and neurological conditions. Abnormalities or imbalances in these waves can indicate various psychological or neurological issues, making EEG an invaluable tool for diagnosis and understanding of the human mind.

Verses from the Bible

Luke 3:38
King James Version

38 Which was the son of Enos, which was the son of Seth, which was the son of Adam, which was the son of God.

Acts 2:22
New International Version

22 "Fellow Israelites, listen to this: Jesus of Nazareth(A) was a man accredited by God to you by miracles, wonders and signs,(B) which God did among you through him,(C) as you yourselves know.

Hebrews 7:1-17
New International Version
Melchizedek the Priest

7 This Melchizedek was king of Salem(A) and priest of God Most High.(B) He met Abraham returning from the defeat of the kings and blessed him,(C) **2** and Abraham gave him a tenth of everything. First, the name Melchizedek means "king of righteousness"; then also, "king of Salem" means "king of peace." **3** Without father or mother, without genealogy,(D) without beginning of days or end of life, resembling the Son of God,(E) he remains a priest forever.

Hebrews 7:3
King James Version

3 Without father, without mother, without descent, having neither beginning of days, nor end of life; but made like unto the Son of God; abideth a priest continually.

Romans 8:14
New International Version

14 For those who are led by the Spirit of God(A) are the children of God.(B)

John 10:31, 33, 34
New International Version

31 Again his Jewish opponents picked up stones to stone him, **32** but Jesus
said to them, "I have shown you many good works from the Father. For
which of these do you stone me?"

33 "We are not stoning you for any good work," they replied, "but for
blasphemy, because you, a mere man, claim to be God."

34 Jesus answered them, "Is it not written in your Law, 'I have said you
are "gods"'[d]? **35** If he called them 'gods,' to whom the word of God
came—and Scripture cannot be set aside— **36** what about the one whom
the Father set apart as his very own and sent into the world? Why then do
you accuse me of blasphemy because I said, 'I am God's Son'? **37** Do not
believe me unless I do the works of my Father. **38** But if I do them, even
though you do not believe me, believe the works, that you may know and
understand that the Father is in me, and I in the Father." **39** Again they
tried to seize him, but he escaped their grasp.

Deuteronomy 6:4
King James Version

"Hear, O Israel: The LORD our God, the LORD is one."

Mark 12:29
King James Version

"The most important one," answered Jesus, "is this: 'Hear, O Israel: The Lord our God, the Lord is one."

Genesis 6:2
King James Version

2 That the sons of God saw the daughters of men that they were fair; and they took them wives of all which they chose.

Quranic verses in Arabic that are used in this book

All the Quranic verses (*ayat*) mentioned in this book are presented in the original Arabic language. The beauty of Islam is that the original message is preserved in its original language, allowing you to always refer back to it to verify if anyone is misinterpreting it due to ignorance or for any other purpose.

فَاطِرُ السَّمَاوَاتِ وَالْأَرْضِ جَعَلَ لَكُم مِّنْ أَنفُسِكُمْ أَزْوَاجًا وَمِنَ الْأَنْعَامِ أَزْوَاجًا يَذْرَؤُكُمْ
فِيهِ **لَيْسَ كَمِثْلِهِ شَيْءٌ** وَهُوَ السَّمِيعُ الْبَصِيرُ ﴿١١﴾

"[He is] Creator of the heavens and the earth. He has made for you from yourselves, mates, and among the cattle, mates; He multiplies you thereby. **There is nothing like unto Him**, and He is the Hearing, the Seeing." – Surah Ash-Shura (42:11)

وَالسَّمَاءَ بَنَيْنَاهَا بِأَيْدٍ وَإِنَّا لَمُوسِعُونَ

"And the heaven We constructed with strength, and indeed, We are [its] expander" – Surah Al-Jariayat (51:47)

بَدِيعُ السَّمَاوَاتِ وَالْأَرْضِ وَإِذَا قَضَىٰ أَمْرًا فَإِنَّمَا يَقُولُ لَهُ كُن فَيَكُونُ ﴿١١٧﴾

"Originator of the heavens and the earth. When He decrees a matter, He only says to it, "Be," and it is." Surah Al-Baqarah (2:117)

سَكَنًا وَالشَّمْسَ وَالْقَمَرَ حُسْبَانًا ذَٰلِكَ تَقْدِيرُ الْعَزِيزِ الْعَلِيمِ ﴿٩٦﴾

"[He is] the cleaver of daybreak and has made the night for rest and the sun and moon for calculation. That is the determination of the Exalted in Might, the Knowing" – Surah Al-An'am (6:96)

قُلْ أَرَأَيْتُمْ إِنْ جَعَلَ اللَّهُ عَلَيْكُمُ النَّهَارَ سَرْمَدًا إِلَىٰ يَوْمِ الْقِيَامَةِ مَنْ إِلَٰهٌ غَيْرُ اللَّهِ يَأْتِيكُمْ
بِلَيْلٍ تَسْكُنُونَ فِيهِ أَفَلَا تُبْصِرُونَ ﴿٧٢﴾

"Say, "Have you considered: if Allah should make for you the day continuous until the Day of Resurrection, what deity other than Allah could bring you a night in which you may rest? Then will you not see?" – Surah Al-Qasas (28:72)

هُوَ الَّذِي جَعَلَ الشَّمْسَ ضِيَاءً وَالْقَمَرَ نُورًا وَقَدَّرَهُ مَنَازِلَ لِتَعْلَمُوا عَدَدَ السِّنِينَ وَالْحِسَابَ مَا
خَلَقَ اللَّهُ ذَٰلِكَ إِلَّا بِالْحَقِّ يُفَصِّلُ الْآيَاتِ لِقَوْمٍ يَعْلَمُونَ ﴿٥﴾

"It is He Who made the sun to be a shining glory and the moon to be a light (of beauty), and measured out stages for her; that ye might know the number of years and the count (of time). Nowise did Allah create this but in truth and righteousness. (Thus) doth He explain His Signs in detail, for those who understand." – Surah Yunus/Jonah (10:5)

وَٱللَّهُ خَلَقَ كُلَّ دَآبَّةٍ مِّن مَّآءٍ فَمِنْهُم مَّن يَمْشِى عَلَىٰ بَطْنِهِۦ وَمِنْهُم مَّن يَمْشِى عَلَىٰ رِجْلَيْنِ
وَمِنْهُم مَّن يَمْشِى عَلَىٰٓ أَرْبَعٍ يَخْلُقُ ٱللَّهُ مَا يَشَآءُ إِنَّ ٱللَّهَ عَلَىٰ كُلِّ شَىْءٍ قَدِيرٌ ﴿٤٥﴾

"Allâh has created every moving (living) creature from water. Of them there are some that creep on their bellies, some that walk on two legs, and some that walk on four. Allâh creates what He wills. Verily! Allâh is Able to do all things." - Surah Al-Noor (24:45)

أَوَلَمْ يَرَ ٱلَّذِينَ كَفَرُوٓا۟ أَنَّ ٱلسَّمَـٰوَٰتِ وَٱلْأَرْضَ كَانَتَا رَتْقًا فَفَتَقْنَـٰهُمَا ۖ وَجَعَلْنَا مِنَ ٱلْمَآءِ كُلَّ شَىْءٍ
حَىٍّ ۖ أَفَلَا يُؤْمِنُونَ ٣٠

“Have not those who disbelieve known that the heavens and the earth were joined together as one united piece, then We parted them? And We have made from water every living thing. Will they not then believe?” - Surah Al-Ambiya (21:30)

كَيْفَ تَكْفُرُونَ بِاللَّهِ وَكُنْتُمْ أَمْوَاتًا فَأَحْيَاكُمْ ثُمَّ يُمِيتُكُمْ ثُمَّ يُحْيِيكُمْ ثُمَّ إِلَيْهِ تُرْجَعُونَ ٢٨

“How can you disbelieve in Allah when you were lifeless and He brought you to life; then He will cause you to die, then He will bring you [back] to life, and then to Him you will be returned.”- Surah Al-Baqarah (2:28)

وَإِذْ قَالَ رَبُّكَ لِلْمَلَائِكَةِ إِنِّي جَاعِلٌ فِي الْأَرْضِ خَلِيفَةً قَالُوا أَتَجْعَلُ فِيهَا مَنْ يُفْسِدُ فِيهَا
وَيَسْفِكُ الدِّمَاءَ وَنَحْنُ نُسَبِّحُ بِحَمْدِكَ وَنُقَدِّسُ لَكَ قَالَ إِنِّي أَعْلَمُ مَا لَا تَعْلَمُونَ ٣٠

“And [mention, O Muhammad], when your Lord said to the angels, "Indeed, I will make upon the earth a successive authority." They said, "Will You place upon it one who causes corruption therein and sheds blood, while we declare Your praise and sanctify You?" Allah said, "Indeed, I know that which you do not know." - Surah Al-Baqarah (2:30)

أَوَلَمْ يَرَ الَّذِينَ كَفَرُوا أَنَّ السَّمَاوَاتِ وَالْأَرْضَ كَانَتَا رَتْقًا فَفَتَقْنَاهُمَا وَجَعَلْنَا مِنَ الْمَاءِ كُلَّ
شَيْءٍ حَيٍّ أَفَلَا يُؤْمِنُونَ ٣٠

"Do not the Unbelievers see that the heavens and the earth were joined together (as one unit of Creation), before We clove them asunder? We made from water every living thing. Will they not then believe?" - Surah Al-Ambiya (21:30)

وَاللَّهُ خَلَقَ كُلَّ دَابَّةٍ مِّن مَّاءٍ ۖ فَمِنْهُم مَّن يَمْشِي عَلَىٰ بَطْنِهِ وَمِنْهُم مَّن يَمْشِي عَلَىٰ رِجْلَيْنِ وَمِنْهُم
مَّن يَمْشِي عَلَىٰ أَرْبَعٍ ۚ يَخْلُقُ اللَّهُ مَا يَشَاءُ ۚ إِنَّ اللَّهَ عَلَىٰ كُلِّ شَيْءٍ قَدِيرٌ ﴿٤٥﴾

"Allah has created every [living] creature from water. And of them are those that move on their bellies, and of them are those that walk on two legs, and of them are those that walk on four. Allah creates what He wills. Indeed, Allah is over all things competent." - Surat An-Noor (24:45)

خَلَقَ الْإِنسَانَ مِن صَلْصَالٍ كَالْفَخَّارِ ﴿١٤﴾

"He created man from clay like [that of] pottery"- Surat Al-Rahman (55:14)

الَّذِي خَلَقَكَ فَسَوَّاكَ فَعَدَلَكَ ﴿٧﴾ فِي أَيِّ صُورَةٍ مَّا شَاءَ رَكَّبَكَ ﴿٨﴾

"Who created you, proportioned you, and balanced you? In whatever form He willed has He assembled you." - Sura Al-Infitr (82:7-8)

وَمَنْ أَعْرَضَ عَن ذِكْرِي فَإِنَّ لَهُ مَعِيشَةً ضَنكًا وَنَحْشُرُهُ يَوْمَ الْقِيَامَةِ أَعْمَىٰ ﴿١٢٤﴾

"And whoever turns away from My remembrance - indeed, he will have a depressed life, and We will gather him on the Day of Resurrection blind." – Surah Ta-Ha (20:124)

وَمَنْ أَعْرَضَ عَن ذِكْرِي فَإِنَّ لَهُ مَعِيشَةً ضَنكًا وَنَحْشُرُهُ يَوْمَ الْقِيَامَةِ أَعْمَىٰ ﴿١٢٤﴾

"And whoever turns away from My remembrance - indeed, he will have a depressed life, and We will gather him on the Day of Resurrection blind." – Surah Ta-Ha (20:124)

ظَهَرَ ٱلْفَسَادُ فِى ٱلْبَرِّ وَٱلْبَحْرِ بِمَا كَسَبَتْ أَيْدِى ٱلنَّاسِ لِيُذِيقَهُم بَعْضَ ٱلَّذِى عَمِلُوا۟ لَعَلَّهُمْ
يَرْجِعُونَ ﴿٤١﴾

"Mischief has appeared on land and sea because of (the meed) that the hands of men have earned that (Allah) may give them a taste of some of their deeds: in order that they may turn back (from Evil)." - Surah Al-Rum (30:41)

فَبِمَا رَحْمَةٍ مِنَ اللَّهِ لِنْتَ لَهُمْ وَلَوْ كُنْتَ فَظًّا غَلِيظَ الْقَلْبِ لَانْفَضُّوا مِنْ حَوْلِكَ فَاعْفُ عَنْهُمْ
وَاسْتَغْفِرْ لَهُمْ وَشَاوِرْهُمْ فِي الْأَمْرِ فَإِذَا عَزَمْتَ فَتَوَكَّلْ عَلَى اللَّهِ إِنَّ اللَّهَ يُحِبُّ الْمُتَوَكِّلِينَ

"...and consult them in the matter. And when you have decided, then rely upon Allah. Indeed, Allah loves those who rely [upon Him]" – Surah Al-Imran (3:159)

يَٰٓأَيُّهَا ٱلَّذِينَ ءَامَنُوا۟ كُونُوا۟ قَوَّٰمِينَ لِلَّهِ شُهَدَآءَ بِٱلْقِسْطِ ۖ وَلَا يَجْرِمَنَّكُمْ شَنَـَٔانُ قَوْمٍ عَلَىٰٓ أَلَّا
تَعْدِلُوا۟ ۚ ٱعْدِلُوا۟ هُوَ أَقْرَبُ لِلتَّقْوَىٰ ۖ وَٱتَّقُوا۟ ٱللَّهَ ۚ إِنَّ ٱللَّهَ خَبِيرٌۢ بِمَا تَعْمَلُونَ ﴿٨﴾

"O you who believe! Stand out firmly for Allâh as just witnesses and let not the enmity and hatred of others make you avoid justice. Be just: that is nearer to piety, and fear Allâh. Verily, Allâh is Well-Acquainted with what you do." - Surah Al-Ma'idah (5:8)

يَٰٓأَيُّهَا ٱلَّذِينَ ءَامَنُوا۟ لَا يَسْخَرْ قَوْمٌ مِّن قَوْمٍ عَسَىٰٓ أَن يَكُونُوا۟ خَيْرًا مِّنْهُمْ وَلَا نِسَآءٌ مِّن نِّسَآءٍ
عَسَىٰٓ أَن يَكُنَّ خَيْرًا مِّنْهُنَّ ۖ وَلَا تَلْمِزُوٓا۟ أَنفُسَكُمْ وَلَا تَنَابَزُوا۟ بِٱلْأَلْقَٰبِ ۖ بِئْسَ ٱلِٱسْمُ ٱلْفُسُوقُ
بَعْدَ ٱلْإِيمَٰنِ ۚ وَمَن لَّمْ يَتُبْ فَأُو۟لَٰٓئِكَ هُمُ ٱلظَّٰلِمُونَ ﴿١١﴾

"O you who believe! Let not a group scoff at another group, it may be that the latter are better than the former; Nor let (some) women scoff at other women, it may be that the latter are better than the former, Nor defame one another, nor insult one another by nicknames. How bad is it, to insult one's brother after having Faith [i.e. to call your Muslim brother (a faithful believer) as: "O sinner", or "O wicked"]. And whosoever does not repent, then such are indeed wrong-doers. "- Surah Al-Hujurat (49:11)

كُلُوا مِن طَيِّبَاتِ مَا رَزَقْنَاكُمْ

"Eat from the good things with which We have provided you."- Al-Baqarah (2:57)

يَا أَيُّهَا النَّاسُ كُلُوا مِمَّا فِي الْأَرْضِ حَلَالًا طَيِّبًا

"O mankind, eat from whatever is on earth [that is] lawful and good..."- Al-Baqarah (2:168)

كُلُوا مِن طَيِّبَاتِ مَا رَزَقْنَاكُمْ

"Eat from the good things with which We have provided you."- Al-Baqarah (2:172)

قُلْ أُحِلَّ لَكُمُ الطَّيِّبَاتُ

"Say, 'Lawful for you are [all] good foods..."- Al-Maaida (5:4)

وَكُلُوا مِمَّا رَزَقَكُمُ اللَّهُ حَلَالًا طَيِّبًا

"And eat of what Allah has provided for you [which is] lawful and good."- Al-Maaida (5:88)

كُلُوا مِن طَيِّبَاتِ مَا رَزَقْنَاكُمْ

"Eat from the good things with which We have provided you."- Al-A'raaf (7:160)

فَكُلُوا مِمَّا رَزَقَكُمُ اللَّهُ حَلَالًا طَيِّبًا

"That eat of what Allah has provided for you [which is] lawful and good."- An-Nahl (16:114)

كُلُوا مِن طَيِّبَاتِ مَا رَزَقْنَاكُمْ

"Eat from the good things with which We have provided you."- Taa-Haa (20:81)

يَا أَيُّهَا الرُّسُلُ كُلُوا مِنَ الطَّيِّبَاتِ

"[Allah said], 'O messengers, eat from the good foods…"- Al-Mu'minun (23:51)

إِنَّ الْمُسْلِمِينَ وَالْمُسْلِمَاتِ وَالْمُؤْمِنِينَ وَالْمُؤْمِنَاتِ وَالْقَانِتِينَ وَالْقَانِتَاتِ وَالصَّادِقِينَ وَالصَّادِقَاتِ
وَالصَّابِرِينَ وَالصَّابِرَاتِ وَالْخَاشِعِينَ وَالْخَاشِعَاتِ وَالْمُتَصَدِّقِينَ وَالْمُتَصَدِّقَاتِ وَالصَّائِمِينَ
وَالصَّائِمَاتِ وَالْحَافِظِينَ فُرُوجَهُمْ وَالْحَافِظَاتِ وَالذَّاكِرِينَ اللَّهَ كَثِيرًا وَالذَّاكِرَاتِ أَعَدَّ اللَّهُ لَهُمْ
مَغْفِرَةً وَأَجْرًا عَظِيمًا ﴿٣٥﴾

"Indeed, the Muslim men and Muslim women, the believing men and believing women, the obedient men and obedient women, the truthful men and truthful women, the patient men and patient women, the humble men and humble women, the charitable men and charitable women, the fasting men and fasting women, the men who guard their private parts and the women who do so, and the men who remember Allah often and the women who do so - for them Allah has prepared forgiveness and a great reward."- Surah Al-Ahzab (33:35).

ٱلْوَٰلِدَيْنِ وَٱلْأَقْرَبِينَ ۚ إِن يَكُنْ غَنِيًّا أَوْ فَقِيرًا فَٱللَّهُ أَوْلَىٰ بِهِمَا ۖ فَلَا تَتَّبِعُوا۟ ٱلْهَوَىٰٓ أَن تَعْدِلُوا۟ ۚ وَإِن
تَلْوُۥٓا۟ أَوْ تُعْرِضُوا۟ فَإِنَّ ٱللَّهَ كَانَ بِمَا تَعْمَلُونَ خَبِيرًا ﴿١٣٥﴾

"O you who have believed, be persistently standing firm in justice, witnesses for Allah, even if it be against yourselves or parents and relatives. Whether one is rich or poor, Allah is more worthy of both. So, follow not [personal] inclination, lest you not be just. And if you distort [your testimony] or refuse [to give it], then indeed Allah is ever, with what you do, Acquainted. "– Surah Al-Nisa (4:135)

يَٰٓأَيُّهَا ٱلَّذِينَ ءَامَنُوا۟ كُونُوا۟ قَوَّٰمِينَ لِلَّهِ شُهَدَآءَ بِٱلْقِسْطِ ۖ وَلَا يَجْرِمَنَّكُمْ شَنَـَٔانُ قَوْمٍ عَلَىٰٓ أَلَّا
تَعْدِلُوا۟ ۚ ٱعْدِلُوا۟ هُوَ أَقْرَبُ لِلتَّقْوَىٰ ۖ وَٱتَّقُوا۟ ٱللَّهَ ۚ إِنَّ ٱللَّهَ خَبِيرٌۢ بِمَا تَعْمَلُونَ ﴿٨﴾

"O ye who believe! stand out firmly for Allah, as witnesses to fair dealing, and let not the hatred of others to you make you swerve to wrong and depart from justice. Be just: that is next to Piety: and fear Allah For Allah is well-acquainted with all that ye do."- Surah Al-Maidah (5:8)

يَٰٓأَيُّهَا ٱلَّذِينَ ءَامَنُوا۟ لَا يَسْخَرْ قَوْمٌ مِّن قَوْمٍ عَسَىٰٓ أَن يَكُونُوا۟ خَيْرًا مِّنْهُمْ وَلَا نِسَآءٌ مِّن نِّسَآءٍ
عَسَىٰٓ أَن يَكُنَّ خَيْرًا مِّنْهُنَّ ۖ وَلَا تَلْمِزُوٓا۟ أَنفُسَكُمْ وَلَا تَنَابَزُوا۟ بِٱلْأَلْقَٰبِ ۖ بِئْسَ ٱلِٱسْمُ ٱلْفُسُوقُ
بَعْدَ ٱلْإِيمَٰنِ ۚ وَمَن لَّمْ يَتُبْ فَأُو۟لَٰٓئِكَ هُمُ ٱلظَّٰلِمُونَ ﴿١١﴾

"O you who believe! Let not a group scoff at another group, it may be that the latter are better than the former; Nor let (some) women scoff at other women, it may be that the latter are better than the former, Nor defame one another, nor insult one another by nicknames. How bad is it, to insult one's brother after having Faith. And whosoever does not repent, then such are indeed wrong-doers. "- Surah Al-Hujurat (49:11)

يَٰٓأَيُّهَا ٱلَّذِينَ ءَامَنُوا۟ ٱجْتَنِبُوا۟ كَثِيرًا مِّنَ ٱلظَّنِّ إِنَّ بَعْضَ ٱلظَّنِّ إِثْمٌ ۖ وَلَا تَجَسَّسُوا۟ وَلَا يَغْتَب بَّعْضُكُم بَعْضًا ۚ أَيُحِبُّ أَحَدُكُمْ أَن يَأْكُلَ لَحْمَ أَخِيهِ مَيْتًا فَكَرِهْتُمُوهُ ۚ وَٱتَّقُوا۟ ٱللَّهَ ۚ إِنَّ ٱللَّهَ تَوَّابٌ رَّحِيمٌ ﴿١٢﴾

"O you who believe! Avoid much suspicion, indeed some suspicions are sins. And spy not, neither backbite one another. Would one of you like to eat the flesh of his dead brother? You would hate it (so hate backbiting). And fear Allâh. Verily, Allâh is the One Who forgives and accepts repentance, Most Merciful."- Surah Al-Hujurat (49:12)

يَا أَيُّهَا النَّاسُ إِنَّا خَلَقْنَاكُمْ مِنْ ذَكَرٍ وَأُنْثَى وَجَعَلْنَاكُمْ شُعُوبًا وَقَبَائِلَ لِتَعَارَفُوا إِنَّ أَكْرَمَكُمْ عِنْدَ اللَّهِ أَتْقَاكُمْ إِنَّ اللَّهَ عَلِيمٌ خَبِيرٌ ﴿١٣﴾

"O mankind, indeed We have created you from male and female and made you peoples and tribes that you may know one another. Indeed, the most noble of you in the sight of Allah is the most righteous of you. Indeed, Allah is Knowing and Acquainted"- Surah Al-Hujurat (49:13)

ظَهَرَ ٱلْفَسَادُ فِى ٱلْبَرِّ وَٱلْبَحْرِ بِمَا كَسَبَتْ أَيْدِى ٱلنَّاسِ لِيُذِيقَهُم بَعْضَ ٱلَّذِى عَمِلُوا۟ لَعَلَّهُمْ يَرْجِعُونَ ﴿٤١﴾

"Mischief has appeared on land and sea because of (the meed) that the hands of men have earned that (Allah) may give them a taste of some of their deeds: in order that they may turn back (from Evil)."- Surah Al-Rum (30:41)

يَٰبَنِيٓ ءَادَمَ خُذُواْ زِينَتَكُمۡ عِندَ كُلِّ مَسۡجِدٖ وَكُلُواْ وَٱشۡرَبُواْ وَلَا تُسۡرِفُوٓاْۚ إِنَّهُۥ لَا يُحِبُّ
ٱلۡمُسۡرِفِينَ ٣١

"O children of Adam! Wear your beautiful apparel at every time and place of prayer; eat and drink, but waste not by excess. For Allah loves not the wasters."- Surah Al-A'raf (7:31)

زُيِّنَ لِلنَّاسِ حُبُّ ٱلشَّهَوَٰتِ مِنَ ٱلنِّسَآءِ وَٱلۡبَنِينَ وَٱلۡقَنَٰطِيرِ ٱلۡمُقَنطَرَةِ مِنَ ٱلذَّهَبِ وَٱلۡفِضَّةِ
وَٱلۡخَيۡلِ ٱلۡمُسَوَّمَةِ وَٱلۡأَنۡعَٰمِ وَٱلۡحَرۡثِۗ ذَٰلِكَ مَتَٰعُ ٱلۡحَيَوٰةِ ٱلدُّنۡيَاۖ وَٱللَّهُ عِندَهُۥ حُسۡنُ ٱلۡمَـَٔابِ ١٤
۞قُلۡ أَؤُنَبِّئُكُم بِخَيۡرٖ مِّن ذَٰلِكُمۡۖ لِلَّذِينَ ٱتَّقَوۡاْ عِندَ رَبِّهِمۡ جَنَّٰتٞ تَجۡرِي مِن تَحۡتِهَا ٱلۡأَنۡهَٰرُ
خَٰلِدِينَ فِيهَا وَأَزۡوَٰجٞ مُّطَهَّرَةٞ وَرِضۡوَٰنٞ مِّنَ ٱللَّهِۗ وَٱللَّهُ بَصِيرُۢ بِٱلۡعِبَادِ ١٥

"Fair in the eyes of men is the love of things they covet: women and sons; heaped-up hoards of gold and silver; horses branded (for blood and excellence); and (wealth of) cattle and well-tilled land. Such are the possessions of this world's life; but in nearness to Allah is the best of the goals (to return to). (14) Say: shall I give you glad tidings of things far better than those? For the righteous are Gardens in nearness to their Lord with rivers flowing beneath; therein is their eternal home; with companions pure (and holy) and the good pleasure of Allah. For in Allah's sight are (all) His servants. - (15) "- Surah Al-Imran (3:14-15)

كُلُّ نَفۡسٖ ذَآئِقَةُ ٱلۡمَوۡتِۗ وَإِنَّمَا تُوَفَّوۡنَ أُجُورَكُمۡ يَوۡمَ ٱلۡقِيَٰمَةِۖ فَمَن زُحۡزِحَ عَنِ ٱلنَّارِ وَأُدۡخِلَ ٱلۡجَنَّةَ
فَقَدۡ فَازَۗ وَمَا ٱلۡحَيَوٰةُ ٱلدُّنۡيَآ إِلَّا مَتَٰعُ ٱلۡغُرُورِ ١٨٥

"Everyone shall taste death. And only on the Day of Resurrection shall you be paid your wages in full. And whoever is removed away from the

Fire and admitted to Paradise, he indeed is successful. *The life of this world is only the enjoyment of deception (a deceiving thing)"* - Surah Al-Imran (3:185)

ٱعْلَمُوٓا۟ أَنَّمَا ٱلْحَيَوٰةُ ٱلدُّنْيَا لَعِبٌ وَلَهْوٌ وَزِينَةٌ وَتَفَاخُرٌۢ بَيْنَكُمْ وَتَكَاثُرٌ فِى ٱلْأَمْوَٰلِ وَٱلْأَوْلَـٰدِ ۖ كَمَثَلِ غَيْثٍ أَعْجَبَ ٱلْكُفَّارَ نَبَاتُهُۥ ثُمَّ يَهِيجُ فَتَرَىٰهُ مُصْفَرًّا ثُمَّ يَكُونُ حُطَـٰمًا ۖ وَفِى ٱلْـَٔاخِرَةِ عَذَابٌ شَدِيدٌ وَمَغْفِرَةٌ مِّنَ ٱللَّهِ وَرِضْوَٰنٌ ۚ وَمَا ٱلْحَيَوٰةُ ٱلدُّنْيَآ إِلَّا مَتَـٰعُ ٱلْغُرُورِ ﴿٢٠﴾

"Know that the life of this world is but amusement and diversion and adornment and boasting to one another and competition in increase of wealth and children - like the example of a rain whose [resulting] plant growth pleases the tillers; then it dries and you see it turned yellow; then it becomes [scattered] debris. And in the Hereafter is severe punishment and forgiveness from Allah and approval. *And what is the worldly life except the enjoyment of delusion."*- Surah Al-Hadeed (57:20)

وَزُخْرُفًا ۚ وَإِن كُلُّ ذَٰلِكَ لَمَّا مَتَـٰعُ ٱلْحَيَوٰةِ ٱلدُّنْيَا ۚ وَٱلْـَٔاخِرَةُ عِندَ رَبِّكَ لِلْمُتَّقِينَ ﴿٣٥﴾

"And adornments of gold. *Yet all this (i.e. the roofs, doors, stairs, elevators, thrones of their houses) would have been nothing but an enjoyment of this world.* And the Hereafter with your Lord is (only) for the Muttaqûn."- Surah Al-Zukhruf (43:35)

وَإِذَا قِيلَ لَهُمُ اتَّبِعُوا مَا أَنْزَلَ اللَّهُ قَالُوا بَلْ نَتَّبِعُ مَا أَلْفَيْنَا عَلَيْهِ آبَاءَنَا أَوَلَوْ كَانَ آبَاؤُهُمْ لَا يَعْقِلُونَ شَيْئًا وَلَا يَهْتَدُونَ ﴿١٧٠﴾

"And when it is said to them, "Follow what Allah has revealed," they say, "***Rather, we will follow that which we found our fathers doing." Even though their fathers understood nothing, nor were they guided?***"- Surah Al-Baqarah (2:170)

وَٱللَّهُ خَلَقَ كُلَّ دَآبَّةٍ مِّن مَّآءٍ ۖ فَمِنْهُم مَّن يَمْشِى عَلَىٰ بَطْنِهِۦ وَمِنْهُم مَّن يَمْشِى عَلَىٰ رِجْلَيْنِ
وَمِنْهُم مَّن يَمْشِى عَلَىٰٓ أَرْبَعٍ ۚ يَخْلُقُ ٱللَّهُ مَا يَشَآءُ ۚ إِنَّ ٱللَّهَ عَلَىٰ كُلِّ شَىْءٍ قَدِيرٌ ﴿٤٥﴾

"Allah has created every [living] creature from water. And of them are those that move on their bellies, and of them are those that walk on two legs, and of them are those that walk on four. Allah creates what He wills. Indeed, Allah is over all things competent."- Surat An-Noor (24:45)

إِنَّ رَبَّكُمُ ٱللَّهُ ٱلَّذِى خَلَقَ ٱلسَّمَٰوَٰتِ وَٱلْأَرْضَ فِى سِتَّةِ أَيَّامٍ ثُمَّ ٱسْتَوَىٰ عَلَى ٱلْعَرْشِ يُغْشِى
ٱلَّيْلَ ٱلنَّهَارَ يَطْلُبُهُۥ حَثِيثًا وَٱلشَّمْسَ وَٱلْقَمَرَ وَٱلنُّجُومَ مُسَخَّرَٰتٍۭ بِأَمْرِهِۦٓ ۗ أَلَا لَهُ ٱلْخَلْقُ وَٱلْأَمْرُ ۗ
تَبَارَكَ ٱللَّهُ رَبُّ ٱلْعَٰلَمِينَ

"*Indeed, your Lord is Allah, who created the heavens and earth in six days and then established Himself above the Throne*. He covers the night with the day, [another night] chasing it rapidly; and [He created] the sun, the moon, and the stars, subjected by His command. Unquestionably, His is the creation and the command; blessed is Allah, Lord of the worlds."- Surah Al-A'raf (7:54)

End Notes with References

[1] "Declining birth rate in Developed Countries: A radical policy re-think is required." Retrieved from:
https://www.ncbi.nlm.nih.gov/pmc/articles/PMC4255510/

[2] "List of American Nobel Laureates." Retrieved from
https://en.wikipedia.org/wiki/List_of_American_Nobel_laureates

[3] "Shifting Baseline". Retrieved from:
https://en.wikipedia.org/wiki/Shifting_baseline

[4] "The Native American Experience". Retrieved from
https://www.pbs.org/wgbh/americanexperience/collections/native-americans/

[5] "Inmate Race, Federal Bureau of Prisons". Retrieved from:
https://www.bop.gov/about/statistics/statistics_inmate_race.jsp

[6] "Understanding Racial Restrictive Covenants and their Legacy by the Racial Restrictive Covenants Project Washington State." Retrieved from https://depts.washington.edu/covenants/segregation.shtml

[7] "History of Fair Housing." Retrieved from:
https://www.hud.gov/program_offices/fair_housing_equal_opp/aboutfheo/history

[8] "Historically denied 'pivotal' loans, Black farmers still struggle to get support. Dec 7, 2021." Retrieved from:
https://www.pbs.org/newshour/show/historically-denied-pivotal-loans-black-farmers-still-struggle-to-get-support

[9] "Black farmers struggle in face of structural racism and economic headwinds." Retrieved from:
https://www.pbs.org/newshour/show/black-farmers-struggle-in-face-of-structural-racism-and-economic-headwinds

[10] "Black Farmers in America, 1865-2000. The Pursuit of Independent Farming and the Role of Cooperatives. United States Department of Agriculture." Retrieved from: https://www.rd.usda.gov/files/RR194.pdf

[11] "Charts that Explain Wealth Inequality in the United States. October 19, 2022. Shehryar Nabi." Retrieved from:
https://www.aspeninstitute.org/blog-posts/charts-that-explain-wealth-inequality-in-the-united-states/

[12] "Distribution of Household Wealth in the U.S. since 1989." Retrieved from:
https://www.federalreserve.gov/releases/z1/dataviz/dfa/distribute/chart/#quarter:0;series:Net%20worth;demographic:networth;population:1,3,5,7;units:levels;range:2005.2,2020.2

[13] "Alcohol-Related Emergencies and Deaths in the United States." Retrieved from:
https://www.niaaa.nih.gov/alcohols-effects-health/alcohol-topics/alcohol-facts-and-statistics/alcohol-related-emergencies-and-deaths-united-states

[14] "Key Substance Use and Mental Health Indicators in the United States: Results from the 2019 National Survey on Drug Use and Health." Retrieved from:
https://www.samhsa.gov/data/sites/default/files/reports/rpt29393/2019NSDUHFFRPDFWHTML/2019NSDUHFFR090120.htm

[15] "Deaths from Excessive Alcohol Use in the United States." Retrieved from:
https://www.cdc.gov/alcohol/features/excessive-alcohol-deaths.html

[16] "Committee on Nutrition. American Heart Association. Diet and Heart Disease." American Heart Association; Dallas, TX, USA: 1968

[17] Pelletier, X., P. Thouvenot, S. Belbraouet, J. A. Chayvialle, B. Hanesse, D. Mayeux, and G. Debry. "Effect of Egg Consumption in Healthy Volunteers: Influence of Yolk, White, or Whole-Egg on Gastric Emptying and on Glycemic and Hormonal Responses." Annals of Nutrition & Metabolism 40 (1996): 109-115. https://doi.org/10.1159/000177903

[18] "The Fifty Year Rehabilitation of the Egg." Retrieved from:

https://www.ncbi.nlm.nih.gov/pmc/articles/PMC4632449/#B1-nutrients-07-05429

[19] Villaume, C., B. Beck, R. Rohr, J. P. Pointel, and G. Debry. "Effect of Exchange of Ham for Boiled Egg on Plasma Glucose and Insulin Responses to Breakfast in Normal Subjects." Diabetes Care 9 (1986): 46-49. https://doi.org/10.2337/diacare.9.1.46.

[20] Song, W. O., and J. M. Kerver. "Nutritional Contribution of Eggs to American Diets." Journal of the American College of Nutrition 19 (2000): 556S-562S. https://doi.org/10.1080/07315724.2000.10718980.

[21]Kearns, Cristin E., Laura A. Schmidt, and Stanton A. Glantz. "Sugar Industry and Coronary Heart Disease Research: A Historical Analysis of Internal Industry Documents." JAMA Internal Medicine 176, no. 11 (2016): 1680–1685.
https://www.ncbi.nlm.nih.gov/pmc/articles/PMC5099084/

[22] Stamler, Jeremiah, Rose S. Stamler, and Joseph D. Stoll. "Dietary Fats, Carbohydrates and Atherosclerotic Disease." New England Journal of Medicine 276, no. 1 (1967): 39-47.
https://doi.org/10.1056/NEJM196701052760108

[23] "'Inclusive' view of obesity and metabolic dysfunction." Retrieved from:
https://robertlustig.com/wp-content/uploads/2020/08/Inclusive-View.pdf

[24] "Facts & Figures by International Diabetes Federation." Retrieved from:
https://idf.org/about-diabetes/facts-figures/

[25] "Hypertension. World Health Organization." Retrieved from:
https://www.who.int/news-room/fact-sheets/detail/hypertension

[26] "Risk Factors for Coronary Artery Disease." Retrieved from:
https://pubmed.ncbi.nlm.nih.gov/32119297/

[27] "2022 Heart Disease & Stroke Statistical Update Fact Sheet." Retrieved from:
https://professional.heart.org/-/media/PHD-Files-2/Science-News/2/2022-Heart-and-Stroke-Stat-Update/2022-Stat-Update-factsheet-GIobal-Burden-of-Disease.pdf

[28] "Worldwide cancer data." Retrieved from:
https://www.wcrf.org/cancer-trends/worldwide-cancer-data/

[29] "Trends in health care spending." Retrieved from: https://www.ama-assn.org/about/research/trends-health-care-spending

[30] "U.S. Health Care from a Global Perspective, 2022: Accelerating Spending, Worsening Outcomes." The Commonwealth Fund. Retrieved from:
https://www.commonwealthfund.org/publications/issue-briefs/2023/jan/us-health-care-global-perspective-2022

[31] "Metabolical" by Dr. Robert Lustig.

https://robertlustig.com/metabolical/
32 "Sugar, The Bitter Truth with Robert Lustig." Retrieved from: https://robertlustig.com/sugar-the-bitter-truth/
33 "The Fructose Epidemic" by Robert H. Lustig, MD. Retrieved from: https://cdn.media.freedomainradio.com/feed/Bariatrician_Fructose.pdf
34 "Coronavirus Cases." Retrieved from: https://www.worldometers.info/coronavirus/#countries
35 "U.S. Depression Rates Reach New Highs." Retrieved from: https://news.gallup.com/poll/505745/depression-rates-reach-new-highs.aspx
36 "Population projection of US adults with lifetime experience of depressive disorder by age and sex from year 2005 to 2050". Retrieved from: https://www.ncbi.nlm.nih.gov/pmc/articles/PMC3207493/
37 "Mental Health Conditions Can Contribute to Suicide Risk." Retrieved from: https://www.pewtrusts.org/en/research-and-analysis/articles/2022/05/02/mental-health-conditions-can-contribute-to-suicide-risk
38 "Broken hearts: A rundown of the divorce capital of every state by John Harrington and Cheyenne Buckingham." Retrieved from: https://www.usatoday.com/story/money/economy/2018/02/02/broken-hearts-rundown-divorce-capital-every-state/1078283001/
39 "The impact of family structure on the health of children: Effects of divorce." Retrieved from: https://www.ncbi.nlm.nih.gov/pmc/articles/PMC4240051/
40 "Loneliness in U.S. Subsides From Pandemic High" Retrieved from: https://news.gallup.com/poll/473057/loneliness-subsides-pandemic-high.aspx
41"America has a loneliness epidemic. Here are 6 streps to address it." Retrieved from: https://www.npr.org/2023/05/02/1173418268/loneliness-connection-mental-health-dementia-surgeon-general
42 "Slave Code for the District of Columbia." Retrieved from https://www.loc.gov/collections/slaves-and-the-courts-from-1740-to-1860/articles-and-essays/slave-code-for-the-district-of-columbia/

[43] "Annual 2023 Global Climate Report." Retrieved from: https://www.ncei.noaa.gov/access/monitoring/monthly-report/global/202313
[44] "Arctic sea ice minimum at sixth lowest extent on record." Retrieved from: https://nsidc.org/arcticseaicenews/2023/09/arctic-sea-ice-minimum-at-sixth/
[45] "Sea Level Rise and Implications for Low-Lying Islands, Coasts and Communities." Retrieved from: https://www.ipcc.ch/srocc/chapter/chapter-4-sea-level-rise-and-implications-for-low-lying-islands-coasts-and-communities/
[46] "Household air pollution." Retrieved from: https://www.who.int/news-room/fact-sheets/detail/household-air-pollution-and-health
[47] "2017 UN World Water Development Report, Wastewater: The Untapped Resource." Retrieved from: https://www.unep.org/resources/publication/2017-un-world-water-development-report-wastewater-untapped-resource
[48] "What is the sixth mass extinction and what can we do about it?" Retrieved from: https://www.worldwildlife.org/stories/what-is-the-sixth-mass-extinction-and-what-can-we-do-about-it
[49] "Food Waste FAQs." Retrieved from: https://www.usda.gov/foodwaste/faqs
[50] "Average U.S. House and Household Size infographics. Retrieved from: https://populationeducation.org/resource/average-u-s-house-and-household-size-infographic/
[51] "After Sandy Hook, More Than 400 People Have Been Shot in Over 200 School Shootings. By Jugal K. Patel. Feb 15, 2018." Retrieved from: https://www.nytimes.com/interactive/2018/02/15/us/school-shootings-sandy-hook-parkland.html
[52] "K-12 School Shooting Statistics: 52 years of Data." Retrieved from: https://www.campussafetymagazine.com/safety/k-12-school-shooting-statistics-everyone-should-know
[53] "Giffords Law Center To Prevent Gun Violence. Statistics." Retrieved from: https://giffords.org/lawcenter/gun-violence-statistics/
[54] Willoughby, B. J., Carroll, J. S., Busby, D. M., & Brown, C. C. (2016). Differences in pornography use among couples: Associations with satisfaction, stability, and relationship processes. Archives of Sexual Behavior, 45(1), 145-158
[55] "American Psychological Association. (2016). Understanding the Behavioral and Emotional Consequences of Child Abuse." Retrieved from:
https://www.apa.org/pi/prevent-violence/resources/child-abuse

[56] "National Center for Missing and Exploited Children. (2019). 2019 Annual Report." Retrieved from:
https://www.missingkids.org/content/dam/netsmec/en_us/documents/annual_reports/2019_Annual_Report.pdf

[57] Grubbs, J. B., Kraus, S. W., & Perry, S. L. (2019). Self-reported addiction to pornography in a nationally representative sample: The roles of use habits, religiousness, and moral incongruence. Journal of Behavioral Addictions, 8(1), 88-93

[58] Landripet, I., & Štulhofer, A. (2015). Is pornography use associated with sexual difficulties and dysfunctions among younger heterosexual men? Journal of Sexual Medicine, 12(5), 1136-1139.

[59] "Middle Ages." Retrieved from:
https://en.wikipedia.org/wiki/Middle_Ages

[60] "Renaissance." Retrieved from:
https://en.wikipedia.org/wiki/Renaissance

[61] "How Islam Saved Western Civilization" by Dr. Roy Casagranda. Retrieved from:
https://youtu.be/C8M4i9fvq1M?si=WElcjpFghkFj69wa

[62] "Ibn al-Haytham." Retrieved from:
https://en.wikipedia.org/wiki/Ibn_al-Haytham

[63] "Scientific Control." Retrieved from:
https://en.wikipedia.org/wiki/Scientific_control

[64] "Ibn al-Haytham." Retrieved from:
https://en.wikipedia.org/wiki/Ibn_al-Haytham

[65] "Ancient Greek Astronomy and Cosmology." Retrieved from:
https://www.loc.gov/collections/finding-our-place-in-the-cosmos-with-carl-sagan/articles-and-essays/modeling-the-cosmos/ancient-greek-astronomy-and-cosmology

[66] "The Early Middle Ages, 284 – 1000 (HIST 210)" by Professor Freedman, year 2012, Open Yale Courses. Retrieved from:
https://oyc.yale.edu/history/hist-210

[67] "Tetrarchy." Retrieved from: https://en.wikipedia.org/wiki/Tetrarchy

[68] Lecture of Professor Paul Freedman of Yale, titled, "The Early Middle Ages, 284 – 1000 with Paul Freedman" in 2012 available from YaleCourses. Lecture titled: "06. Transformation of the Roman Empire"

[69] "How Islam Saved Western Civilization" by Dr. Roy Casagranda. Retrieved from:

https://youtu.be/C8M4i9fvq1M?si=WElcjpFghkFj69wa
[70] "Why doesn't Judaism Encourage Conversion?" Retrieved from: https://intranet.birmingham.ac.uk/student/multi-faith-chaplaincy/about/news/why-doesn't-judaism-encourage-conversion.aspx
[71] "Superdeterminism." Retrieved from: https://en.wikipedia.org/wiki/Superdeterminism
[72] "Richard Dawkins in Conversation with Jim Al-Khalili on Free Will." Retrieved from: https://youtu.be/735o-d62FGE?si=AzYbFHOT04Y__OAr&t=2374 at 40:00 minutes
[73] "Drug Overdose Death Rates." Retrieved from: https://www.drugabuse.gov/drug-topics/opioids/opioid-overdose-crisis
[74] "Charles B. Davenport". Retrieved from: https://collections.countway.harvard.edu/onview/exhibits/show/galtonschildren/galton-s-children/charles-b--davenport
[75] "Religious Landscape Study." Retrieved from: https://www.pewresearch.org/religion/religious-landscape-study/
[76] "The Burmingham Quran." Retrieved from: https://www.birmingham.ac.uk/facilities/cadbury/birmingham-quran-mingana-collection/birmingham-quran/
[77] "The Origins Myth." Retrieved from: https://www.americanacademy.de/the-origins-myth/
[78] "Tuberculosis (TB) Test." Retrieved from: https://my.clevelandclinic.org/health/diagnostics/22751-tuberculosis-tb-test
[79] "Can Quantum-Mechanical Description of Physical Reality Be Considered Complete?" By Einstein, Podolsky, and N. Rosen. Retrieved from: https://cds.cern.ch/record/405662/files/PhysRev.47.777.pdf
[80] "Entangled states – from theory to technology." Retrieved from: https://www.nobelprize.org/prizes/physics/2022/press-release/
[81] "The Unknown Universe Explained By Neil DeGrasse Tyson." Retrieved from: https://youtu.be/6RXobWpXEpo
[82] "The Origin of the Universe – Prof Stephen Hawking at Hong Kong University of Science & Technology." Retrieved from: https://youtu.be/c7MO3up5bZs

[83] "The Origin of the Universe – Prof Stephen Hawking at Hong Kong University of Science & Technology." Retrieved from: https://youtu.be/c7MO3up5bZs

[84] "Press Release: the 2017 Nobel Prize in Physiology or Medicine." Retrieved from: https://www.nobelprize.org/prizes/medicine/2017/press-release/

[85] "The Quran:An Theists Perspective." Retrieved from: https://youtu.be/2AvepssBwzY

[86] "Prehistoric Warfare." Retrieved from: https://en.wikipedia.org/wiki/Prehistoric_warfare

[87] "Human." Retrieved from: https://en.wikipedia.org/wiki/Human

[88] "Hominin." Retrieved from: https://www.britannica.com/topic/hominin

[89] "The origin of Homo Sapiens & timeline of human evolution." Retrieved from: https://reasonandscience.catsboard.com/t2596-the-origin-of-homo-sapiens-timeline-of-human-evolution

[90] "Human Migration:" Out of Africa Theory." Retrieved from: https://www.scribd.com/article/510755708/Human-Migration-Out-Of-Africa-Theory

[91] "Professor Paul Freedman. "16. The Early Middle Ages, 284-1000: The Splendor of the Abbasid Period" under the course, "The Early Middle Ages, 284—1000 (HIST 210)" at Yale in 2012. Retrieved from: https://youtu.be/ji8kKMSLEQo

[92] Professor Paul Freedman. "17. The Early Middle Ages, 284-1000: The Crucial Seventh century" titled "Chapter 1. Geography and Medicine under the Abbasids" under the course, "The Early Middle Ages, 284—1000 (HIST 210)" at Yale in 2012. Retrieved from: https://youtu.be/afmnB0o8-jI

[93] Professor Paul Freedman. "14. Mohammed and the Arab Conquests" under the course, "The Early Middle Ages, 284—1000 (HIST 210)" at Yale in 2012. Retrieved from: https://youtu.be/cXF7RkgANNo

[94] Lang, Jeffrey (1997). Even Angels Ask: A Journey to Islam in America (1st ed.). In "Don't We Need Another Prophet" (p. 78)

[95] "Average teen circadian cycle." Retrieve from: https://images.nigms.nih.gov/pages/DetailPage.aspx?imageid2=6611

[96] "Autophagy fights disease through cellular self-digestion." Retrieved from:

https://www.ncbi.nlm.nih.gov/pmc/articles/PMC2670399/pdf/nihms101429.pdf

[97] "The Effect of Prostration (Sajdah) on the Prefrontal Brain Activity: A Pilot Study." Retrieved from:
https://www.ncbi.nlm.nih.gov/pmc/articles/PMC6712630/

[98] "The effects of grounding (earthing) on inflammation, the immune response, wound healing, and prevention and treatment of chronic inflammatory and autoimmune diseases." Retrieved from: https://www.ncbi.nlm.nih.gov/pmc/articles/PMC4378297/

[99] "How this chart explains Americans' wealth across income levels." Retrieved from https://usafacts.org/articles/how-this-chart-explains-americans-wealth-across-income-levels/

[100] "The inauguration speech of Abu Bakr, the first caliph of Muslims in Madinah." Al-Bidaayah wan-Nihaayah 6:305, 306

[101] "Global trends in incidence, death, burden and risk factors of early-onset cancer from 1990 to 2019." Retrieved from:
https://bmjoncology.bmj.com/content/2/1/e000049

[102] "Press Release. The Nobel Prize." Retrieved from:
https://www.nobelprize.org/prizes/medicine/2016/press-release/

[103] "A review of the therapeutic effects of using miswak (Salvadora Persica) on oral health." Retrieved from:
https://www.ncbi.nlm.nih.gov/pmc/articles/PMC4436748/

[104] "The Neurobiology Shaping Affective Touch: Expectation, Motivation, and Meaning in the Multisensory Context." Retrieved from:
https://www.ncbi.nlm.nih.gov/pmc/articles/PMC4701942/

[105] "The Proposition 65 List, California Office of Environmental Health Hazard Assessment." Retrieved from:
https://oehha.ca.gov/proposition-65/proposition-65-list

[106] "Disposable paper cups release tiny plastic particles, harmful ions." Retrieved from:
https://www.nature.com/articles/nindia.2020.173

[107] "Per- and Polyfluoroalkyl Substance Toxicity and Human Health Review: Current State of Knowledge and Strategies for Informing Future Research." Retrieved from:
https://www.ncbi.nlm.nih.gov/pmc/articles/PMC7906952

[108] "Dopamine, Smartphones & You: A battle for your time." Retrieved from:

https://sitn.hms.harvard.edu/flash/2018/dopamine-smartphones-battle-time/

[109] Christmas Lecture at The Royal Institution's titled: "Waking up in the Universe" in 1991. Retrieved from: https://youtu.be/jY_hJUm__78

[110] "Richard Dawkins vs Piers Morgan On Religion and Gender. Piers Morgan Uncensored." Retrieved from https://youtu.be/505UazMNgLg

[111] "Militant Atheism by Richard Dawkins." Retrieved from: https://youtu.be/VxGMqKCcN6A

[112] "Al-Quran (Full) – Mishary Alafasy [Eng Subs]." Retrieved from: https://youtube.com/playlist?list=PLoqNzfHlA__knCeUoKUHjQfZpUL6mj64w

[113] "Full Quran Recitation by Mishary Rashid Alafasy." Retrieved from https://open.spotify.com/album/485V9nMD70JTzbdYpxPp4W

[114] "Ibn al-Haytham." Retrieved from: https://en.wikipedia.org/wiki/Ibn_al-Haytham

[115] "Medieval Studies: An Introduction, Second Edition" by James M. Powell. Published by Syracuse University Press; 2nd edition (August 1, 1992) (p.354-355)

[116] "History of the Moorish Empire in Europe" by S. P. Scott. Published by Bloomsbury Academic (January 28, 2021)

[117] "The House of Wisdom: How Arabic Science Saved Ancient Knowledge and Gave Us the Renaissance" by Jim Al-Khalili"

[118] "Library of Alexandria." Retrieved from: https://en.wikipedia.org/wiki/Library_of_Alexandria

[119] "Deconstructing Racism and Sexism in the Envisagement of Western Civilization" by Dr. Roy Casagranda. Retrieved from: https://youtu.be/lk4ncpkstAw?si=93Zo2oTtDXWUhV0y

[120] "The University of Al Karaouine." Retrieved from https://en.wikipedia.org/wiki/Islamic_Golden_Age#cite_note-55

[121] "Islamic Golden Age." Retrieved from: https://en.wikipedia.org/wiki/Islamic_Golden_Age

[122] "Mathematics in in the Medieval Islamic World." Retrieved from: https://en.wikipedia.org/wiki/Mathematics_in_the_medieval_Islamic_world

[123] "Physics in the Medieval Islamic World." Retrieved from: https://en.wikipedia.org/wiki/Physics_in_the_medieval_Islamic_world

[124] "The Canon of Medicine." Retrieved from:

https://en.wikipedia.org/wiki/The_Canon_of_Medicine
[125] "Maragheh Observatory." Retrieved from:
https://en.wikipedia.org/wiki/Maragheh_observatory
[126] "Astronomy in the Medieval Islamic World." Retrieved from:
https://en.wikipedia.org/wiki/Astronomy_in_the_medieval_Islamic_world
[127] "Brocchi's Cluster." Retrieved from:
https://en.wikipedia.org/wiki/Brocchi%27s_Cluster
[128] "The House of Wisdom: How Arabic Science Saved Ancient Knowledge and Gave Us the Renaissance" by Jim Al-Khalili
[129] "Alhambra and Generalife." Retrieved from:
https://www.alhambra-patronato.es/en/discover/alhambra-y-generalife

Made in the USA
Middletown, DE
28 July 2024

58100163R00181